THE JURY

THE
JURY

—

Disorder in the Courts

STEPHEN J. ADLER

MAIN
STREET
BOOKS

DOUBLEDAY
New York London Toronto Sydney Auckland

A Main Street Book

PUBLISHED BY DOUBLEDAY

a division of Bantam Doubleday Dell Publishing Group, Inc.
1540 Broadway, New York, New York 10036

Main Street Books, Doubleday, and the portrayal of a
building with a tree are trademarks of Doubleday, a division of
Bantam Doubleday Dell Publishing Group, Inc.

The Jury was originally published in hardcover by Times Books,
a division of Random House, Inc., in 1994. The Main Street
Books edition is published by arrangement with Times Books,
Random House.

Library of Congress Cataloging-in-Publication Data

Adler, Stephen J.
The jury: disorder in the courts/Stephen J. Adler.
—1st Main Street books ed.
p. cm.
Originally published: New York: Times Books, c1994.
"A Main Street book"—T.p. verso.
Includes bibliographical references and index.
1. Jury—United States. I. Title.
KF8972.A735 1995
347.73'752—dc20
[347.307752] 95-2734
CIP

ISBN 0-385-47969-7
First Main Street Books Edition: October 1995

1   3   5   7   9   10   8   6   4   2

FOR LISA GRUNWALD ADLER

Acknowledgments

When I set out four years ago to write a book about the jury, I anticipated that lawyers, judges, and jurors would be reluctant to speak honestly about actual cases. Lawyers, I figured, would shade events to favor themselves and their clients. Judges would be distant and uninformative. And jurors would guard their privacy by refusing to be interviewed, or would echo the usual postverdict clichés. Some of this turned out to be true. But, to my delight, I found that most participants in jury trials were eager to contribute to public understanding of what they had just been through. This meant that many lawyers were willing to reveal in detail how they had picked, and then tried to persuade, particular juries. Judges submitted to interviews and in some cases directly assisted me in gaining access to jurors and court records. Court clerks provided jury records and an array of insights. Jurors let me into their homes and workplaces, shared with me diaries and notes that were invaluable in helping me reconstruct deliberations, sat through multiple interviews, and in the Liggett case even included me in their weekend-long reunion a year after the verdict. I'd like to offer my thanks to all of them.

ACKNOWLEDGMENTS

Lawyers, judges, and other jury experts who provided assistance though they were not involved in the trials discussed in the book include Beth Bonora, Fred Cate, Philip Corboy, Thomas Demetrio, Amitai Etzioni, Marc Galanter, Ira Gammerman, Nancy Gertner, Stephen Gillers, Norman Goodman, Erwin Griswold, Valerie Hans, Stephen Herzberg, Judith Kaye, Richard Lempert, Daniel Margolis, Colleen McMahon, Arthur Miller, Newton Minow, Lawrence Mitchell, G. Thomas Munsterman, Richard Roth, William Schwarzer, Neil Vidmar, Donald Vinson, Harvey Weitz, Ted Wells, and the late Hans Zeisel.

I also wish to thank Norman Pearlstine and Paul Steiger, successive managing editors of *The Wall Street Journal,* for generously granting me the flexibility to develop this book while continuing my work as law editor at the *Journal;* and the *Journal*'s law staff—especially deputy editor Ellen Joan Pollock—for covering for me so graciously and so well.

Steven Brill, editor-in-chief of *The American Lawyer,* who reported on jury deliberations before anyone else, sparked my interest in the subject. My agent, Kathy Robbins, was an invaluable editor, sounding board, and cheerleader throughout the project. Peter Osnos at Random House and Times Books immediately embraced the idea of a book on the jury, then relentlessly pushed me to sharpen my thinking and my manuscript. Peter Smith of Times Books offered numerous important organizational and copy suggestions.

My wife, novelist and editor Lisa Grunwald Adler, read and critiqued each chapter more times than anyone should have to read anything. From start to finish, she enriched this project with her intellect, wisdom, and love. I could not have done it without her. Finally, I am grateful to my family and friends for their patience and support.

A NOTE ON METHODS

Much of the action of this book takes place inside the jury room. Deliberations in each case are reconstructed based on the memories of the jurors, most of whom I interviewed repeatedly. Where I reproduce dialogue verbatim, I am relying on one or more jurors' accounts of what was said. More often, I paraphrase, again based solely on jurors' recollections. No dialogue is imagined or embellished for dramatic effect. I recount what jurors or lawyers are thinking only when they have related to me what they had in mind at the time.

All the jurors are identified by their real names except two in the New Jersey love triangle murder case described in Chapter 6. In that case, the jurors identified as Lilly Tai and Wendy Meadows requested that pseudonyms be used.

CONTENTS

INTRODUCTION

The American jury system confronts us with a powerful contradiction: We love the idea of the jury but hate the way it
works. We celebrate the jurors' democratic power but no
longer trust the decisions they reach. We say we have the best
system in the world, but when called to serve, most of us do
everything we can to duck out.[1] So what good is the power if
it's exercised so poorly—and by so few? This book explores
the contradiction and tries to answer the question.

I began this project under the influence of the usual myths
and the conventional wisdom. In the Salem witch trials, juries
that embraced the madness ultimately called a halt to it. In
the age of slavery, stubborn Northerners discredited and
defanged the Fugitive Slave Laws by acquitting people who
harbored runaways. In the movie *12 Angry Men* one good man
held out against a quick, careless verdict and guided eleven
others through debate and catharsis and onward to truth and
justice. What's not to like? These are the juries we got to know
in childhood. Check out the *World Book* encyclopedia from
1962: There a jury of solemn men in business suits is pictured
listening "attentively" and trying, the caption reports, "to

reach a fair decision by weighing all of the evidence presented.''

My reporting took me to a much different world. It was a world I had first chosen to look at so I could illustrate the different issues that juries face and study how they handle them. I focused on current cases that introduced me to different regions of the country, to civil and criminal matters, to good lawyers and bad, to careful judges and callous ones. But inside the jury rooms, which I entered through multiple post-trial interviews with nearly all the players, I soon found that the juries had some dismaying characteristics in common.

For one thing, I repeatedly encountered scenes that bore next to no resemblance to the high-minded debates of *12 Angry Men*. There were few Henry Fondas standing up for reasonable doubt and painstakingly reconstructing the evidence. To the juries' credit, there were also almost no Jack Wardens, trying to get out early to make a ball game. Instead, there were lots of sincere, serious people who—for a variety of reasons—were missing key points, focusing on irrelevant issues, succumbing to barely recognized prejudices, failing to see through the cheapest appeals to sympathy or hate, and generally botching the job. I saw a great deal of New Age bonding among jury members. But I searched nearly in vain for evidence that when it came to intelligent decision making, twelve heads were really better than one.

Yet my reaction to each case was never entirely negative. I found myself delighting in the spectacle of entrusting whatever was at issue to a random slice of the community, rather than to a single judge. In New York City a ragtag, multiethnic jury had the proud task of deciding whether two world figures, Imelda Marcos and Adnan Khashoggi, had violated U.S. criminal laws. I imagined the jurors as hastily assembled minutemen aiming their muskets over stone walls: They were there to enforce our rules.

A love triangle murder case in New Jersey came down to

the question of whether the defendant or his two-timing ex-wife was telling the truth. One could never scientifically prove what had happened. I felt better knowing that twelve members of the community, the neighbors who would have to live with the consequences of their verdict, would get to decide whether anyone went to jail.

Even in a North Carolina antitrust case involving two big companies and bizarrely complex legal issues, I came to believe that the community's involvement, via the jury, was invaluable. The centrality of the jury lent weight and credibility and reality and democracy to all these proceedings.

Nonetheless, in these cases and the others I observed I couldn't avoid the contradiction and the question. No matter how uplifting, energizing, and empowering the concept, what was the good of a system that produced the shoddy—and sometimes patently stupid—verdicts that frequently resulted?

For a long time I didn't have an answer. Now I believe I do. A jury system that works as badly as this book shows it does simply shouldn't, and won't, survive. It may never be abolished, given its protected status among our national myths and in our Constitution. But it will certainly erode, a process that is already well under way. The real question is whether the jury system is worth saving in principle and, if so, whether we can improve it sufficiently to make it worth saving in practice.

We need only look around us to see that a jury system isn't necessary to a well-ordered society or even to a representative democracy.[2] Japan had a jury system for a while and dropped it. Israel has never had one. Germany, France, and most of the rest of Europe use a different system of justice, one that relies on small panels of professional and lay judges. India inherited the British jury system from its former colonizers and then dropped it altogether in 1961. Gandhi explained: "I have known juries finding prisoners guilty in the face of no evidence. We must not slavishly copy all that is British."

And what of Britain, the cradle of the modern jury? There the system has been slowly disintegrating. Today only 1 percent of civil trials and 5 percent of criminal trials are decided by juries.

This book will attempt to show that we needn't go the way of Britain, and that we mustn't. In the opening section I explore our peculiarly, powerfully American vision of the jury that stems from its special role in revolutionary times. This heritage sets us apart from the rest of the world and gives us greater reason to preserve the jury and greater hope that we can. The revolutionary ideal is more visible in some modern cases than in others; the Dallas death penalty case reported in the book's first section shows the jury at its contemporary best.

The second section offers the stories of five other juries that functioned far less well. These cases, I've gradually come to realize, are more representative than anomalous. While some American juries perform admirably, a shockingly large number do not, when they are judged by academic studies, lawyers' and judges' anecdotes, and court records of damage awards reduced on appeal as the result of jurors' errors.[3]

The book's final section looks for ways to fix what is so clearly broken. My proposals address various aspects of the system: who gets called for jury duty, who actually serves, how trials are conducted, what goes on in the jury room. All the suggestions stem from the same premise: that if jurors are useful and powerful figures in our democracy, they must be treated that way. They must be given the training, the tools, and the information, along with the comforts and the deference normally provided to people in positions of power. A visionary judge in Phoenix already runs his courtroom this way, and we'll meet him and one of his juries in Part III. If we make the changes suggested in this section, I believe we can save the jury. If we fail, I will argue, we will lose the most potent and ingenious vehicle for self-rule ever invented.

Part I

THE VISION

—

W YOMING'S most famous lawyer, Gerry Spence, tells the story of a woman named Maude who was on trial for pistol-whipping a man named Benny. It seems that Maude had a powerful motive: Benny had sewn up the mouth of Maude's horse, which had taken a liking to Benny's hay. The judge in the case sternly instructed the jury that a person couldn't take the law into his or her own hands. But the jury acquitted Maude nonetheless. Afterward, recounts Spence, who prosecuted the case, the jury foreman explained: "The judge trusted us to do justice. . . . That judge knew we wouldn't go along with all that legal horseshit as he was readin' us."[1]

Maude's case is quintessentially American, and it reveals what we imagine and want our jury system to be. It shows the little guy speaking for all of us, justice handed up from the community, not down from some gilded hilltop legislature. It illustrates how a jury, told what the written law is, can nonetheless disregard it when circumstances require. It celebrates justice that's particular to the facts and to the individual. And it displays the jury as more powerful than the high-and-mighty judge (whose legal instructions are ignored) and the imposing prosecutor (who has brought the charges and sought the conviction). Finally it reminds us that jury duty can open our eyes, make us citizens who recognize "all that legal horseshit" when we see it.

This is our idealized view of the American jury. The jury is powerful, it is wise, it is flexible, and it is ours. This has always been so. One hundred sixty years ago, Alexis de Tocqueville observed of jury service: "By obliging men to turn their attention to other affairs than their own, it rubs off that private selfishness which is the rust of society. . . . I think that the practical intelligence and political good sense of the Americans are mainly attributable to the long use that they have made of the jury."[2]

The jury, of course, wasn't born in the U.S.A.[3] In fact, it had evolved in Britain hundreds of years before the American Revolution, at first to settle disputes over who should be taxed for particular parcels of land, and later to resolve a broader range of conflicts. In these matters jurors were sometimes ordered to reach particular results and were targets of physical reprisals if they did not. But political currents shifted over time, and British courts in the seventeenth century granted juries the power to reach their verdicts freely. So, when the system was imported to America, it was ready-made to serve as a counterweight to the king's power, a subversive vehicle through which the colonists could prevent royal decrees from being carried out.

The most talked-about case that tested the jury's power was the trial of John Peter Zenger, a printer in colonial New York who published a muckraking newspaper that regularly criticized and taunted the corrupt governor, William Cosby. The governor was particularly detested because he freely used the colonial courts to benefit himself and his cronies, and he tried to use them to silence Zenger and his cohorts as well. In 1734 Zenger was arrested and in 1735 prosecuted under a law that made it illegal to criticize government officials even if the accusations were true. But the New York jury in the case wasn't buying. Written law or no written law, it took just a few minutes to decide that Zenger was not guilty. The British mas-

4

ters were furious, but the verdict stood. Both the king's men and the colonists understood thereafter that juries could put severe limits on any ruler's use of power.[4]

But juries don't just prevent the government from acting; more often, by convicting a defendant, they allow the government to proceed with the punishment of someone who has violated the written law. In this role, too, the ideal jury plays an important and inspiring role. First, it puts the government's evidence to the test. Then, by endorsing the charges, it reassures the rest of the community that the government has acted fairly and that the punishment, however severe, is just. The jury's role is similar in civil cases, which resolve private disputes. If Smith must give up his property to Jones, at least Smith, Jones, and their neighbors can rest assured that the outcome is the result not of some judge's favoritism but of the common judgment of a local jury.

Federal appellate judge John J. Gibbons characterized this aspect of the jury's ideal function: "The jury is a sort of ad hoc parliament convened from the citizenry at large to lend respectability and authority to the process. . . . Any erosion of citizen participation in the sanctioning system is in the long run likely, in my view, to result in a reduction in the moral authority that supports the process."[5]

Perhaps the most surprising and distinctive task of the American jury is to serve as official historian in any case in which facts are in dispute. In the public perception the real story of an alleged crime is hidden in the courtroom among a clutter of lies, alibis, mistaken identities, and selective memories. The assumption is that the jurors use their common sense to sort through the confusion. Whether they do their jobs well or poorly, what they decide is typically perceived as true, both legally and historically. Once a jury speaks, journalists no longer refer to an accused person as the "alleged" slayer; "murderer" suffices.

Literalists may argue that juries don't decide what is true; they merely decide whether the government has presented its facts convincingly. A not-guilty verdict, they say, doesn't mean a person is innocent, only that the government has failed to meet its burden of proof. Still, this is so only in a formal sense. As a practical matter the not-guilty person leaves the courthouse with all his freedoms and most of his privileges intact, while the guilty person goes to prison and, if he emerges, continues to suffer the consequences of having been found guilty. Depending on the nature and severity of his crime, he may be legally barred from voting or serving on a jury, denied occupational licenses, prevented from holding public offices, rejected for automobile insurance, or denied parental rights. Informally the stigma of a felony conviction can cause him countless other problems. Licensing boards, employers, or landlords won't buy the excuse of a false accusation; the jury's verdict has determined the truth. Boxer Mike Tyson will live his life as a convicted rapist. Physician William Kennedy Smith will not. Their juries didn't just evaluate the government's proof; they wrote history.[6]

It seems wonderfully in keeping with our democratic ideals that we allow juries of ordinary people to have this power. By doing so, we deny powerful judicial officials who may have political agendas from shaping this history for us. And we stay far removed from the most totalitarian regimes, in which official history—whether declaring a dissident insane or a scholar guilty of subversion—is subject to revision whenever a new regime emerges. It's no accident that the Communist-era Soviet Union did without a jury system and, as it fought in 1993 to develop as a democracy, Russia was working to establish one.[7]

We're speaking here, of course, of the ideal of the jury, of the theory we venerate rather than the reality that we often scorn and of which we'll see much more in the second part of the book. But first we will see the jury operating much as it was meant to, in a case in which the stakes for the defendant could not have been higher and in which the jurors' task evokes echoes of de Tocqueville and Gibbons, Zenger, and Maude.

1

THE AWFUL COURT
OF JUDGMENT

—

O NE moment the scene was idyllic: Two young men were fishing for catfish in a backyard creek just north of Dallas. The next moment one of the men shot the other in the back of the head and then sneaked inside the house to execute the victim's eighty-one-year-old grandmother. Nine days later, on August 28, 1989, twenty-one-year-old Mark Allen Robertson was arrested in Las Vegas, where he'd driven a Cadillac belonging to the woman. He quickly, even boastfully, confessed. The only concern he expressed to police was whether he'd been featured on the TV show *America's Most Wanted*. Back in Dallas he was charged with murder under a law providing the death sentence to someone who deliberately kills in the course of a robbery. A year later jury selection began. By the time it was over, a collection of twelve quite ordinary people—with no special training, expertise, or social cachet—possessed the greatest power any government can assert over a citizen: the power to put him to death.

In most nations, throughout most of history, this is a power that has belonged to the head of government and his proxies. In the United States we've come to rely almost entirely on juries to exercise this ultimate authority, and we've done so for some very good reasons.

One reason is that in death penalty cases, certainly more than in disputes over horses and their hay, we want verdicts to be carefully tailored to the people and circumstances, and this is a specialty of juries. In the privacy of their deliberations, jurors can transcend inflexible laws to reveal the more human face of justice. Judges, bound to their written opinions, typically cannot.

Secondly, especially when life is at stake, we also want justice done by members of the community who are awed by their assignment, rather than by professional judges who have heard every alibi dozens of times before. The problem with judges, as the British essayist G. K. Chesterton put it, "is not that they are wicked (some of them are good), not that they are stupid (several of them are quite intelligent), it is simply that they have got used to it. . . . They do not see the awful court of judgment; they only see their own workshop."[1]

Particularly in a nation that's perpetually ambivalent about executions, the element of personal concern that a jury brings to the decision is distinctly reassuring. Our greatest modern jury mythmaker, the movie *12 Angry Men*, wildly idealizes the jury in many respects. But in one particular the movie had it absolutely right: Jurors who know that a defendant is facing the death penalty can become personally involved, even obsessed, with the defendant, the victim, the crime, and their own unparalleled responsibility.[2]

A third reason we rely on juries to mete out death sentences is that on a deep level we simply believe that the most important decisions should be made as democratically as possible. It's true that people without some special claim to influence or fame don't usually play much of a role in our contemporary government. Yet despite the growth of bureaucracy, the power of money in politics, the statistical insignifi-

9

cance of the individual vote, the near impossibility of fighting city hall, we still refer to ourselves as a democracy. It's in jury rooms such as the one in which Mark Robertson was on trial in Dallas—where ordinary people together must exercise extraordinary power—that we may come closest to being one.

Mark Robertson seemed to be just the sort of cold-blooded, sociopathic killer who'd earn a quick trip to death row. He'd killed easily, then shown no remorse. He'd played the slot machines and eaten ice cream and popcorn while the victims' family had grieved. He'd offered no motive beyond off-handed greed. And thus he was just the sort of criminal defendant most in need of a fair, careful trial by decision makers committed to protecting his rights as well as society's.

The most articulate opponents of capital punishment argue that the criminal justice system is racially biased and that juries are unreliable; as a result, they say, innocent people are too frequently convicted and put to death.[3] But these opponents are calling for the abolition of capital punishment, never for the replacement of juries with professional judges. As the Robertson case shows, juries in capital cases are picked, in fact, with surprising care. The complex and lengthy process seems to reflect simultaneously our respect for the lives of even the nastiest defendants and our commitment, at great expense, to the ideal of the impartial jury.

To find twelve members of the Dallas community who could provide Mark Robertson with a sufficiently dispassionate hearing, court officials figured they would need to start with a vast pool of five hundred. For an ordinary trial, so wide a call would have been unnecessary, even absurd; one tenth as many would have been closer to the standard. But in a capital case anyone who ultimately is allowed to serve has to be certified as "death-qualified," and membership in this ominously named club is strictly limited.

The reason is that many people oppose the death penalty in principle, and if those people are permitted to serve without question, they may refuse to condemn regardless of the circumstances. Simply by holding out and producing hung juries, these people can prevent most executions from occurring, and that isn't a result either the pro–death penalty majority or the state's prosecutors can accept. Exclude all death penalty opponents, however, and you remove roughly 25 percent of the population from the jury pool—and generally the 25 percent most concerned about civil liberties. Those who remain will be more conservative, more likely to support the police and to presume a defendant is guilty just because he's been arrested. They're more likely to convict than are the excluded jurors and then much more likely to sentence the defendant to death.[4]

Death qualification is a way to steer a middle ground: to let juries reflect their communities' diverse viewpoints on capital punishment without standing in the way of all executions. As the U.S. Supreme Court has directed, each prospective juror has to agree in advance that he or she will be able to consider issuing a death sentence; anyone who refuses to make such a leap is excluded, though death penalty opponents who agree to follow the law despite misgivings are included.[5]

Compare this system with the chief alternative: letting a judge decide the sentence on his own, as only Arizona, Idaho, Montana, and Nebraska currently do. The judge may have been elected or appointed precisely because he favors, or doesn't favor, the death penalty. He operates on his own rather than in a group that might temper any of his prejudices. And at the time of trial no one inquires into whether he holds the kinds of views that easily would disqualify jurors. A jury, in contrast, first must be death-qualified and then must decide on the death sentence unanimously.

For the five hundred potential Robertson jurors, the laborious selection process began in September 1990 with the completion of questionnaires that sought detailed information about their views on capital punishment, then moved on to personal interrogations by the lawyers and the judge. These interviews, each from one to three hours, stretched impressively, if exhaustingly, through the fall and into the winter. As illustrated in later chapters, jury selection is frequently unfair and capricious, with lawyers relying on stereotypes and snap judgments to disqualify people with whom they've barely exchanged a word. In a death penalty case such as Robertson's, however, such problems seem to be reduced somewhat by the extraordinary time and attention devoted to the process.

During the interviews the court-appointed defense team of Brook Busbee and Mike Byck studied each potential juror closely, seeking those who might be soft on capital punishment. The calculus was delicate: They wanted jurors with sufficient emotion to feel sorry for the defendant and his family and, perhaps, to be merciful. But if an emotional juror felt the pain of the victim's family instead, the case would be lost.

Also studying the possible jurors—of course, with opposite intentions—was prosecutor Howard Wilson. He wasn't looking, for the most part, for law and order zealots. Because this was a death penalty case, scrutiny on appeal would be intense, and he didn't want anybody who might later be found to be biased. Nonetheless, he wanted to exclude anyone who seemed queasy about making the choice to condemn. So Wilson described for each prospective juror the details of a Texas execution: the prisoner taken from his cell, the prisoner strapped down, the needle probing for a vein, the IV dripping glucose into the vein until the fatal drug was added to the flow. Wilson invariably paused then and said, "He will exist no more." Any prospective juror who blanched became a candidate for removal. Many blanched.

Seeing the defendant, who had a right to attend the interviews, was also part of the exercise. During jury selection

Mark Robertson showed up in a polo shirt and khaki pants or a business suit instead of his white prison jumpsuit. Invariably prospective jurors were startled by his youth and conservative appearance—like Howdy Doody but better-looking, with his red hair shorter and neater than it had been in years. Several jurors later remembered their astonishment upon realizing that the meek young fellow at the defense table was the man on trial for murder.

As is often the case, the death qualification process didn't weed out everyone with immediate and strong feelings about the case. Sue Warner, an opinionated thirty-five-year-old bank officer with a liberal arts education, was vigorously opposed to capital punishment except in the most extreme cases and was convinced it didn't deter others from committing similar crimes. She was also worried, she told the lawyers, that the defendant might not be guilty and that once he was executed, there'd be no way to make up for the mistake. Anna Emmons, a petite twenty-seven-year-old Delta Air Lines stewardess with long red fingernails who seemed to have been transported from a 1960s airlines ad, was a different story. Conservative, shy, and deeply religious, she shuddered both at the thought of Robertson's crime and at the notion of playing a role in executing him; she wanted no part of either. In her interview with the lawyers she said it was her Christian belief that one must not kill, even for retribution, but that she also believed people should pay a penalty for murder and not be allowed out of prison under any circumstance.

But she and Sue Warner promised to follow the law despite their own opinions, as the death qualification rules require, and they landed among the final twelve. Their presence on the jury guaranteed that those in control of Robertson's fate would have to face up to the arguments of at least two death penalty doves. More broadly, in keeping with our vision of the ideal jury, this meant the jury would reflect the divisions

13

within the community. And if nothing else, the involvement of Anna Emmons and Sue Warner would ensure that the deliberations would be lively as well as painful.

In Texas, as in all thirty-six states with capital punishment laws, any death penalty case is heard in two stages. First the jury decides guilt or innocence. Then, if it finds the defendant guilty, the jury hears more testimony on whether the defendant should receive the death penalty or a life sentence, the only choices available.

In the Robertson trial the guilt or innocence phase passed quickly and efficiently. At least to the courtroom regulars, the case seemed to offer few interesting twists. State Judge Pat McDowell watched stone-faced and at times appeared distracted by paperwork at the bench. The bailiffs, court reporters, police officers, clerks, and lawyers all seemed somewhat bored by the proceedings. The familiar courtroom fostered their shoptalk, sparked their romances and feuds, paid their bills. Like the court officials described by G. K. Chesterton in the early part of this century, they seemed barely aware of the consequences of their work.

One of the greatest virtues of the jury system is that the same can almost never be said of jurors, who are perpetually new to the scene and attuned to its human dimension. Many of the Robertson jurors had hoped to avoid jury duty—nationally, a majority of people make some effort to be excused —but they became hooked on the case immediately, and they were acutely aware that they had the sole power to condemn a man to death. This was no distant democracy in which one voted, if one cared, to elect others to govern the nation or community. This was, as Aristotle wrote about the very first juries, the way the people "become sovereign in the government."[6] These jurors were paying attention; at night they were brooding and even dreaming about the terrifying case.

They listened carefully to Janice Warder, the forty-year-old prosecutor who took over from Howard Wilson at the trial and was crisp and convincing. She showed that Mark's confessions had been voluntary and that his elderly victim, Edna Brau, had been killed by a bullet from his gun. What more was there to say? There had been no drugs found in Mark's system that might have reduced his level of responsibility, and there had been no evidence of insanity.

The defense team was skilled and experienced—Mike Byck had tried a dozen death penalty cases in seventeen years and liked to call them "the Grand Prix" of the law—but along with cocounsel Busbee he had precious little with which to work. They had researched the case thoroughly and had even subjected their client to a last-minute brain scan just to make sure there wasn't some medical excuse that could be offered. And even though psychiatric tests had uncovered no clear signs of mental illness, they had carefully considered, then rejected, an insanity plea.

Creatively, if desperately, the defense lawyers hit on one technical legal point that offered some small promise of removing the possibility of a death sentence. Texas defined the crime of capital murder as murder committed "in the course of" some other serious crime, such as robbery, kidnapping, burglary, sexual assault, or arson. The aim was to give the jury some guidance by making distinctions between garden-variety murder, for which a death sentence wasn't appropriate, and even more heinous crimes: murder plus. Taking advantage of the distinction, Byck vehemently pressed the notion that Mark had intended to kill but that the robbery had been an afterthought. Hence no murder plus.

Juror Emily Bennett, a perceptive twenty-eight-year-old inventory manager at General Instrument, privately scoffed at this suggestion; the lawyer was obviously grasping at straws. For his part, juror Jack Smith, a calm, broad-shouldered fifty-one-year-old former Air Force officer, saw Byck's argument as

15

confirmation that the lawyers could come up with no defense on the merits. To Smith, it was a classic lawyer's sleight of hand: Because solid facts were against Byck, he was relying on the slimmest wisp of law. On Tuesday morning, January 29, after just three days of testimony and arguments, the twelve jurors were dispatched to the jury room to decide whether Byck's argument made any sense at all.

To most of them, the decision they now faced was like an exam question that seemed just a bit too easy. The man had robbed, and the man had murdered. If ever there was reason to take a quick vote and return with a verdict, wasn't this it? The next stage, after they had found him guilty, would involve court testimony on what his sentence should be, followed by another round of their deliberations. That was where the case would get tough, not here on the question of guilt.

But the jurors still held surprises for one another because they had dutifully followed the judge's directions and hadn't spoken to one another about the case during the trial. And there were twelve of them—a sizable number with which to reach a quick, unanimous verdict on so important a case. This was, after all, "the awful court of judgment"; not all of them were ready to convict just yet.

Ray Truesdell, a fifty-six-year-old hospital supplies sales manager who had previously been a foreman in a murder case, was one of those remarkable individuals who populate our mythic juries and occasionally our real ones. When Truesdell learned that he'd be serving in a death penalty case, he had geared up as if he were preparing for a major sales presentation. In the local library he'd found several books that offered guidance on how to perform as a juror, and he'd taken careful notes. As a result, by the time deliberations began, he had developed firm ideas about how the process should work. Already a stickler for order, he seized on the books' recommendations that each juror speak in turn, without interruption, and that all the issues in the case be discussed thoroughly before anyone committed himself or herself to a position and before any vote was taken.

The general method he espoused is known as evidence-driven deliberation, in which each piece of evidence is examined and analyzed for its significance. In contrast, verdict-driven debate aims at identifying the minority members of the jury and then convincing them to change their minds. The evidence-driven method is supposed to be less divisive, to produce more thoughtful discussion and keep the jurors working together.

Though Truesdell wasn't the foreman, he easily convinced the other jurors to go along with his recommendation and not put the case to a vote right away. An open-ended evidence-driven discussion followed, and it left at least two of the jurors doubting whether Mark had actually had robbery in mind when he killed Mrs. Brau—the prerequisite for capital murder. Mike Byck's self-assured argument along these lines seemed, astonishingly, to have struck at least a minor chord.

Juries are sometimes criticized for taking such legal technicalities seriously when the facts seem to point clearly to a guilty verdict. The most famous contemporary example is the suburban state court jury that in 1992 failed to convict four white Los Angeles police officers for assaulting black motorist Rodney King, a verdict that seemed absurd to anyone who watched the videotape of the officers repeatedly clubbing and kicking him. But one man's legal technicality is another's constitutional right to a fair trial, and jurors in that case insisted afterward that they were simply hewing to the legal instructions they'd received on what constitutes excessive force.

Whatever the truth in the King case, in the Robertson trial it was clear that the jurors' questioning of the seemingly obvious stemmed from a good-faith effort to tread cautiously where a man's life was at stake. They certainly didn't feel unduly sympathetic to Robertson or to his lawyers, and they had no ulterior motives. And though the other jurors considered the questions pretty bizarre, they respected the questioners and dutifully pulled out the floor plan to the Brau house and reviewed Mark Robertson's actions on the night of the murders.

They traced his path as he walked into the house after killing his buddy, proceeded to the living room to shoot Mrs. Brau, and, instead of fleeing, purposefully inspected a filing cabinet to find the title to Mrs. Brau's car. There in itself was evidence of his intention to rob. In addition, some jurors noted, none of his fingerprints had been found in the house, suggesting that he might have worn gloves or wiped surfaces down to avoid detection of the robbery. That might mean he had contemplated robbery from the start.

The house tour quickly satisfied thirty-eight-year-old medical office manager Tamara Bell, one of the two early doubters. An hour or so later Carlton Roark, a tall, artsy thirty-two-year-old marketer for the Postal Service, also relented. The very obvious, but carefully reached, verdict was "guilty."

Testimony in the so-called penalty phase of the trial began the same afternoon, Tuesday, January 29. For the jury, it was an eye-opening experience. During the guilt or innocence phase, the usual narrow evidentiary rules had applied: Evidence of past crimes hadn't been admissible because it might have prejudiced the jury; character witnesses hadn't been presented because since Robertson hadn't taken the stand, only his behavior at the Brau house, not his credibility, had been at issue. And lacking even the hint of an alibi, the defense had rested without offering evidence of its own. A portrait of the crime had emerged, but not of the criminal.

In the penalty stage the blinders were lifted. Under Texas law the jury now had two distinct questions to answer: whether the murder had been "deliberate"—that is, committed "with the reasonable expectation" that death would occur—and whether there was "a probability" that the defendant would commit future violent acts that would make him "a continuing threat to society." If the jury voted yes on both, Mark Robertson would be sentenced to death. The scheme was designed in part as a sort of executioner's hood for the jurors; they would only have to answer the two questions, not pronounce the actual death sentence.[7]

There was a loophole in Texas's two-question format that made the jurors' role a bit more confusing: The Supreme Court had required that a jury always be permitted to consider any evidence the defense wanted to present to show that a death sentence was inappropriate. Such mitigating factors might include a defendant's age, good works, hard-luck past, the influence of drugs, or even a mother's plea for mercy. The Court's requirement had to be grafted onto Texas's earlier two-question scheme, and trial judges did so by instructing jurors that they could spare the defendant on the basis of mitigating factors—even if they thought the accurate answers to the two jury questions was yes.

This rather bizarre setup made the penalty phase a freewheeling affair, with the prosecution trying to show that Robertson was a violent man and likely to remain so, and the defense aiming to reveal his warmer side as well as the extent of his past suffering. Though many of the jurors had already become emotionally involved in the case, all were jarred, and ultimately haunted, by what they now heard.

First Janice Warder, the no-nonsense prosecutor who had already impressed the jury with her clarity and efficiency, embarked on a brisk but exhaustive two-and-a-half-day presentation. On day one the jury learned that Mark had first been arrested at age twelve for spray-painting cars and that later in the year he had brought a loaded gun to school. On day two the prosecution revealed an attempted robbery at age fifteen and, ten days before the Brau killing, the murder of a 7-Eleven clerk, a crime to which Robertson had also confessed but for which he hadn't yet been tried. Net gain in the 7-Eleven robbery-murder: fifty-five dollars and a bag of potato chips. That made three killings—Edna Brau, her grandson, Sean, and the store clerk—between August 9 and August 19, 1989.

Day three, January 31, brought testimony regarding Robertson's attempt to escape from his cell in Las Vegas; he had dismantled a table to use as a battering ram and was chipping away at a plate-glass window when he was apprehended. Witnesses also revealed that he had boasted to other prisoners about the three Dallas murders. To some of the jurors, Mark's innocent appearance began to seem menacing in itself as they realized how much violence it concealed. Judith Holmes, a forty-one-year-old secretary, found it chilling that the defendant appeared so emotionless. Jack Smith saw it as a sign of Mark's lack of conscience. "This guy will just as soon kill you as order a cheeseburger," he thought as Warder closed the prosecution case. Gentle Anna Emmons, however, saw sorrow, rather than evil, in Mark's placid face.

The conscientious defense team had done some serious legwork of its own and had assembled a group of witnesses from all over the country to plead for Mark's life. Day four, February 4, 1991, would be make or break. Robertson's two older sisters, Carol and Denise, opened with the harrowing story of their father's drunken rages. When he was on a tear, they said, he had made his children stand at the foot of his bed for long stretches, usually until he passed out. He had made the girls bend over and touch their ankles as he hit them with a four-inch-thick board, while his favorite, Mark, had been forced to watch. Mark had sometimes been beaten, too, but not as often, they said. The girls would cry together afterward, but Mark had just withdrawn. "He'd let it go, and he never would show many expressions," Carol told the jury. Their mother had finally fled California for the Dallas area when Mark was eight, and she soon married school custodian Gary Runnels, who adopted the children when Mark was nine and treated them well, both sisters said.

Robertson had been in and out of drug clinics, and the defense lawyers wanted some of the counselors to testify about his hard work in trying to stop using drugs. But the lawyers decided they couldn't risk such testimony, because the prosecution would be able to elicit on cross-examination that Mark had discussed with the counselors some of his unsavory practices, such as killing cats for sport. Instead, cousins and a neighbor testified to Mark's strong efforts to adjust to a stable home and his mostly innocent youth, punctuated only by pranks and rebellions typical of adolescence.

Then his twenty-three-year-old ex-girlfriend, Circle Lisa Tallant, came forward to explain what might have triggered his murderous rage in August 1989. Blond and attractive, Circle cried through much of her testimony. Mark was working at a bowling alley when they met around Christmas 1988, she said, and they quickly became lovers and then housemates. She spoke glowingly of their early relationship. "He was great," she told the jury. "I mean, I never had a boyfriend like him. He gave in the relationship. He didn't take." There was never any violence, she said.

But Mark couldn't hold a job for very long, and sometimes he smoked marijuana with a friend while claiming to be job hunting. Meanwhile, she was supporting them both. For these reasons, she said, she decided at the end of May 1989 to kick him out. Shortly afterward Mark returned to the mobile home they had rented to pick up his things and saw a home pregnancy kit on the table, showing a positive result.

The realization that Circle was pregnant (and that he was apparently the father) stunned and excited Mark, who began calling her a hundred times a day, she said, and begging her to let him come back and marry her. "He said that I didn't have to do anything," she testified. "He would take care of the baby if I kept the baby." But she insisted she would have an abortion, and in July she told him she had done so, although she hadn't yet. Mark was crushed; his murderous spree began barely two weeks later. The last time he called her, the murders had already begun. Her mother had picked up the phone. "My mom said he was crying," Circle sobbed, "but I didn't get a chance to talk to him."

The pivotal day of testimony was capped by Mary Lou Runnels's plea for her son's life. Mark's mother described her first husband's drunken tirades each night, his belligerence, his constant abuse of her and the children. She spoke of her decision to flee, her fight to retrieve her children from their father, Mark's pain and confusion as an eight-year-old in a new home. She described his first use of marijuana in the fifth grade and his later efforts to kick his drug habit. She told of his kindness. "That's why I can't understand it. He would kiss us good-night. Hug us good-night every night," she said, sobbing. Though Judge McDowell had been impassive through most of the trial, now even he seemed moved, and he called for a break. When everyone returned, Mrs. Runnels's pain seemed only deeper. "Please let him live," she begged the twelve jurors, turning in their direction as both she and her son dissolved into tears.

The jurors' reactions were intense. Anna Emmons was deeply moved by Mrs. Runnels's words. "God, too, loves Mark," Anna later remembered thinking, "and he could still be saved." Judith Holmes, who had chosen to sit in a far corner of the jury box so that she could avoid looking at Robertson through her big red-rimmed glasses, felt desperately sorry for his mother. Judith was the divorced mother of a son who had also gone astray, and she knew the heartache firsthand, but did that mean a killer should be spared? Ray Truesdell, the oldest and most meticulous of the jurors, was taking notes each night and later described this day's testimony as painful. But he was a rational thinker, and to him a mother's love wasn't relevant to the rules on sentencing. Still others on the jury had their own reactions: sadness, anxiety, disgust, impatience, sympathy for the murderer's family or for the victim's.

That night many of the jurors couldn't think of anything else. Mark made another unscheduled appearance in juror Emily Bennett's dreams, as he had on previous nights, just walking through like a cameo actor. Her boss at General Instrument called her at six the next morning to talk about work, but although she was an ambitious young manager, she couldn't muster any interest. "Handle it, just handle it. Who cares?" she thought as she was asked to address problems that suddenly seemed ridiculously insignificant.

Judith Holmes didn't dream about Mark, but she saw his face in day reveries, staring at her emotionlessly but somehow mockingly. Meanwhile, in her garden apartment, Sue Warner collapsed on a couch and was seized by a sense of unreality. "The reality is the courthouse and sitting there," she thought. "The rest isn't real."

The two days that followed the Runnels plea added little of significance, except for the fact that Mark's favorite drug counselor had died of a brain tumor just as Mark appeared to be making progress. That, thought Judith Holmes, was a particularly bad break. The penalty phase of the trial culminated in a closing speech by defense lawyer Brook Busbee, who urged the Dallas jurors to concentrate not on the murder but on the image of Mark Robertson facing his own death. "I want you to imagine that you're in that death chamber and this man is strapped to a gurney and he's about to be lethally poisoned," she said, looking right into Judith's eyes, then Sue's and Anna's and the others'. "I want you to watch the life go out of him in your mind." Could they condemn a man to that fate?

At 12:45 P.M. on February 11 the Dallas jury retired to its small, tidy jury room to begin considering the profound questions of retribution and forgiveness that were before them. Much more anxious than during the guilt or innocence phase, the jurors weren't as amenable this time to Ray Truesdell's suggestions that they follow his rules of deliberation. Instead of holding a long discussion first, someone called for a quick vote on whether Mark Robertson had "deliberately" acted to put his victim to death. There was no doubt there. "You shoot someone in the back of the head, and you know that person will die," said Sue Warner. A unanimous tally followed.

Then, after a very short discussion, they jumped to a preliminary vote on question two: whether there was a probability that Mark would pose a future danger to society. It was a curious question on at least two grounds. First, the words *probability* and *society* weren't defined anywhere in the instructions. How probable did the probability have to be? Slightly more likely than not, or something greater? And where was society? Did it include prison? Or was it just the world outside the prison gates? In 1976 the Texas criminal appeals court had considered whether the question was too murky to be answered responsibly. Its conclusion: "We hold the phrase 'a probability' . . . is not so vague that men of common intelligence must guess as to its meaning and differ as to its application."[8]

But how were the jurors to predict dangerousness? There had been no testimony on acceptable or useful methods of prediction. Moreover, although the jurors didn't know this, extensive academic and clinical studies have shown that even the most sophisticated prediction methods by psychiatrists and psychologists are largely ineffective.

But courts have brushed off such results in ruling that jurors have the innate ability to make a prediction of dangerousness that is sufficiently accurate to warrant a sentence of death. For better or worse, efforts at scientific precision have to yield to an age-old faith: that the common sense of the common man—and woman—can produce a correct and just result. Such faith may seem anachronistic in an increasingly technical age. On the other hand, it's much the same faith that we place in voters to predict (on the basis of campaign advertising, candidate rhetoric, and old-fashioned character judgment) how the president they elect will behave in times of crisis.

In a secret ballot the Dallas jurors voted 9–3 that Robertson posed a future danger to society. Medical office manager Tamara Bell and Anna Emmons quickly identified themselves as having voted no. The third dissenter remained anonymous for a time. But when asked, Sue Warner—from the start, the most adamant opponent of capital punishment on the jury—acknowledged that she, too, would seek a life sentence instead of death.

It was about 2:00 P.M. In an attempt to shock the dissenters into relenting, some jurors called for the exhibits and spread them out on the table. There was the bullet that had killed Edna Brau, Sean's fishing pole, the gun, and the gruesome photos of Sean and Mrs. Brau with the backs of their heads blown off. Anna Emmons tried to avoid looking at the pictures, but when she did, she began to sob quietly. Judith Holmes also forced herself to look, as an antidote to the sympathy she felt for Mark's mother. Looking at the pictures required courage, and the demands of jury service in such a case had given these two jurors an extra dose. The fact that Judith's grandmother had died the week before the trial made her even more sensitive to Mrs. Brau's death. Staring at the photographs, Judith exclaimed, "I don't ever want to see that again, and this boy will do it." Still, she wasn't altogether certain Mark had to be executed to be kept from doing it.

With emotions running high, Ray Truesdell won back some of his authority by steering the conversation toward the mitigating circumstances they were supposed to consider. Was there anything they had heard in the past few days that made Mark's crime seem less terrible, that rendered him worthy of the chance to outgrow his baby face and his postadolescent violence?

Judith Holmes, the single mother of two boys, had already thought deeply about this question. She had favored capital punishment strongly at the start of trial, considering it a deterrent for at least some potential murderers. But having heard the testimony and dealt with the reality that Robertson might die—having seen and appreciated "the awful court of judgment"—she took the matter much more seriously than before. "It's one thing to believe in it, another to sit on a jury and have to decide," she reflected later.

She had avoided looking at Mark as much as possible during the trial—in some ways, he reminded her too much of her younger son, who had been in trouble with drugs—but she had watched him enough to see that he seemed to have neither sympathy nor remorse. He cried when his mother and ex-girlfriend spoke, she noted, but he never showed a glimmer of feeling when members of the victim's family testified or when gruesome photos of the murdered woman were shown. On the other hand, he was so very young.

When Ray suggested listing each potentially mitigating factor on a display board, Judith quickly took up the marker and started to write, eager to grapple actively with the issue. Child abuse. Drug abuse. Rejection by his girlfriend. His girlfriend's abortion. The death of his favorite drug counselor. His youth at the time of the crime. There was no objective way to evaluate these factors. All that mattered was how they influenced these twelve individuals, with their separate attitudes, backgrounds, and perceptions. This made the jurors' discretion virtually absolute. It also made their interaction more crucial.

Did Anna Emmons, Tamara Bell, and Sue Warner have the conviction or the stubbornness to remain holdouts? Did Ray Truesdell or Jack Smith have the moral authority to muffle the dissenters' opposition? Would someone with peacemaking skills nurtured at home or in an office find a way to unite the two sides? Such considerations might seem to cast doubt on the integrity of the jurors' decision making, since friendships and rivalries appear to say more about the little jury room world the jurors have created for themselves than about the facts of the case they have to decide. But these factors also can be understood as contributing to our most exalted vision of the jury room as a place where members of a group, by challenging one another's ideas, values, and loyalties, can achieve a coherent result.

The abuse that Mark had both endured and witnessed as a child was one potentially mitigating factor over which the jurors initially disagreed and about which they had to arrive at some sort of consensus. Society's attitudes toward childhood sexual abuse have changed markedly over the past century and again, perhaps, in the past decade. Freud dismissed many allegations of child sexual abuse as products of his female patients' fantasy lives. But by the early 1980s child abuse prosecutions were cropping up all over the country: against parents, day care operators, priests, teachers, cops. Lately there has been a backlash as some of the most sensational allegations—from those against Woody Allen to those against the proprietors of the McMartin Preschool in Southern California

—haven't held up in court.[9] Meanwhile, suspicions have grown that some children have been coaxed by parents or therapists to make unfounded charges and that some criminal defendants have made up or exaggerated instances of childhood abuse to justify violent acts. Three years after the Robertson trial, two juries in Los Angeles deadlocked over the question of whether Lyle and Erik Menendez had been guilty of murder when they'd shot their wealthy parents at pointblank range. The reason for the hung jurors' indecision: The Menendez brothers had claimed that their father had abused them for years, causing damage that defense lawyers argued had mitigated, if not negated, the brothers' crimes.

Jurors in the Robertson case, having been selected roughly at random from the community, could be expected to reflect some of the community's ambivalence on the issue. Stories of childhood abuse particularly haunted Sue Warner, who had taken psychology courses in college and had once been married to a psychologist. Mark hadn't been abused as badly as his sisters, she acknowledged. But she pointed out that the special treatment may have been even worse for Mark, infecting him with so-called survivor guilt. "I think it made Mark hate himself and want to die," she surmised. "He can't kill himself, so he'll let the state do it." Anna, listening quietly, thought this made some sense.

But Emily Bennett, and most of the others, weren't impressed. Allegations of child abuse were in vogue, Emily said; it was too easy an excuse. Besides, she said, Mark had left his abusive father by the age of eight. His stepfather had treated him kindly. At some point, she insisted, an individual becomes responsible for his acts regardless of past traumas. At age twenty-one, thirteen years after the last childhood beatings, surely Mark Robertson could be held accountable for murder. Clyde Stanley, thirty-five, a tanned, clean-cut cable maintenance worker, agreed. Living on the wrong side of the tracks, on a street lined with ramshackle houses and rusting pickup trucks, Clyde had nonetheless managed to straighten out his life. He didn't get into trouble anymore, as he had as a teen, and he was quietly proud of his stable lifestyle. The state-of-the-art video and sound system that was the centerpiece of a littered living room attested to what could be attained through hard work and clean living. Mark had messed up; he'd lost his chance. "The guy had so many breaks," Clyde said. "So many people tried to help him. He'd walk out. He didn't want the help."

For now Sue Warner was holding firm. But Anna Emmons was prepared, reluctantly, to acknowledge that Mark had had a chance to transcend his bad upbringing and that they couldn't spare him merely because he had once been abused. However, Mark's drug abuse and his attempts at rehabilitation did strike a chord with her. Here, suggested Anna, was a way out. Maybe, even though no supporting evidence had been offered, Mark had been under the influence of drugs when the crime occurred. Maybe he could get his drug problem under control and make something of his life, even in prison. But Judith Holmes knew all too much about drugs from her experience with her son, and that experience made her tougher on Mark than Anna could be, and ultimately much more convincing.

In our vision of the ideal jury, Judith Holmes's insights into her own life experiences would combine with those of eleven other jurors to make the group more knowledgeable, and perhaps wiser, than a single judge could ever be. In the Robertson case that ideal came close to being realized. After putting up with her younger son's drug use and disobedience for more than two years, Judith told the jurors, she had joined a tough-love group that had helped her insist that her son leave the house and not return unless he agreed to follow all the rules. Her son had drifted between his father's house and friends' apartments and had even landed on the streets for a while. But she'd held fast, and he had quit using drugs and eventually had returned home.

"He got down in the gutter and he was by himself and he supported himself and he just grew up. He realized that's no way to live," she had told the lawyers during jury selection. Now she reminded the jury that Mark had been given plenty of opportunities for drug rehabilitation and had chosen to walk away from them. Wasn't his trouble his responsibility now? Anna Emmons, who hadn't had any experiences like Judith's, was impressed enough to start searching for yet another argument for sparing the defendant.

None of the remaining mitigating factors that were proposed, however, managed to generate much support from Anna or the others. The discussion succeeded, instead, in solidifying Judith's view that she had to vote for death; it also convinced Tamara Bell to join the pro-execution side. Tamara had begun the deliberations believing that Mark's murders had been part of a single spree and that he had had no time to reflect in between. His earlier crimes had been insignificant. "He spray-painted cars. Whoop-de-doo," she said. Considering what he had just been through, including the recent rejection by his girlfriend, perhaps his violence had been an aberration. Perhaps he wouldn't turn violent again.

As is often the case in jury deliberations, Tamara needed a guide—someone she trusted and respected—to lead her to the majority view without making her feel as if she had abandoned her principles. Ray was rigorous but perhaps too rigid for the role of conciliator; he could direct but not necessarily persuade. Emily Bennett, the forewoman, was strong-willed, snappy, and smart, but not always sympathetic. Anyway, she had backed off from the heat of battle, choosing for long stretches to sit at a desk away from the jury's table. Clyde Stanley, the cable technician, was earnest and well liked but not very articulate. Cliff McBryde, a thirty-one-year-old building maintenance man who played solitaire in the jury room during slack time, was adamantly, and impatiently, in favor of the death penalty. Two of the youngest jurors, Diane Gibbs and Denise Duguay, were followers in the jury room, never leaders.

That left Jack Smith, who at fifty-one was the second-oldest juror. A specialist in client satisfaction as a manager for the local phone equipment company, he projected both competence and modesty. Seated next to Tamara, he gently pointed out that Robertson had committed his murders over a ten-day period—the same number of days, he noted, that the jurors had been listening to testimony in this case. "Look how long that has seemed," he said. From the time of Mark's 7-Eleven murder to the killings of Sean and Mrs. Brau, he'd had plenty of time to come to his senses. Three murders demanded more mitigation than just one, Jack reasoned. Nothing in Mark's background could explain away his behavior.

"That's what convinced me," Tamara said later. "He had the opportunity to walk away from each murder, and he didn't. Had we tried him for the first murder [at the 7-Eleven], I don't think I could have voted death because that could have been precipitated by things in his life that just put him over the edge."

Because Anna Emmons was the first identified dissenter after Tamara switched sides and perhaps also because she seemed easier to sway than Sue, all eyes now turned to her. What was her problem? Cliff McBryde wanted to know. What part of the case wasn't she sure of?

Anna said she knew that the murder had been deliberate and that Mark would probably kill again. Even so, she said softly, she wanted to avoid the death penalty and wanted to seek another option. Keeping him in prison might protect society, she said, and would certainly punish him enough. It would also give him the chance to redeem himself, to reform and repent.

Judith Holmes had struggled with this issue too and, though much more battle-worn than Anna, was similarly religious and deeply sympathetic toward her. Now Judith tried to take advantage of Anna's obedient nature to convince her to change her vote. "You have to answer the questions as they're put by the law, even though it results in death. You need to answer each separately," Judith suggested.

Anna held fast. "I don't believe in the death penalty," she said. "You can talk until you're blue in the face. I'm just not going to sentence someone to death."

Because she knew she was one of only two holdouts, Anna felt she would bear extra responsibility for Mark Robertson's death if she changed her mind. And she couldn't help thinking that while Mark might be dangerous right now, he could still make something of his life. "There's some good in everyone," she kept saying.

So the others changed tacks, having noticed that Anna had appeared scared of Mark. Even if he were never released, Emily Bennett said, he might murder an innocent prison guard or another inmate. A prison official had testified that Mark couldn't be isolated entirely; therefore, he'd remain dangerous. Moreover, they had no assurance that he wouldn't escape or somehow get out. Several jurors asked Anna how she'd feel if she ran into him in a shopping mall parking lot or on a dark street. Anna knew they were suggesting that he'd be paroled someday, and she believed them.

Feeling on shaky ground, Anna said that nevertheless, she didn't want to be responsible for killing Mark. Jack Smith listened sympathetically, but he thought that Anna was being too weak. With the firmness of a longtime military man, he felt he had a responsibility to make sure the jury came to grips with its duty, however harsh. "I'm not here to give mercy. I'm here to give justice. If justice means death, that's what we should do," he said.

Like the others, Anna had given her oath that she "would make true answers to such questions as may be propounded to you . . . so help you God." So, in addition to being afraid of Mark—she'd already had terrible nightmares about the crime—she recognized a moral obligation to follow the jury instructions, her views on the death penalty notwithstanding. In her mind the true answer to both jury questions was yes. The mitigating factors weren't sufficient to alter those answers. Ray Truesdell, the juror she respected the most, suggested gently that she answer the questions honestly and leave the consequences to others in the legal process.

At around 7:00 P.M. she reluctantly agreed. Ray, feeling fatherly, went over to comfort her. "Anna is such a considerate individual," he said later. "I thought she wouldn't hurt a fly."

There was only one dissenter left, Sue Warner. Where Anna had been mostly weepy and docile, Sue was combative. Her arsenal included a firm belief that the death penalty didn't deter crime and the knowledge that regardless of the proper answers to questions one and two, she had the power as a juror to refuse to join the others in their vote—to refuse, in effect, to play by the rules.

That Sue Warner knew this was surprising because it's a well-kept secret of our justice system. But part of what gives juries their strength is the surprisingly wide range of information to which one member or another becomes privy over a dozen lifetimes. In Sue Warner's case she had read in *The Wall Street Journal* the previous month that a jury rights group, the Fully Informed Jury Association, had been created to spread the word to jurors that they have an absolute power to refuse to follow the law if they consider it unjust. This power, known as jury nullification, has been used often in death penalty cases throughout history, most notably in Britain in the

nineteenth century when juries rebelled against capital punishment for petty theft and other minor offenses. It also was
used by the colonial jury that in 1735 acquitted John Peter
Zenger of the crime he'd clearly committed, speaking ill of a
government official. And it was used by the Wyoming jury
that rejected a country judge's "legal horseshit" in reaching
the decision that Maude shouldn't be punished for giving
Benny a bashing that he deserved.[10]

The power helps keep the justice system flexible and open
to acts of mercy. And as long as jury deliberations are secret
and not open to judicial scrutiny, the power of nullification
cannot be taken away. It also was—and is—a unique part of
our legal system that could not be preserved if the jury system
was abolished and power was turned over to judges duty
bound to follow the law.

Sue knew that she couldn't be punished for insisting on
remaining a holdout and that she could vote no even if all the
facts of the case dictated the answer yes. She had even mentioned this power when the other jurors were trying to convince Anna that she had to follow the rules, but no one had
believed her. The judge hadn't mentioned this power in his
instructions (indeed, judges almost never do because they
want the law to be followed), and the other jurors had never
heard about it.[11]

Given her views, there wasn't much the other jurors could
say to try to sway Sue, and their impotence made some of
them angry. Cliff McBryde asked over and over what she
needed to hear to convince her. "Would you want Mark living
next door to you?" Cliff asked. "What if you ran into him on
the street? What if he killed someone?"

She responded by shouting at Cliff and the others, "Shut
up. Leave me alone. I won't say another word." Stubbornly
she added, "There's nothing you can say that will change my
mind."

———

But Cliff, despite his stridency, was on to something. And he and the others kept hammering away at it. While Sue didn't believe that the death penalty deterred others from committing crimes, she knew it certainly put the defendant out of action; at least Mark Robertson would never kill again. And as she reviewed the case, while the evening wore on, she became more and more convinced that he would kill if given the chance. She decided she didn't care much about the jail population, only about whether Mark would be released. Since she assumed he would be paroled at some point, she finally agreed, reluctantly, to join the others. "What swayed me was, if he did it again, how would I feel?" she said after the trial.

At about 8:00 P.M. Emily tallied the votes: unanimous on deliberateness, unanimous on future dangerousness. She contacted the bailiff, who alerted the judge, who called the court back into session. The bailiff handed the verdict form to Judge McDowell, who read out the answers to the two questions. Then the judge called each juror's name and asked if this was his or her verdict. Each in turn said yes. Tears streamed down Anna's face. Sue frowned. Mark Robertson looked calm, but his eyes widened suddenly, and he jumped a little as the result hit home. Then the jurors were ushered back into the jury room, so they wouldn't hear the judge formally translate their answers into a sentence of death.

For Robertson, this was just the beginning of the legal process. It would take close to a year for a trial transcript to be printed. Then a new appeals attorney would review the record, looking for errors by the trial judge. The case would be appealed through the state court system, where it would be entitled to an automatic review by the Texas Court of Criminal Appeals, the top criminal court in the state. After that court upheld the sentence, Mark's lawyer would proceed up the federal court ladder, arguing violations of Mark's federal constitutional rights. If it got that far, last-minute stays would be sought from the U.S. Supreme Court. New arguments would likely be made that hadn't been made in lower courts: perhaps that Mark hadn't been competently represented at trial, perhaps that the judge had been biased in some way, perhaps that some new evidence had emerged. If all these hurdles were cleared, by the turn of the new century the jury's action in February 1991 might result in Mark Robertson's death.[12]

The verdict ended the jurors' active role in the trial, but it didn't stop affecting their lives. Talking to them after the trial was like having a conversation with someone who was just back from Nepal or who'd just had sex for the first time. They betrayed the same sense of wonder at having been to a new place and having seen life differently. There was enormous excitement, an eagerness to talk about the experience at the slightest provocation, and a great deal of worry about the consequences of their actions.

In the last century de Tocqueville had described jury service as a peerless teacher of citizenship, and that role seemed powerfully alive in Dallas in 1991. With the exception of Anna Emmons and Sue Warner, all the jurors had been quite comfortable with the idea of capital punishment prior to the trial. Now, having sentenced a man to death, they saw the issue far more personally and didn't think it was at all clear. Although the Dallas jurors were the only people among their friends, families, and colleagues who had ever sentenced someone to death, suddenly they were the softest-hearted, least callous, least militant people in their circles.

Carlton Roark, who had believed all along that a person forfeits his right to live if he commits a heinous crime, nonetheless blanched at the thought of the execution itself. "I couldn't kill somebody, no matter what the reason," he said shortly after he and the others had mandated such a killing. He now considered the decision to sentence Robertson the most important of his life, and by far the most sobering. When he returned to work, people asked him, "Did you fry the sucker?" It was the kind of comment Carlton might unthinkingly have made before his jury experience. Now he responded angrily, "That's no attitude."

Tamara Bell found her friends at work and church far more understanding. Still, some people asked, "Did you hang him?"

"Yes," she answered tersely. "It made me so mad because they were so cavalier," she explained. "It was a really tough decision that shouldn't be taken lightly." After the case she took to reading the newspapers closely for news of executions. "They just seem to jump off the page," she said.

Emily Bennett, who liked to come across as tough and irreverent, found that the case had made her much more fearful of crime and significantly more sober about criminal justice issues. "I've always been very flippant about criminal cases, that we should take criminals out and shoot them," she reflected shortly after the trial. "But I'm more serious about it now."

The experience seemed to have scarred Sue Warner, who became even more militantly anti–death penalty. Although she didn't regret the way she had voted, she felt bitter about having had to serve and said she would attempt never to serve on such a case again. Although she had gotten along well with Emily and Judith, two strong, independent women, she did not ask for their phone numbers, as many jurors who make friends do. The case had made her feel tainted, she said, as if she and the other jurors had been involved in some wrongdoing together.

Sue Warner's reaction was far from unusual among jurors

in high-stakes cases, researchers have found. Indeed, jury service in such cases often triggers a range of stress-related problems, including upset stomachs, heart palpitations, headaches, sexual inhibitions, depression, chills, and fever. Some court systems now even provide counseling to jurors after emotionally wrenching cases.

No one offered therapy sessions to the Robertson jurors, although some of them might have benefited from a chance to talk with a counselor about what they had been through. The first two weeks after the case, Judith Holmes said, she was "a blithering idiot" in her secretarial job. "I couldn't type or think straight. I thought, 'Who cares?' " But at home, having struggled to understand the factors that had contributed to Mark's drug abuse and having thought deeply about the pain of growing up, she somehow became more understanding of her nineteen-year-old son than she had been in years. He, in turn, respected her more for having served on the case and having taken on so important a responsibility. "He understands why I'm against drugs so much, that it can lead to murder," she said. "We can talk better. He thinks Mom's not so dumb after all."

Of all the jurors, Anna Emmons, predictably, had the strongest reaction to the case. At first she fantasized about writing an anonymous letter to Mark in prison, telling him that God loved him and would forgive him. But she decided that that would be too dangerous. He might figure out who she was, and she didn't want him to develop any kind of fixation on her. So she ventured to a friend's church which had a prison ministry and told the head of the ministry about Mark. She asked him to go to Huntsville, where the death row inmates are imprisoned, to seek Mark out and to try to steer him toward God. The minister, she said, agreed. "I think about Mark 'most every other day. I pray for him. I worry about him," Anna said a month after the trial. "Mark seems sad.

But God is forgiving and merciful. Anyone can start over anew.''

Nonetheless, thoughts of Mark filled her with fear as well as charity. Shortly after the trial ended, Anna became so frightened that she felt compelled to drive by the Brau house at night to look at the crime scene. She had nightmares about the crime. She put new locks on her doors. Even many months later she'd walk through a shopping mall in some strange city where her Delta plane had landed and think she saw Mark and be terrified. Then she'd feel a wave of relief, knowing not only that he was safely tucked away in prison, not only that he'd never get out, but also that someday he would be gone forever.

None of these jurors' reactions would have seemed all that strange to American jurors one hundred, two hundred, or even three hundred years ago. Our juries have always sprung up from our communities and reflected our communities' weaknesses and their strengths. They have groped toward a common understanding of the facts, sought to make their verdicts just as well as lawful, and then gone back to the places they had been. Like other citizen soldiers, jurors have often felt different upon their return.

In 1920 author John Galsworthy got to the heart of the institution, as Anna Emmons, Judith Holmes, and the other Robertson jurors came to know it, in a story called "The Juryman." He described the effects of jury service on a respected businessman who comes to identify with the plight of the troubled defendant, a soldier who attempts suicide because he misses his wife. Coming home from court, the businessman "had a yearning, not for his wife's kisses, but for her understanding. He wanted to go to her and say: 'I've learnt a lot to-day—found out things I never thought of. Life's a wonderful thing, Kate, a thing one can't live all to oneself; a thing one shares with everybody, so that when another suffers, one suffers too. It's come to me that what one *has* doesn't matter a bit—it's what one does, and how one sympathises with other people. It came to me in the most extraordinary vivid way, when I was on that jury watching that poor little rat of a soldier in his trap; it's the first time I've ever felt—the—spirit of Christ, you know.' "[13]

Whatever one thinks of the death penalty, the Robertson trial was a jury success story, and not just because of its impact on the jurors. Because there was a jury, Mark Robertson's lawyers got to help pick the people who were to decide his fate. The defense lawyers didn't like the result, of course, but the jury they helped select at least paid attention to every detail. Even a farfetched legal argument had been taken seriously before it was properly rejected. Deliberations during the sentencing phase had engaged the jurors' heads and hearts, as befits a discussion of another man's life.

The Robertson jury had a great deal going for it that many of today's juries—the ones we second-guess and so often despise—do not. The stakes were so high that no one dared daydream or doze off. The facts were straightforward; the legal issues, relatively clear. The case was of manageable length. The lawyers were equally matched. But in the chapters to come, as we meet other juries whose work falls disappointingly short, it's worth remembering the Robertson jury and then returning to consider the vision it reflects and the hope it still may inspire.

Part II

THE
DISAPPOINTMENT

—

The jury system puts a ban upon intelligence and honesty, and a premium upon ignorance, stupidity, and perjury. It is a shame that we must continue to use a worthless system because it *was* good a thousand years ago.

—Mark Twain, *Roughing It*[1]

W e sense, rather than know, that the jury isn't working properly. We don't know for certain because no one can measure how many jury verdicts are "correct" and how many are "wrong." One reason is that there are more jury trials each year than could possibly be studied. Another is that truth and justice are elusive commodities. There are no absolute authorities on how to determine the former or achieve the latter.

Perhaps as a result, worries about the performance of juries have been expressed ever since the first juries delivered the first verdicts. Even the classical precursor to the modern jury, the 501-member dicastery of ancient Greece, was the subject of ridicule. Aristophanes peopled his play *The Wasps* with jurors who were drunk with power and suckers for flattery. The character Philocleon positively gloats as he describes his role in a trial: "Tremblingly the father sues for grace and pardon then/As though I were a god to grant forgiveness unto men."[2]

Over time the critical themes have been quite consistent. Juries have been derided as lazy, biased, easily inflamed, and, most frequently, incompetent. In 1603 a British judge refused to let a jury decide a complicated case because, according to a report from the time, "the Court was better able to judge then [*sic*] a jury of ploughmen."[3]

In recent years such age-old concerns about the jury have

been supplemented by some significant new ones. Commercial lawsuits have become much more complex than business disputes of the eighteenth and nineteenth centuries, stretching and often overwhelming the capacity of jurors to comprehend. The emergence of legal doctrines providing for cash awards for numerous psychological harms has given jurors new opportunities to punish the rich, and many juries seem to have leaped at the chance. And marketers and social scientists have entered the scene, bringing new forces into play. These jury consultants have proved, ominously, that they can harness social science methods to help select juries that will serve the interests of whichever party pays for the consultants' services. Truth and justice are hardly the aim.

People who are disappointed with the work of American juries are starting to move beyond the worrying and complaining stage. State legislators who believe that juries are antibusiness are pushing through new laws that bar jurors from awarding more than a particular sum to injured individuals. And some corporate groups are trying to convince appeals courts to repeal the right to a jury trial in complex commercial cases. One business lawyer, Patrick Lynch, has argued the point this way: "Whatever criticisms might be leveled at the intellectual qualifications of the average federal judge, each of them has such minimal intellectual equipment as to have passed a bar examination, and presumably to have completed college and law school. This alone creates a probability that the powers of comprehension of a federal judge will exceed those of the average juror."[4]

Such efforts should not be taken lightly. In some countries following the British legal model, concerns such as those now being voiced in the United States (along with cost considerations) led to the gradual removal of juries from almost all types of civil disputes during the past fifty years. And the U.S. mass media's intense interest in court cases guarantees that any apparent misstep by any jury in any big case will receive immediate national attention and feed our sense of pessimism and disappointment.

We are, after all, already veterans of the absurd $10.5 billion jury award against Texaco in a takeover-related battle with Pennzoil in a Houston court in 1986. In that case jurors explained afterward that they had added $1 billion to the award for each of the Texaco witnesses they had most despised. Following appeals involving some of the best lawyers in the country, the parties settled for $3 billion, after Texaco landed temporarily in bankruptcy court. To the business community, the case remains a potent symbol of what one jury can do at any time to any company.[5]

Then there was Bensonhurst. The trial centered on a mob's beating and shooting of a young black man named Yusuf Hawkins in a mostly white neighborhood in Brooklyn, New York. Two of the defendants were tried together for murder, and two juries were seated so that either one could be asked to leave when testimony relevant to only one of the defendants was heard. After a monthlong trial defendant Joseph Fama was convicted of murder charges on the theory that he had acted "in concert" with the triggerman. But the other defendant, Keith Mondello, who'd confessed that he'd been the ringleader of the gang, was acquitted under the same standard. The split verdicts simply didn't make sense, and in the avalanche of newspaper columns and street demonstrations that followed, the jury system came across as an awfully feeble force for criminal justice and racial healing.[6]

Most famously, of course, there was the Rodney King case, which became a lightning rod for criticism of the American jury. After the acquittal of the white police officers who kicked and beat King and after the Los Angeles riots that the verdict sparked, jurors in the case attempted to explain their verdict as a rational application of the law to the relevant facts. But the beating had been clearly visible to millions of Americans who had viewed the amateur videotape of the scene on TV. How could the white suburban jurors have acquitted the police officers, millions wondered, unless racism had played at least a part?[7]

Of course, these were just isolated, well-publicized verdicts —a handful among the one million or more jury verdicts nationwide between 1986 and 1993.[8] And like a team that never seems to win the big games, the jury surely owes some of its Cubs-like reputation to its dismal performance in these few extraordinary cases. But other disappointing news about the jury has emerged in recent years from dozens of academic studies of ordinary cases. In these studies observers have identified inadequacies in the ways juries are selected, trained, and instructed—and terrible flaws in the way they reach their decisions.

The best of the studies was conducted by the American Bar Association's section on litigation and released in 1989. The researchers convinced a number of judges to allow extra alternate jurors to be seated for trials of complicated cases. Afterward the alternates were sent off to deliberate separately from the actual jurors and were videotaped. This method enabled the ABA to circumvent the usual prohibition against taping real jury deliberations and provided a unique look at four almost real deliberations. (Indeed, in at least one case the alternates thought they were actually deciding the case.)[9]

The committee's conclusion was that "many jurors were confused, misunderstood the instructions, failed to recall evidence, and suffered enormously from boredom and frustration." Viewers of the videotapes of the deliberations might conclude that this was an understatement. Many of the jurors, like many of those we meet in this section of the book, were simply out of their league. But if they were failing the jury system, perhaps the jury system—by neglecting to explain in a concise, comprehensible way the facts and the law, not to mention the jury's function—was failing them too. One juror who sat in one of the cases the ABA studied left a note in the jury room that seemed to reflect the frustration of many mystified, cooped-up American jurors:

> *Oh, give me a break, just a ten-minute break,*
> *When I don't have to sit and listen to this shit,*
> *Oh, give me a chance to get up and dance,*
> *For it's such a bore, I long for the door.*

2

LAWYERS' POKER

—

I MELDA Marcos was famous worldwide for throwing the most extraordinary parties. As First Lady of the Philippines she had mixed power with extravagance, descending on one continent after another to dazzle and cajole prime ministers, presidents, and kings. She had whirled on countless dance floors, ordered up glittering festivals amid the poverty of Manila, and invariably found an opportunity to belt out one plaintive love song after another.

But the party Imelda hosted in New York City on July 14, 1990, while comparatively modest, may have been her most astonishing. It took place eleven days after a federal jury in New York had cleared her of charges that she'd stolen and spent hundreds of millions of dollars belonging to her own people. Now the renowned Iron Butterfly, widowed and exiled at the age of sixty, was throwing the doors open to two hundred friends and supporters in the elegant community room atop her home in Manhattan's Dag Hammarskjöld Plaza.

It was an uproarious affair, all the more so because there had been so little to celebrate for so long. A belly dancer, courtesy of codefendant Adnan Khashoggi, gyrated across the floor. Imelda, who claimed to have sung for General Douglas MacArthur when she was a young beauty back in the Philippines, looked radiant again as she tore into "God Bless America," the Philippine national anthem, and, of course, the ubiquitous "Feelings." There was roast pig and wine and dancing; there were congratulations and hugs. And the guests of honor were none other than ten of the twelve jurors who had set Mrs. Marcos free to shop again—and perhaps someday to reclaim the power she and her late husband, Ferdinand, had lost.

Dressed in their finest clothes, the jurors arrived by subway from steaming hot apartments in less elegant quarters of the city, most bringing along a mother or a husband or a daughter to share in the splendor. They were quickly seated at a dais commanding a view of the room and the skyline beyond, and the stately Imelda greeted them one by one, assuring them that they were all one family now. To emphasize the point, she gave each an autographed photograph of herself, signed "with love and appreciation always," and a pin of the American and Philippine flags, which she solemnly affixed to their clothes.

Later the jurors were ushered one by one toward the microphone, where each thanked Imelda for her hospitality and wished her well. She returned the compliments by singing a song that had been written just for them. "It was so beautiful," marveled juror Yvonne Granberry, a forty-eight-year-old teacher's aide from Harlem. "It was swank; it was plush. I don't think I'll ever go to a bash like that again." Said another juror, fifty-five-year-old postal worker Anna Sneed: "I can't get over what a simply lovely person Mrs. Marcos is."

When word of the party filtered back to the Philippines, it was denounced by Marcos opponents as evidence that the trial had been fixed, that the American jurors had joined the

Marcos clique, and even that they had been on the take. This wasn't true, of course. Imelda hadn't bought the jurors' affection and loyalty. They were freely, even eagerly given. But why? What had a jury of lower-middle-class people from New York—who together couldn't have bankrolled a single day of decent shopping for Imelda—found so appealing about her? Why had they sided with her at her trial, and why had they been moved to celebrate with her rather than quietly go back to their lives?

Answering these questions means coming to grips with some of the jury system's greatest inadequacies and tracing them to their source. As the Marcos trial will illustrate, some jurors succumb all too easily to emotional appeals. Some are stymied by the least bit of complexity. Many filter facts through such a thick mesh of prejudice that the facts become unrecognizable. Common sense mutates into mutual delusion. And the unfortunate reality is that this isn't always an accident. Through the deceptive, frequently cynical process of jury selection, lawyers can and often do steer some of the least capable and least fair-minded people on to some of the most important cases.

In the Marcos case we'll witness in unusual detail how one jury in one high-profile case was picked. But the selection techniques involved are more or less standard throughout the country, in big cases and small. They go a long way toward explaining what makes so many jury verdicts and the deliberations that produce them so disappointing. It's also worth remembering that the use of these techniques is hardly inevitable. They've developed through common practice, court rules, and legislation. They're nowhere in the Constitution, and they can be changed.

How should a jury be composed? Our vision is of a cross section of the community, people of all backgrounds, a variety of occupations, a range of income levels and educational attainments. The jury attracts the fairest people, excludes or discourages the biased and easily manipulated. And it is capable of performing the basic tasks of jury service. As one federal court has put it, "The law presumes that a jury will find facts and reach a verdict by rational means. It does not contemplate scientific precision but does contemplate a resolution of each issue on the basis of a fair and reasonable assessment of the evidence and a fair and reasonable application of the relevant legal rules."[1]

Picking any jury, ideal or otherwise, begins with identifying the people who are potentially eligible to serve and summoning them to appear. In federal cases, such as the Marcos trial, the overall pool is derived primarily from voter registration records and is relatively free of restrictions, thanks in large measure to a 1968 law that bars discrimination "on account of race, color, religion, sex, national origin, or economic status."[2] There are some basic requirements: citizenship, English-language literacy, lack of a criminal record. And there are some automatic ways out: current work as a soldier, firefighter, police officer, or public official. Then there's a vast, amorphous zone of possible exits under the category of "undue hardship or extreme inconvenience."

Squeezing into the friendly "hardship" category is an art form practiced by many busy, well-educated people who otherwise would make excellent jurors in cases such as Marcos's. The ease with which people can remove themselves from consideration is one reason that while 80 million Americans have been called for jury duty in state or federal court, fewer than half of those called have ever sat on a jury. The biggest category of excuses: work-related conflicts. It was not surprising, then, that about half the 150 people who showed up for Marcos jury duty on March 15, 1990, made a beeline to the jury clerk's office to plead to be excused. About 50 got off on the spot.[3]

The prosecutors in the case, who were present in the room, shrugged knowingly; lots of college graduates who'd be good at sorting through the complex financial evidence in the case were, as expected, already racing for the exits. Though records weren't kept of the precise breakdown of those excluded in the Marcos case, such results were documented with shocking clarity in the Watergate-related Mitchell-Stans trial in the same New York federal court in 1974. Of the 196 people who were initially called, 88 had attended some college. But by the time 85 had been let go after claiming some hardship that precluded service, 38 had been excused for showing signs of prejudice, and others had been excluded for various reasons by the lawyers, the jury included only a single person who had advanced past high school.[4]

The flight from jury service is as old as the jury system itself; indeed, a seventeenth-century British pamphlet bemoaned it.[5] But it seems to have intensified in recent years, in part because jury duty has lost much of its aura of honor. Earlier in the century many courts selected jurors through a so-called keyman method, under which community leaders identified capable members of their churches and social clubs to be included on the jury rolls. The system made jury service a mark of distinction and helped fill jury rooms with better-educated people. It also was racist and elitist. The selection method was properly scrapped, but the one that's replaced it has been nearly comically lenient about letting many potentially competent jurors off the hook.

Even those who aren't let off at the outset may be excluded later, in the stage of jury selection in which lawyers exercise their so-called peremptory challenges. These challenges let lawyers exclude a limited number of prospective jurors—generally between three and fifteen, depending on the type of case—without having to give a reason. And this permits lawyers to reject people who they suspect are predisposed against their client but who haven't said anything extreme enough to qualify for automatic, or for-cause, exclusion. The Supreme Court has said the purpose of peremptory challenges is "to assure the parties that the jurors before whom they try the case will decide on the basis of the evidence placed before them, and not otherwise."[6]

But the Supreme Court's vision of peremptory challenges, and the reality that jurors and lawyers know, are entirely different. The truth is that trial lawyers with cases to win don't necessarily want conscientious juries; they want favorable juries. And often, particularly when their cases are weak, the best approach may be to seat jurors who are readily swayed by their feelings or easily confused. This approach turns the Supreme Court's theory on its head, because it leads inevitably to the removal of many of the most capable and impartial jurors from the panel. A sizable industry of lawbook publishers, videotape producers, and consultants has emerged to profit from lawyers' hunger for tips on how to do this. One advertisement for a jury selection primer reminds lawyers that "a lawyer who can pack the jury with persons whose life experiences, values, and personality incline them to the lawyer's position has won a significant battle in the overall war." The publisher assures lawyers that its book "shows you how to assemble your winning jury, step-by-step." The ad emphasizes that the "impartial juror" is a myth.[7]

Most experienced lawyers think they know how to spot favorable jurors without the help of how-to books. Over the years the legal profession has perpetuated a vast, mostly secretive lore concerning what sorts of people make what sorts of jurors, and these classifications usually weigh heavily toward ethnic, class, and racial stereotypes. Fabled criminal defense lawyer Clarence Darrow gave the public a rare peek at some of these in a May 1936 article in *Esquire* magazine titled "Attorney for the Defense." In it Darrow revealed his prime candidates for peremptory challenges, among them the "cold as the grave" Presbyterian, the "almost always sure to convict" Scandinavian, the "solemn" Christian Scientist, and, worst of all, the very rich because, wrote Darrow, "next to the Board of Trade, for him, the Penitentiary is the most important of all public buildings." Darrow acknowledged that he wasn't seeking justice in the abstract. "The lawyer's idea of justice," he declared with an honesty that's still refreshing, "is a verdict for his client, and really this is the sole end for which he aims."

In the Marcos case the prosecution had six challenges, the defense team ten, to be divided between Marcos and her co-defendant, Saudi Arabian arms merchant Khashoggi. Whom would the lawyers seek to unseat and to seat? On the defense side, Khashoggi lawyer James Linn, a lean, elegant sixty-year-old with a Clark Gable mustache, would be looking, first and foremost, at a juror's race. He'd found in past cases that blacks had generally been more sympathetic to criminal defendants than had whites. Also, he had discovered that blacks had displayed a healthy mistrust of the government, which was to bear a particularly heavy burden in this politically sensitive prosecution.

In addition, Linn planned to try to avoid seating engineers or mathematicians. These people, he thought, must be excluded because they tended to be too exacting, not seeing the gray areas of life, the ambiguities inherent in all behavior. Although of Irish lineage himself, Linn was also skeptical of Irish-American jurors because they generally supported police and prosecutors. Age and sex mattered to Linn as well. Middle-aged women, he believed, would be best. They'd be sympathetic to the defendants, suspicious of the male authorities who had ordered the indictment, and perhaps more readily enticed than men would be by Linn's own charm, gallantry, and good looks.

Although Imelda's lawyer, Gerry Spence of Jackson, Wyoming, insisted on wearing western boots, a fringed suede jacket, and a cowboy hat amid the canyons of Wall Street, many attorneys considered him the most sophisticated trial lawyer in America. Openly derisive of Ivy League lawyers who went by the book, he was often coarse and bombastic in court and out. But he nonetheless commanded wide respect for his powerful instincts and showstopping oratory—not to mention his record of not having lost a jury trial in twenty-one years.

Spence, too, had his favored collection of stereotypes, which differed somewhat from Linn's. When representing a criminal defendant, he preferred men to women because he believed men had more experience with hell-raising and were more forgiving of it. He also liked fat people more than thin ones because he believed that fat people lacked self-control and wouldn't demand as much law-abiding discipline from others. The old were preferable to the young because older people had more understanding of human frailties. Yuppies were the worst jurors: They feared crime, loved property, and hadn't suffered enough to be sympathetic to the accused.

The Marcos defense team had a special interest in identifying jurors who said they knew little, if anything, about the defendants. Pretrial publicity had been heavy, and the attention devoted to Imelda Marcos had been consistently negative, even gloating in tone. A columnist had dubbed the case "the last of the great Evil Women Trials." Cartoons had made merciless fun of Imelda's fondness for shoes. Anyone aware of the media's version, Spence would explain later, "had a preconceived prejudice against my client. Even I did. This was the universal view."

Chief prosecutor Charles LaBella, a tough customer with

little glitz, couldn't afford to be as choosy as the defense lawyers because he had fewer challenges at his disposal. The imbalance is customary in federal criminal cases and is meant to redress what seems a greater imbalance: the fact that many people assume a defendant is guilty merely because the government has gone to the trouble of charging him with a crime. The defendants' four extra peremptory challenges in the Marcos case presumably would compensate a bit for the prosecution's head start.

While LaBella was alert to the familiar juror stereotypes, he'd probably only have enough peremptories to exclude jurors who appeared to be dead set against the government. To the extent that he could choose further, he'd prefer seating intelligent jurors who would be able to keep up with the complex documentary evidence in the case and levelheaded people not easily swayed by appeals to sympathy.

The challenges would all be exercised after completion of the judge's and lawyers' interviews with each prospective juror, the so-called voir dire, translated variously as "to speak the truth" or "true talk." These interviews, which usually lasted about twenty minutes each, began in Judge John F. Keenan's robing room on Tuesday, March 20, 1990. There were still quite a few alert and well-informed juror candidates left on March 20; the voir dire would eliminate most of them.

One was chemist David Gong. Like the other prospects, he had filled out a thirty-two-page questionnaire to provide the lawyers with information about his background, interests, and attitudes. It revealed that he liked to read *Science* magazine and didn't watch much TV. He knew that Ferdinand Marcos was the former president of the Philippines, that Corazon Aquino was the current leader, and that Imelda Marcos owned an abundance of shoes. But he said in his interview that he wouldn't hold this against her because the whole subject was trivial. He said he didn't think wealthy people were more likely than poorer people to be guilty of crimes. He was intelligent, respectful, and articulate.

He didn't make it. After the judge sent him home for the day, the defense team marked him down as a likely juror to exclude, and they later removed him through a peremptory challenge. Gong was too analytic, like an engineer or an accountant, figured T. Barry Kingham, a clean-cut big-firm lawyer from New York who was working as local counsel with Linn. Another mark against Gong was that he was Asian, an indication, according to Spence, that a juror would believe in hierarchies and respect such authorities as the federal prosecutors. A thoughtful juror, probably, but not a favorable one for the defense.

Zachary Berman was another potential juror who didn't stand a chance. Interviewed on the second day of voir dire, Wednesday, March 21, Berman, forty-nine, seemed well equipped to decide a complex case of great public importance. He told the judge he had a graduate degree in urban planning and a job with a child protection agency, investigating abuse. He was active in the Corporate Outreach program for disadvantaged children and had played Santa Claus at a Christmas party for the kids the previous year. He had read about the Marcos case in *The New York Times,* and he knew that Khashoggi was purported to be among the world's wealthiest men. But he said he had no preconceived ideas about guilt or innocence. Asked twice about whether he had any ill feelings toward Arabs, he said that he had none.

When the defense team caucused, the Khashoggi lawyers immediately insisted that Berman be struck. The reason? Because he was Jewish. Explained one defense lawyer involved in the case: "When an American Jew thinks of an Arabian arms trader, he doesn't think of a friend." Later the defense marked down another prospect, Peter Kreuter, to be challenged for the same reason. Because Marcos and Khashoggi were being tried together, however, their lawyers had to agree on each defense exclusion. Spence, representing Marcos, wanted to keep Berman, and later Kreuter, because both seemed sympathetic to the plight of the mistreated and thus defense-oriented. Like Linn with blacks, Spence favored having Jews on his juries because he viewed them as sensitive to persecution and suspicious of government power. "We had a problem on Jews," Spence said later. "They wanted to kick off all the Jews, and we wanted the Jews on it." Ultimately the compromise among the defense lawyers was that two of the three Jews would be excluded.

Denying a Jew any other government post would violate federal civil rights laws. And excluding a Jew, or any member of an identifiable group, including women, blacks, and Hispanics, from the overall jury pool would run afoul of the 1968 federal jury selection law. Yet peremptory challenges based on race or ethnicity traditionally haven't been subject to review. Only recently, in the 1986 case of *Batson* v. *Kentucky,* has the Supreme Court banned prosecutors from systematically removing blacks from cases with black defendants. The Court's prohibition on racial challenges was extended to attorneys in civil cases in 1991 and to criminal defense lawyers in 1992.[8] Challenges based solely on sex, though not those based on religion, were finally barred in 1994. But lawyers still could easily skirt such prohibitions by articulating a neutral, nondiscriminatory reason for any particular challenge.

It wasn't only the defense that removed qualified candidates from the jury pool. Among the people prosecutor LaBella excluded was Glynis Burnham, a thirty-nine-year-old black woman who had majored in English in college and now worked for AT&T designing phone networks for companies. Not only did she fit the defense profile—black, female, nearly middle-aged—but she was particularly forceful and articulate, a potential leader. She knew that Imelda Marcos was called the Iron Butterfly, but she didn't consider the term pejorative. Imelda, and she, had started out with little and, through toughness and willpower, had made more of themselves. One precious prosecution challenge went to ridding the jury of her.

In contrast with some of the candidates who were to be excluded from the case via peremptory challenges, some of those who were ultimately seated on the jury came across in voir dire as less than ideal—at least when considered for competence and impartiality. In most instances the defense lawyers were pleased with the choices. The prosecution, because it had only those six challenges with which to oust objectionable jurors, was often less so.

A common characteristic of many of the prospects who made it onto the jury was that they were ill informed about public affairs and uninterested in the topic, just as the defense team had hoped. One of them was Ted Kutzy, a mild-mannered twenty-five-year-old electrical engineer who liked to watch *The Simpsons* and worked for a defense contractor. Kutzy said he had never bought a newspaper, never watched TV news, never heard of Khashoggi or, more surprisingly, of Imelda Marcos. He noted in a barely audible voice during voir dire that "I wasn't even sure if she was a female or not." He knew vaguely that Ferdinand Marcos had been president of the Philippines, but he told the judge and the lawyers that he'd heard "nothing really. Never interested me that much."

A similarly isolated candidate who was to get on the Marcos jury was Rochelle Gore, a twenty-nine-year-old college graduate who worked as a computer operator for a legal publishing company. She had marked on her questionnaire that she had never heard of any of the key players, including Ferdinand Marcos. Indeed, she seemed to care so little about public matters that Judge Keenan became suspicious in voir dire about whether she was telling the truth:

59

Keenan: You said that you never heard of someone by the name of Ferdinand Marcos. Now that you have been to court and you have heard me introduce some of the people in the case, I just want to ask you again: Are you sure? . . . I am not arguing with you. I just want to make sure, okay?

Gore: Yes, I have never heard of him.

Keenan: Never heard of him.

Gore: Never.

Keenan: Have you ever heard of a man by the name of Adnan Khashoggi?

Gore: Never.

Keenan: Have you ever heard of a lady by the name of Imelda Marcos?

Gore: Never.

Keenan: You saw Mr. Khashoggi stand up there in court this morning. He is the man over there in the corner. And you saw Mrs. Marcos stand up this morning. Is that right?

Gore: Yes, I did.

Keenan: Do you think you ever saw either of them on television ever?

Gore: I have never seen them on television before.

The defense lawyers, of course, were delighted.

Then there was Llewellyn White, who was also coveted by the defense team, in his case because they were nearly certain that he *couldn't* be impartial. A forty-nine-year-old native of Montserrat in the Caribbean, White was one of the few prospects who came to court in a business suit, and he seemed in full command as he detailed his background and assured the court of his fair-mindedness. A subway motorman with the city transit agency, he was also an entrepreneur who ran two small businesses in the suburban community of Mount Vernon. He knew a little about the Marcoses and nothing about Khashoggi. But most significant, as far as the defense lawyers were concerned, was that he had recently suffered a loss: His brother had been shot and killed less than three months earlier, while driving on a crowded highway near Kennedy Airport. The killer had not been caught. White had written on his questionnaire that the event wouldn't affect his ability to consider the Marcos case objectively. Asked the same question by Judge Keenan, White seemed firm when he said, "No, Your Honor, not at all."

But academics who study the jury system, as well as most lawyers, have long understood that prospective jurors seldom admit their biases and indeed often aren't aware of them.[9] The defense lawyers were willing to bet that White would emerge in deliberations as a powerful advocate for the defense. As they saw it, White would view the case as a misuse of the criminal justice system that diverted resources away from street crime. After all, four FBI agents had spent six months generating information to place on a single chart that the prosecution would display in the Marcos case. Meanwhile, the killer of Lew White's brother remained at large, and it seemed unlikely that law enforcement authorities would be going to very great lengths to solve this run-of-the-mill murder. How could White not make the connection and resent the prosecutors?

In addition, the lawyers figured, since White had lived for twenty years in a Third World country, he would know that U.S. standards of political corruption weren't necessarily those of other cultures. He might prefer not to impose American laws on foreign defendants. The defense lawyers planned to attack the prosecution's case partly on the ground that it was a waste of taxpayers' money and courtroom time when real crime was rampant. "We all agreed he had to stay on the jury because he would understand the 'Why are we here?' argument," said defense lawyer Kingham. "Why is the U.S.

government spending millions of dollars on this prosecution?"

Two other prospects who became jurors reflected different defense priorities. Catherine Balton, a sixty-two-year-old retired office manager with a taste for good food, fine wine, and travel, was, in jury selection parlance, a hanger—someone who might hold out and force a hung jury and a mistrial. Such a person benefits the defense more than the prosecution because just one can prevent the government from getting the unanimous verdict needed for a conviction. Spence in particular desperately wanted one or two hangers on the jury, for insurance.

A petite woman with light brown hair and a wary look, Balton made an instant impression in voir dire because she could barely contain her impatience with questions that other prospects had answered respectfully. Asked if she'd heard of Ferdinand Marcos, Balton huffed, "Well, I imagine everyone has." Told this wasn't so, she shot back, "Well, some people have lived very sheltered lives then."

Judge Keenan looked down at her questionnaire and noted that when asked about her attitudes toward wealth, she had written that her friends were middle class and that she had no interest in anybody's bankbook but her own. She had given that rather tart answer, she acknowledged to the judge, because "I was a little tired of waiting around." But later, under further questioning, she reiterated the point, saying, "Well, I think all this talk about money is very boring. I don't see what that has to do about anything."

Spence said later that he hadn't known which way she'd come down on the evidence, but he'd thought there was at least a chance she'd favor the defense because she wore a big cross around her neck, perhaps a sign that she was forgiving. That was why, he said, "Balton was the juror I picked to hang the case."

Another potential hanger was Alan Belofsky. Bearded, thin, and extremely intense, he looked a decade younger than his listed age of forty. On his questionnaire he had described his parents' national background as "Jewish/European," an obvious red flag to the Khashoggi lawyers. The voir dire did nothing to improve Belofsky's standing in the eyes of most of the defense lawyers. He described Khashoggi as "one of the richest men in the world," and he was well aware that Khashoggi was a Saudi arms trader. He also knew about Marcos's wealth and her reputation for lavish spending, especially on clothes. In addition, his tone of voice and body language were all wrong in a case in which the defense needed sympathy. He was constantly frowning, and he showed no hint of humor.

But Belofsky was a union man, and Spence was vehemently prounion. The lawyer believed he could communicate with Belofsky, that they would understand each other. Moreover, Spence wanted to make sure he got one Jew on the jury. In addition, Belofsky seemed stubborn, angry, argumentative. Put two possible hangers on the jury—Balton and Belofsky—and the defense would increase the chance that at least one of them would vote to acquit and would stick to that position. Spence ultimately insisted that, everyone else's misgivings to the contrary, Belofsky must serve.

The trial began on April 3, 1990. The charges that were outlined in a nearly impenetrable ninety-page indictment came down to this: Imelda Marcos had joined her late husband, the longtime president of the Philippines, in looting the Philippine economy and stashing the money in secret Swiss bank accounts. Then she had spent some of the untold millions on dazzling jewelry and prime Manhattan real estate. Her purchases had included such New York City extravagances as a $30 million Fifth Avenue office tower and a $205,000 sapphire necklace from Van Cleef & Arpels. The reason her actions were allegedly a crime in the United States was that she had transferred some of her dirty money to U.S. banks and had done the profligate spending here. After fleeing to Hawaii to escape the People Power revolt in the Philippines in 1986, the Marcoses had transferred buildings and artwork in the United States to a friend, codefendant Khashoggi, in an apparent effort to evade a U.S. court freeze on those assets. And documents had been backdated—one signed by Khashoggi and one by a Marcos aide—apparently to make it look as if Khashoggi had owned the assets before the freeze.

Opening for the government was Debra Livingston, a tall, thin, precise thirty-one-year-old Harvard Law School graduate whom the jurors quickly nicknamed Olive Oyl. (Fittingly La-Bella, her thirty-nine-year-old fellow prosecutor, had huge forearms and a bit of a strut.) Livingston rose in a jammed courtroom and laced into Imelda, declaring that the case was about "theft, fraud, and deceit on an incredible scale." As the prosecutor acidly outlined the scheme, she periodically gestured accusingly toward Imelda. But though Livingston's words were powerful—at one point she called the Philippine government bank Imelda's "personal piggy bank"—her presentation was not. The jurors came to find her dry approach extremely tedious as the trial dragged on.

Imelda's lawyer, Gerry Spence, was nothing like Livingston. With his coarse wit and sagging trousers, he swept like a crazy country wind into the orderly world of the New York courtroom. Alternately whispering and shouting, exhorting and cajoling, Spence began his opening statement by presenting a portrait of a woman who wasn't capable of crime. According to Spence, Imelda had been so poor as a child that she had drunk water from foxholes during World War II. When the Japanese invaded, he said, she had witnessed the beheadings of a family member and many other townspeople, "the heads stacked up on trucks, truckloads of heads." She loved jewelry,

Spence declared, because as a child she had been entrusted with the family's only asset, a necklace that the family had been forced to sell off, jewel by jewel, for food. She had survived the war, worked her way through school, and fallen instantly in love with a dashing young politician, whom she married eleven days later, Spence said. Imelda had been shy, Ferdinand worldly; he had been powerful, she generous.

Although news stories had consistently depicted the marriage as a troubled one because of Ferdinand's highly publicized philandering, Spence told a story of a woman who loved her husband above all else and would refuse to blame even the tiniest crimes on him just to save herself.[10] But having promised to carry on her fight for the reputation of Ferdinand Marcos, Spence proceeded to distance his client from any of her husband's doings. Imelda was a wife, not a financier, Spence said. She had asked Marcos about his transactions, but he had told her little. He had instructed others to keep her in the dark. She had been the little woman, showered with gifts and insulated from the family business. She was ignorant but lovable and even pitiable.

This was history boldly rewritten to benefit jurors who were not privy to any other version. That was why the defense team had worked so hard to pack the jury with the likes of Ted Kutzy, Rochelle Gore, and all the others who before the trial had had so much trouble identifying the Marcoses. It ignored Ferdinand Marcos's much-documented election fraud when Corazon Aquino ran against him for the presidency in 1986. And it passed over the popular uprising that had ousted the Marcoses and given the presidency to Mrs. Aquino while many in the world—but not the twelve mostly oblivious New Yorkers who later became these jurors—had looked on and cheered.

Prosecutors, apparently astonished at the audacity of Spence's glowing portrait of the Marcoses, objected frequently. These objections were often sustained by Judge Keenan, who repeatedly and angrily admonished Spence to stick to issues relevant to the case. But Spence wasn't easily intimidated, and while he feigned embarrassment at being rebuffed so often by the judge, he knew that this was his golden chance to guide the jurors toward a positive first impression of the defendant.

Spence moved on to raise questions about whether any crimes had been committed. He maintained that Marcos hadn't needed to steal from his people because he had been overwhelmingly rich even before becoming president—thanks to his rather miraculous discovery of a gold hoard supposedly hidden in the Philippines by a Japanese general in World War II. What the government called bribes and kickbacks were merely tax collections, Spence said. The money Marcos funneled out of the country into secret accounts was part of an anti-Communist security fund, not a way to squirrel away cash for personal use.

But most important, Spence insisted, the meek wife, Imelda, "had nothing to do with the payment of any of the moneys," having "never paid a bill in her life." While the government had said she'd made her various purchases through a loyal agent and sidekick named Gliceria Tantoco, Spence said the alleged agent acted on her own behalf or on behalf of Ferdinand—but not on behalf of Imelda. Conveniently this key witness was on the lam in Morocco and not available to testify.

Readers of crime novels know that it's tough to prove a person has done something wrong without explaining why, providing a motive. In this case the Marcoses' motive for alleged crimes would be obvious: to gain power and wealth. But if the government was fabricating its case against them, what was *its* motive? Why would it do something so terribly wrong? For Spence, this was the crucial question. He knew that even if he induced the jurors to be sympathetic to Imelda, they would still have difficulty believing that their own government would accuse her falsely. But if the government had a political motive, an unfair prosecution would make sense, and repudiating it would become the jury's duty.

Spence offered such a motive with particular passion: He told of how the United States had supported a coup by Aquino "against their old loyal friend Mr. Marcos"; how after the coup the United States had wanted above all else to keep Aquino happy so she wouldn't order the removal of U.S. military bases from the Philippines; how the U.S. prosecutors had worked together with the new Philippine government to build the case against Imelda; and how the case was, at bottom, a matter of politics, not law. The government had already tried the Marcoses in the press, he charged, "in the most excoriating campaign that I think history will record has ever been brought against a defendant in this country."

In truth the U.S. government had turned its back on a longtime ally to work closely with the new Philippine government in tracking down funds that the Marcoses allegedly had stolen. And if Imelda was convicted, the U.S. racketeering law required that any stolen funds be forfeited to the U.S. government and ultimately repatriated back to their rightful owners in the Philippines.

Little of this addressed the legal question of whether Imelda had committed the crimes of which she was accused. But after Spence's performance, the case had a shape. Judge Keenan had berated Spence repeatedly, and the lawyer had seemed arrogant to many of the jurors, disobedient, out of control. Nonetheless, he had given Imelda a glow and the government's case a certain taint. As Spence himself said after the case was over, "The only time the jury could hear about political issues was in the opening statement, because the judge hadn't allowed any evidence of it."

*   *   *

In the three months that followed, Livingston and LaBella painstakingly laid out the evidence of Imelda's crimes. Witnesses and documents traced the allegedly tainted money from the Philippines to foreign accounts and then into banks in the United States. Oscar Carino, the head of the New York branch of the Philippine National Bank, testified that when Imelda came to town, he would be ordered by her personal secretary to deliver a hundred thousand dollars in cash to the Waldorf Towers, where she was staying. This happened often enough—as many as four or five times per visit—to help sink the bank into debt. The money was listed on the bank's books as a debt owed by the government to the bank, but the debt was never repaid, Carino testified.

While Spence disputed that Imelda, rather than her various associates, was behind the purchases at issue in the case, witnesses testified that it was Imelda herself who had inspected an eight-million-dollar Park Avenue apartment that was up for sale along with a six-million-dollar art collection. Imelda, it was revealed, had tried to persuade a Sotheby's auction house employee to buy all fourteen million dollars' worth in his name, presumably to disguise her ownership of the property. When the employee refused, the art collection was bought by Marcos aide Tantoco, apparently on Imelda's behalf. (The co-op board wouldn't allow the apartment to be sold to Tantoco.) The art collection later found its way into Khashoggi's hands just as a court was freezing all the Marcos assets.

Participants also made clear that Imelda had been personally involved in the deals concerned with New York office buildings and had chaired an important meeting regarding building refinance in 1984. In addition, the federal case detailed more than $17 million in jewelry purchases, $1.1 million of which had been charged against the profits of the Philippine National Bank. "You can't use money from the

PNB to buy yourself jewelry. If you have any uncertainty what-soever about that, don't,'' LaBella told the jury. He seemed to be succeeding in overcoming the trickiest obstacle in the case: proving that Imelda was directly involved in the transactions at issue and that she knew that the money she was spending had been stolen.

Indeed, by midtrial the case against Imelda appeared so strong and well documented that courtroom reporters began speculating that she might cop a plea to stop the onslaught of damaging evidence. If jury trial was just about the facts and the law and if the jurors were sifting the facts dispassionately, the government was winning, as even some members of the defense team believed.

In fact, though, the jurors weren't buying. For one thing, the case was difficult to follow: One prosecution chart, detailing how the Crown Building in Manhattan had been purchased, offered five boxes in the left-hand column signifying the sources of the funds, flowing to thirteen boxes in the middle representing intermediate accounts, and on to six boxes on the right showing how the funds had been used. Solid and dotted lines darted in all directions among the boxes. Properly read, the chart exposed the network of deceit that had been established to hide the fact that it was the Marcoses who had bought the trophy property on Fifth Avenue. But the net effect on many jurors was panic at their inability to follow the money, a panic that they later papered over with ridicule. "The prosecutors should have been ashamed of themselves," said juror Sandra Alberts, a pleasant thirty-nine-year-old woman with long brown hair and very red lipstick, who worked as a paralegal at the elite law firm Sherman & Sterling. "The lawyers were in their own little thing," she added. "They should have stopped and explained it to us. They're supposed to prove it to us, right?"

The prosecutors compounded their problem by falling into

a common trap: Having painstakingly collected evidence of numerous monetary transactions involving funds from the Philippines, they couldn't resist putting most of the transactions into evidence, even though just a few might have made their case more sharply. The strongest evidence sometimes got lost in the general muddle.

But it wasn't just the complexity of the case that bothered the jurors. It was simply that they liked Imelda Marcos and felt sorry for her. Spence had sketched her as a decent, generous, and persecuted woman, and there she sat each day, dressed somberly in black, fingering her rosary beads, sighing and sometimes dabbing away tears with a black, lace-trimmed handkerchief when the testimony seemed too awful to bear. The day a customs inspector testified about finding in her luggage an anniversary gift to her husband—twenty-four one-kilogram gold bricks inscribed "To my husband on our 24th anniversary"—she sobbed on Spence's shoulder, and the trial was postponed for several days because Imelda's blood pressure had risen perilously high. A few days after that she again began sobbing uncontrollably in the courtroom, and the jury was dismissed. Then, at the end of May, she fainted at the defense table, and some jurors said they saw blood coming from her nose and mouth. A worried Ted Kutzy, the *Simpsons*-watching electrical engineer, wrote in his journal that night: "I hope she feels better next week."

Friends told juror Yvonne Granberry, the teacher's aide, that they believed Imelda had been faking. But, she said after the trial, "I told them, 'No, you wasn't there. I saw the blood.' " She added, "I was very concerned. She was so white. I thought she had died."

By then Yvonne had nothing but warm feelings toward the beleaguered defendant: "I never felt she was a wicked, cruel person. She always seemed warm to me—a person that has deep feelings toward people." Said postal clerk Anna Sneed:

"She didn't seem like a person who would scheme and cheat people. . . . I thought, 'Why are they harassing this sick woman?' "

The jurors' amazingly sympathetic views of the defendant seemed to fuel their suspicions that unseemly political motives might be present in the prosecution's case. Lew White, the longtime New York City transit motorman who had been the defense team's great prize in voir dire, was quickly convinced that Imelda had been set up. Why else would customs officials have searched the Marcos luggage so carefully when the couple first arrived in Hawaii? Why would the government target a former head of state who had been a close ally? "It was shabby, disgusting," he recalled with fresh anger several months later. "From the get-go, I considered, 'Why is she being tried here?' " The defense lawyers had been dead on in predicting that reaction.

The majority of jurors shared White's perspective during most of the trial. "I was mystified to get an answer to why they tried her in this country at all," said Anna Sneed. "All during the trial I was trying to figure out when they were going to get to the point." Sneed ultimately fixed on Spence's theory that the U.S. government was doing the dirty work for Aquino. Lost to her was the detailed description by the prosecution of Imelda's crimes in the United States.

Considering these jurors' opinions of Imelda and of the government's case, it came as no surprise that they were highly susceptible to Spence's efforts to place distance between Imelda Marcos and any wrongdoing. Spence presented no witnesses of his own, relying instead on aggressive cross-examinations of the government's witnesses. He invariably questioned those witnesses' motives—some were Filipinos with much to gain, or to lose, from the Aquino government depending on how they testified—and he reminded the jurors that nobody could state for certain that Imelda knew where the money she spent had come from and whether it had been derived illegally. The government said she must have known, given all of her clear involvement in both political and financial affairs. The defense asked how she could have; she was just the wife of a powerful man who liked to keep secrets. The legal standard: whether she'd actually known or had purposely avoided learning the truth.

One day Ted Kutzy wrote in his journal: "Although the prosecution brought up many interesting points . . . through Spence, it was revealed that no witness could directly link any transaction to Mrs. Marcos. Sometimes I get the feeling that she shouldn't be the one on trial."

Summations took place at the end of June, almost three months after the case had begun. After LaBella restated the government's case, Spence used his closing to reinforce the themes he had developed at trial and to urge the jury to do something with their affection for Imelda and their anger at the government: to acquit. "When you deliberate, you have the power," he reminded them. "This is a case about our jury system. It is a case the whole world watches. It is a case in which the jury system will emerge victorious." Deliberations began late in the afternoon of Thursday, June 28, 1990.

When the jurors filed into their small jury room, they had some mundane matters to which to attend, such as getting to know one another and learning how to work together. During nearly three months of trial these true-to-form New Yorkers hadn't bothered to learn most of the other jurors' names. Smokers had stuck to themselves, racing in nicotine panic to a separate room whenever there were breaks. They hadn't gotten to know some of the nonsmokers well, and vice versa. In addition, race had unquestionably divided the jury: The five white jurors generally sat in one group; the four nonsmoking blacks in another; the three blacks who smoked, plus some alternates, in a third. Small pockets of friendships sprang up, but nothing like group camaraderie.

Catherine Balton, as the first juror selected in the case, was automatically designated forewoman by Judge Keenan, in keeping with his usual practice. In many other courts, including the Dallas state court where the Mark Robertson death penalty case was tried, the jurors pick the foreman at the start of deliberations. But the Marcos jurors had no control over the appointment of Balton, and she was not a fortunate choice. As had been predicted by the lawyers in voir dire, she turned out to be the most intellectual but also the most abrasive of the jurors.

Personal conflicts developed almost immediately. As Balton later recalled it, "As foreman, it was my responsibility to keep conversation going, but a little nucleus of four [black women jurors] didn't want to pay attention. . . . These four had made up their minds, and they didn't want to discuss it." Most of the others remember the circumstances differently. "Catherine was one-sided," says Yvonne Granberry. "You could tell that from the beginning. Plus, she didn't keep control. People talked over one another. It was upsetting."

At Balton's request each juror was provided with a copy of the rather intimidating six-page verdict form that set out the allegations in four separate counts. The first two counts gathered up all the main charges that Imelda had stolen money—for buildings, art, and jewelry—and classified them as racketeering and conspiracy. The third count charged both defendants with obstructing justice by transferring Marcos properties to Khashoggi and thus circumventing the court freeze on funds. The fourth alleged mail fraud against both defendants, for conducting some of their illegal business via the mails.

Alan Belofsky, the Manhattan mail carrier whom Spence

had been so adamant about keeping on the jury, was the first to speak up. "Imelda was spending money like there's no tomorrow, and she went to a lot of trouble to disguise that," Belofsky told the panel confidently. "Even when she'd buy jewelry, she'd have some third party handle the transaction. Why would she do that if she thought it was all legitimate?"

Also, Belofsky said, it was clear that Ferdinand Marcos had skimmed money off the top of government contracts for years. Meanwhile, Imelda Marcos had been mayor of Manila and had been deeply involved in governmental activities. How could she not have known the source of her nearly inexhaustible wealth? "Spence is asking me to believe she's spending all this money and she's not asking where it's coming from," Belofsky said incredulously.

Expecting support for what seemed to him an obvious conclusion, Belofsky was met instead with disagreement, even derision. Reflecting on his own experience growing up in the Caribbean, Lew White scoffed at the notion that it was even illegal for potentates such as Ferdinand Marcos to demand a percentage of businesses' profits. "It's difficult to separate out what's legal and illegal in a Third World country," he explained. "If you're the head of a Third World country, you're it." And if the skimming wasn't illegal, then spending the proceeds in the United States couldn't be illegal either, he concluded.

This was an argument that the prosecution apparently hadn't anticipated, but it had come naturally to Lew White. In the absolute freedom of the jury room such views carry weight and sometimes carry the day. White, who owned a Laundromat and a furniture reupholstering store while holding down a job with the transit authority, also had strong opinions about marriage and about what husbands do and don't tell their wives. He kept his own wife in the dark about the details of his businesses, he told the jurors, and he suspected that Ferdinand Marcos had done the same with Imelda.

Balton couldn't believe the absurdity of what she was hearing. What did White's marriage in Mount Vernon, New York, have to do with the relationship between a foreign head of state and his fearsomely powerful wife? While Balton wasn't sure whether Imelda was guilty, she was certain that White's arguments were nothing more than what she later called "outrageous excuses" for the behavior of the defendant, and she said as much. Then she called for a show of hands on whether the jurors thought that the two defendants were guilty. The initial vote: 10–2 that the government had failed to prove its case. The two dissenters were Belofsky and Balton. They had been good picks as potential hangers, but ironically, it looked as if they might hang the case by denying the defense an acquittal rather than by denying the prosecution a conviction.

The next day deliberations grew testier. While the jurors proceeded to go through each part of the indictment, count by count, discussion never strayed far from the broad issues that seemed of most concern: whether Imelda Marcos was the kind of person who would cheat other people and whether the government had any legitimate grounds to prosecute a sickly, devout, and dignified widow from a foreign land. Mostly the jurors discussed the evidence, but their perceptions were manifestly colored by their strong opinions about those marginally relevant questions. "We argued facts," recalls Ted Kutzy, "but there was a lot of sympathy. There were a lot of bleeding hearts on that jury."

The Marcos jury's sympathies made it difficult for Belofsky, who was articulate, though not diplomatic, to champion the prosecution case. There had been such a flood of evidence that the details of any single transaction had blurred into all the others. So when Belofsky tried to argue that the purchase of one building or another had been clearly traced to tainted Marcos funds and that Imelda had been involved in business transactions concerning the buildings, he was shouted down. "Nothing is proven; nothing is proven," said Charlene Griffin, a strong-minded twenty-seven-year-old night postal supervisor at Kennedy Airport. Belofsky had difficulty finding the proof in the welter of evidence. He was reduced to asserting, again and again, that Imelda simply must have known what was going on. Intense and nervous, he took to leaving the table and pacing. He'd return to admonish the jurors. "Can't you see that Spence was lying?" he'd ask, his voice rising. But some jurors just laughed at Belofsky or whispered to each other that he was "brain dead." Others insisted that Spence's statements didn't reflect on his client. Sandra Alberts, who'd spent eight years observing lawyers in her firm, told Belofsky: "Don't even listen to the lawyers. They sit around and plot all day with smirks on their faces when they come up with a good idea. Spence can tell us anything. He's not on trial; he can lie all he wants."

Meanwhile, Balton was getting angrier and angrier at the proceedings. Separate conversations were sprouting all around the table, and some of them didn't even involve the case. People ignored her when she sought order, so she decided to proceed without them and made her own decisions about which evidence and testimony to request that the bailiff deliver to the jury room. This incensed the group that included Charlene Griffin, Anna Sneed, and Yvonne Granberry. They insisted that Balton include them in her decisions. There was a confrontation between Balton and Griffin, then a shouting match between Balton and White, who had become fed up with what he viewed as arrogance on Balton's part. When another juror asked a question, White said, "Ask Catherine, she knows everything." Balton jumped up and said, "I don't have to take that." Sandra Alberts stepped in to try to calm them down. The jury had already strayed far from the ideal—of jurors' making a "fair and reasonable assessment of the evidence"—and it was only day two of deliberations.

While Balton was unhappy with the other jurors and unimpressed with the level of discourse, she wasn't nearly as pro-prosecution as was Belovsky. She had voted to convict in the first straw vote mostly because she wanted to buy time to sift the evidence and think about the case. She had found the government's presentation confusing and rambling, as it certainly had been, and some of the prosecution's witnesses wholly unconvincing. She had also heard enough evidence to convince her that Ferdinand Marcos had led a life of crime, and she had trouble believing that his savvy wife knew nothing about it.

Ignoring the factual evidence of Imelda's extraordinary involvement in her nation's government and in the U.S. real estate purchases at issue in the case, other jurors whispered among themselves that because Balton wasn't married, she simply didn't understand how many secrets spouses keep from each other. Someone asked Alberts, an affable woman who remained on good terms with everyone despite the commotion, to explain the facts of marriage to Balton. Alberts spoke of her own marriage to a building contractor. Sometimes he'd go off to late meetings, she said, and she wouldn't know for sure what he was doing. "Sandy talked to her real nice," recalls Anna Sneed. "She said it wasn't all cut-and-dried in a marriage. Catherine just loved Sandy and listened to her." By the third day, Saturday, the friendly persuasion seemed to be taking hold. When Belovsky repeated his refrain that on the basis of the evidence in the case, Imelda must have known about her husband's activities, Balton gave him a hard stare and said, "Alan, you're not looking at the facts." The room became quiet as everyone realized that now only

Belofsky remained as a serious obstacle to acquittal. Knowing, without voting formally, that the tally on the racketeering and conspiracy charges was now 11–1, the jurors moved on to by far the strongest count against both Marcos and Khashoggi: obstruction of justice.

This charge involved the allegation that the defendants had arranged to transfer ownership of the six-million-dollar art collection and the four office buildings to Khashoggi after a court in New York had frozen the Marcos assets in the United States. Prosecutors claimed that the defendants had known about the freeze and deliberately thwarted it. There was some dispute about whether Khashoggi had accepted the assets as a favor to the Marcoses or in exchange for cash, but his motive didn't seem to matter.

The evidence was airtight that Khashoggi had gained possession of the properties. The questions were when and under what circumstances. His lawyer, James Linn, had suggested that Khashoggi had agreed to the transfers significantly before the freeze was established. But the prosecution had proved conclusively that documents suggesting an earlier transfer had been backdated. It wasn't absolutely clear that Imelda herself had known about the court freeze—a requirement for conviction—but it was awfully hard to believe that she hadn't. After all, the freeze had been sought in a civil case filed in New York by the new government of the Philippines and would sharply curtail Imelda's ability to spend money; it was the kind of development she was highly likely to have noticed. In addition, the transfer to Khashoggi of the Park Avenue art collection she personally had purchased, a transfer timed perfectly to the freeze on Marcos assets, provided strong circumstantial evidence that she was seeking to evade the court order. In the first vote on the charge even some of the jurors who were deeply sympathetic to Imelda voted to convict, and the panel was about evenly divided.

But most of the support for the prosecution evaporated between Saturday night and Sunday morning largely because jurors realized that they had no desire to punish Imelda Marcos. Something they learned at the hotel where they were sequestered also seems to have influenced some of them, if only by strengthening their resolve to acquit. Earlier Alberts had heard from a coworker that Judge Keenan himself had briefly questioned why the case had been brought in the United States, rather than in the Philippines. In considering the defense's routine motion to dismiss the case on June 20, he had asked, "What's an American court—what am I doing here . . . trying a case involving the theft of money from Philippine banks?" LaBella had explained that the alleged fraud took place when the stolen money was sent to the United States, funneled through a U.S.-based bank, and used to buy property in New York, and the judge had decided that the case must go forward.

Such legal motions and rulings are kept secret from the jury on the theory that it should concentrate on the evidence and that the lawyers' or judge's statements might misdirect or prejudice them. For the same reason, jurors aren't supposed to discuss any aspect of their case with anyone or to read about it in the newspapers. But since Alberts had heard about what Judge Keenan had said inadvertently, she mentioned it in the community room of the hotel where the jury was sequestered, and many of the jurors immediately saw in the judge's question the vindication of their concerns about the government's motives. "All through the trial I didn't believe the case belonged here," said Anna Sneed. "When he said that, it confirmed it for me. I said, 'Hey, kid, you do know something.'" What she missed, of course, was the fact that the judge had not only asked the question but had answered it—in favor of the prosecution, not the defense.[11]

Challenged by Charlene Griffin the next day to prove that

Imelda had known about the court freeze or about any efforts to backdate documents. Belofsky fell short. By the afternoon the jury was still deadlocked at 11–1 on the first three counts. It wasn't clear what, if anything, would induce Belofsky to come around. Some thought a hung jury likely.

The jurors' only hope seemed to be to intensify the personal pressure on Belofsky, and that's what they now attempted. Sunday afternoon and Monday morning their deliberations no longer concerned the facts of the case or even their emotions about it but were a matter of whether Alan Belofsky was certain enough, stubborn enough, and strong enough to withstand the glare of eleven pairs of exhausted and condemning eyes. Sandra Alberts added to the pressure Sunday night, when even she lost her patience and demanded that they finish up and go home.

Belofsky, who had been excited about being a juror, had taken the proceedings perhaps more seriously than anyone else. He had followed the testimony closely and had apparently even sought a little extra edge by surreptitiously (and wholly improperly) perusing newspaper accounts of the case.[12] But by Sunday he was thoroughly disillusioned with the process and incensed that the other jurors were no longer bothering to listen to his arguments, if they ever had. "It was a holiday weekend [just before July 4]. I wanted to get out. I got frustrated that they wouldn't listen," he said afterward. Moreover, he had no idea what would happen if he held out. "I wasn't sure of the law. I didn't know how long I would have to stay." He surmised that the case would have to be retried if he refused to relent, but he didn't know for sure. To get it over with, he said, "I just rolled with the punches." As the nation's leading jury researchers, at the University of Chicago, have suggested, "In an ambiguous situation a member of a group will doubt and finally disbelieve his own correct observation if all other members of the group claim he must have been mistaken." The myth of the jury holdout is Henry Fonda, sticking stubbornly to his convictions in *12 Angry Men* until the others are convinced. The reality, most often, is Alan Belofsky.[13]

The final vote on obstruction of justice was 12–0. All twelve quickly assented to the not-guilty verdicts for racketeering and conspiracy. Mail fraud, which they had never discussed although it was a separate felony charge, was rejected informally, without an actual vote. The case was over. Marcos supporters tearily thanked jurors as they were hustled out the back to waiting government-provided limousines for chauffeured rides home.

Imelda was ready to party. Sitting for an interview in her apartment some months later, she still seemed moved by the affection the jurors had bestowed on her. "Everyone has gone through a painful human experience, of deprivation of one thing or another, of a mother, of love, of material things," she said. In her widowhood, her loss of power, the humiliation of her being dragged into court, the jurors had found a link that transcended differences in wealth and culture, she maintained. In the jurors' minds, Imelda said, "Suddenly [the defendants] are human after all, they're going through the same suffering as us; they just had a different destiny."

On another day in another place jury forewoman Catherine Balton put it this way: "What good would it have done to put her in jail? I thought, 'What do we want from her? She lost her husband, she lost her country, she lost her place. And for a woman like that, that's punishment. Why do we want to put the last nail in the coffin?'"

As Imelda had noted, some of the jurors seemed particularly to identify with her as a fellow sufferer, even though she was rich, possibly even a billionaire, and they were barely getting by. Another common link was religion. Granberry described a moving conversation she had had with Imelda after the trial, in which the defendant had said "she had been in church, praying, when the verdict came in, and Spence went to get her, and she saw a bright light and knew everything would be good for her." Anna Sneed remembers meeting Imelda's sister, Bellarmine Romualdez, who is a nun, and talking about the Marcos camp's concerns about the case, "and I was thinking, 'They must have done some heavy praying.'"

Reflecting on the possibility that Imelda had fooled the jury, Sneed said, "As a religious person she doesn't need us to punish her. She knows God will deal with her. If she really did those things, she'll get hers, and she'll get it in spades." Sneed wasn't betting on it, though.

Why had the jurors become so hopelessly starstruck that they'd been blind to the prosecution's factually strong case against the defendants? Some of the fault surely lay in how the case had been conducted. Prosecutors had made it too complicated by including too many separate counts. And the defense lawyers, two of the best in the nation, had easily outclassed their hardworking but somewhat plodding opponents. Additionally, Judge Keenan had made the common mistake of providing jurors with excessively turgid and lengthy legal instructions, all ninety-seven pages of them. Such problems will be considered in more detail in later chapters.

But the main trouble with the Marcos jury had been the jurors. The pool from which they'd been picked had been narrowed considerably when many of the more articulate pleaders had won excuses from the jury clerk and had been dismissed. Then peremptory challenges had taken their unfortunate toll. The hope—that in America no one is too humble to judge, no one too exalted to be judged—had given way to the disappointment of a verdict driven by ignorance and misplaced sympathy.

Could it have been otherwise? Would a more competent,

fair-minded jury have resulted if it had been picked by lot from the original pool of 150 candidates, with virtually no excuses allowed and no peremptory challenges permitted? The final section of the book will explore these alternatives.

For now, though, consider the view expressed by a barrister from Wales, where, as in the rest of Britain, peremptory challenges have been phased out. Jury selection is supposed to provide "a trial by your peers selected at random from all walks of life," the Welsh lawyer explains. "And I think it's wrong that a person should try and engineer a better jury for himself, by exercising the right of challenges."[14]

3

THE WIZARDS OF ODDS

—

T HE Allentown, Pennsylvania, law offices of Cohen, Feeley & Ortwein provided a warm, dry refuge on a stormy Thursday morning in late October 1991. The postman wandered in and gossiped with the receptionist. A secretary switched on the coffeemaker in the conference room and pulled two boxes of doughnuts from sopping wet plastic bags. Lawyers shook off their raincoats, poured themselves coffee, and chatted amiably about Penn State football and the Pittsburgh Pirates. Everyone seemed relaxed and content. An outsider would never have guessed that the firm had a big trial coming up the following Monday and didn't seem to have a chance in a hundred of winning.

But everyone always took the lead from the office's top gun, Marty Cohen, and the brash forty-nine-year-old personal injury lawyer was projecting his usual ebullience. In the upcoming case Cohen would be representing a teenage boy who had suffered brain damage after being hit by a car. One problem with the case was that the driver had no money for paying any kind of sizable damages. So Cohen was going to try to blame Pizza Hut for the injuries since the driver had allegedly drunk beer at the restaurant before she slammed into the boy. A bigger problem with the case was that there wasn't a single witness who could even place the woman at the Pizza Hut that day, let alone prove she'd been drinking there.

But Cohen wasn't deterred. Like Gerry Spence and Jim Linn, he was a big believer in what could be gained from selecting a favorable jury, no matter how unpromising the case. And unlike the lawyers in the Marcos case, he wasn't relying only on hunches and stereotypes in making the peremptory challenges that would shape the Pizza Hut jury. He had a jury consultant, a social scientist, on his side as well.

Jury consultants were the latest rage among trial lawyers. They brought tools already in wide use in marketing and politics—such as conducting polls and pretesting products and pitches before sample audiences—to the dual tasks of picking and persuading juries. The idea was to leave little to chance. The jury could be shaped through peremptory challenges, and trial strategy could be refined on the basis of a consultant's pretrial analysis of how various approaches would be likely to play.

That social science methods seemed to work even better than lawyers' traditional theories and stereotypes was suggested by the explosive growth of the trial consulting industry. In the year Cohen prepared for trial, jury consultants generated some two hundred million dollars in revenue.[1]

That the consultants were operating in the shadowy middle ground between artfully persuading juries and blatantly rigging them was suggested by the secrecy surrounding the field. Cathy E. "Cat" Bennett of Galveston, Texas, who died in 1992, had achieved a degree of fame for her jury selection work for such well-known clients as William Kennedy Smith, who had been acquitted of rape charges in West Palm Beach the previous year. And Litigation Sciences, then the largest of the consulting companies, had aggressively marketed itself and publicly taken credit for some verdicts. But most consultants labored behind a double screen erected by both client and lawyer, neither of whom typically wanted jurors to know that a Wizard of Odds was in the background evaluating how each potential juror was likely to vote.

Though some consultants were amenable to business-producing publicity, none had ever permitted a journalist to sit in on the pretrial preparations. Typically, if the consultant would agree to allow an observer to be present, the lawyer and the client would not. Neither wanted to appear so unsure of his case—or so untrusting of the decision of a randomly picked jury—that he would need a jury consultant's help. But in the Pizza Hut case Cohen and his jury consultant opened the door to allow an unprecedented look at their preparations. The Pizza Hut case would turn out to illustrate how the new scientific methods of selecting and conditioning juries have contributed, quietly but dramatically, to our disappointment in the contemporary American jury.

Some of the techniques Cohen would have at his disposal had been developed in the early 1970s, when antiwar activists were being tried throughout the country for acts of civil disobedience. Members of the academic community, who were largely sympathetic to the cause, were eager to put their skills to work for the movement. And for social scientists such as Jay Schulman of Columbia University, that meant helping the defendants in those political trials improve their chances of acquittal.

In the case that really launched the whole trial consulting industry, Schulman and several colleagues set out to help Father Philip Berrigan and a group of Catholic war resisters defend themselves against federal charges of conspiring to raid draft boards and, among other things, to kidnap presidential adviser Henry Kissinger.[2]

The government chose Harrisburg, Pennsylvania, for the trial, apparently because of its conservative population. As Schulman described the task, the social scientists' goal was to see if "a few favorable jurors could be found, in a fundamentally conservative area, to try unpopular antiwar activists." The researchers determined that because of the complexity and political explosiveness of the charges, jurors might feel more than the usual temptation to base their verdicts on their ideological preferences. The question was how to predict the way that any given potential juror would approach the case.

The researchers started by conducting an extensive telephone poll of registered voters in the area. Then they trained 45 volunteers to conduct lengthier interviews with more than 250 of the residents. The results proved surprisingly illuminating. Religion correlated closely with attitudes toward the Vietnam War and civil disobedience. Episcopalians, Presbyterians, Methodists, and fundamentalists would be bad for the defense; Catholics, Brethren, and Lutherans would be better bets. Another discovery was that college-educated people in the Harrisburg area were more conservative—and thus more proprosecution—than those with less education. That was because younger, more liberal college graduates had been more apt to desert the conservative region as soon as they could, leaving the jury pool filled with older, mostly prowar degree holders.

The lawyers applied these insights in jury selection and, miraculously, achieved a hung jury on the conspiracy charges in the case, with ten of the twelve jurors voting for acquittal. Triumphant, the social scientists fanned out across the country to help in other trials of antiwar activists, Black Panthers, and sundry revolutionaries. Along the way they developed other techniques, including conducting so-called focus groups of the sort already used by market researchers. Demographically diverse panels were asked to review the facts of upcoming cases and report how they would vote as jurors. Researchers also started interviewing jurors routinely after trials to learn all they could about jurors' methods of decision making.

Schulman and the others saw trial consulting as a useful weapon against the power of a government they perceived as oppressive. But their innovations ironically soon found their way into the commercial arena, where personal injury lawyers and big corporate defendants routinely paid tens of thousands of dollars and occasionally as much as a million for help in civil litigation in which the only issue was money. It was a University of Southern California marketing professor named Donald Vinson who first stumbled on to the amazing possibilities of the field. In 1976 David Boies and Thomas Barr, two hotshot lawyers from New York, were in Los Angeles to defend IBM in an immensely complicated antitrust case. With IBM's preeminence in the industry at stake in a web of such litigation, the firm gave the lawyers from Wall Street's blue-chip Cravath, Swaine & Moore a virtual blank check. The legal bill would mount into the millions; the only thing that mattered was winning.

Boies and Barr, well aware of the effect of market research on the political cases of the past five years, sought out Vinson and asked him to help them solve a problem: how to determine whether the jury in the case was keeping up with them as they delved, day after day, into the minutiae of computer technology and antitrust theory. Focus groups wouldn't suffice; they lasted only a few hours and couldn't measure the cumulative impact of testimony in a trial that would span many months. Similarly, community polling couldn't improve the lawyers' insight into whether their case was working or where it might be going off track as days and weeks went by.

Something else was needed, and Vinson told Boies and Barr that he knew what.

Vinson got their approval to create a surrogate jury, which he dubbed the shadow jury, that would match the actual jury in terms of demographics and, as far as he could determine, psychological traits. Shadow jurors were hired to sit in the spectator section of the courtroom for the entire trial and to report to Vinson each evening on their reactions to the day's developments. Many times during the trial, Boies recalled years later, he learned from Vinson that the shadow jurors had misunderstood a key point, and thus that the real jurors probably had, too. The next day Boies could clarify the point and regain any ground he had lost. The trial never reached a jury verdict because the judge awarded the case to IBM on legal grounds. But Vinson interviewed each of the actual jurors afterward and was impressed with the effectiveness of the shadow jury in predicting their reactions. "We were right on target," he said later.[3] Vinson became enthralled by jury consulting and quit his tenured teaching post to start a business that by 1989 had grown into a twenty-five-million-dollar consulting behemoth employing more than a hundred psychologists, sociologists, marketers, and technicians. Later, in 1991, he split off from the company and helped start a rival firm called DecisionQuest.

Over the years Vinson's methods became increasingly sophisticated and high-tech. He developed more elaborate polling procedures and expanded the use of pretrial focus groups, generally repeating the mock trial procedure several times—often with large groups—so that the lawyers could test variations in their presentations and gain confidence in whatever approach seemed to work best. He and other consultants also began applying social science research to the design and presentation of courtroom visual aids. Before a chart was presented to a jury, it was tested by focus groups. As Vinson's extensive promotional materials explained, "Obviously, an exhibit is not perceived on the basis of the message content but rather by a combination of visual stimuli in the graphic display itself. These include color, size, contrast, contour, luminance, depth, movement, pattern, and form. All of these can be manipulated to make a visual display more effective."

The intent was to take the element of luck out of jury trials; indeed, Vinson once claimed that a purchaser of his full array of services could be 96 percent sure of the outcome before the unwittingly manipulated jury reached its verdict. Marty Cohen, an ambitious young lawyer in Pennsylvania, had been one of the early converts to this kind of social science research. While building a personal injury practice in the decaying industrial town of Easton in the late 1970s, Cohen had learned about the work of jury consultants and become excited about the prospect of making use of it. He had always liked the idea of improving his odds. The skinny, intense young lawyer had gotten off to a fortuitous start by finding an established local practitioner to serve as a mentor and to provide a steady stream of referrals. And by winning a good share of his early cases, Cohen had developed a reputation as a smart, scrappy courtroom lawyer, with a subtler touch than one might expect, given his rough edges and the jarring accent he had brought with him from his childhood in the Bronx. A law practice was an investment, he'd reasoned, and sometimes you had to spend money to make money. A success in his thirties, he had wanted to do better yet.

Cohen had contacted Arthur Patterson, a psychologist who was teaching at Cohen's alma mater, Penn State, and had just established a little trial consulting business on the side. For a few thousand dollars Art Patterson had conducted polls and assembled focus groups whenever Cohen thought that a case was big or complicated enough to warrant the expense. The results at times had been spectacular. And even when Cohen lost a case in which Patterson participated, Cohen had felt he had learned something.

Ten years later Cohen's practice was booming, and so was Patterson's. The consultant's operation in a pleasant neighborhood a few blocks from the Penn State campus was bringing in roughly a million dollars a year, about half of which he kept as profit. A balding man of forty-four, with a reddish brown mustache and a confident handshake, Patterson had left the faculty a few years earlier, and his little side business was now his sole occupation.[4] He didn't really need small cases like Cohen's Pizza Hut matter anymore, but Cohen was a favored client from the old days, and Patterson was charging him only seventy-five hundred dollars for very limited work: a single focus group and then a meeting to analyze the results.

The upcoming case was called *Bochini* v. *Yerkes, Pizza Hut and PepsiCo*. Bruce Bochini, now twenty, was the boy who, while bicycling at dusk, had been run down by the drunk driver five years earlier. For all its weaknesses, from a plaintiff's lawyer's perspective, the case did have some undeniable strengths. Bochini had smashed his foot, fractured his collarbone, broken some vertebrae. He'd needed surgery and physical therapy, for which medical bills had been huge. But the most enduring damage had been to his brain. As a result of the collision, Bochini had lost significant mental ability and, even more devastatingly, a degree of psychological control. He couldn't always appreciate the effect of his actions anymore, and he sometimes said inappropriate things. As a result, doctors predicted, he would have trouble holding down a job and even greater difficulty in personal relationships. If presented in the right case by the right attorney, losses such as those he had suffered could generate millions of dollars in damages.

But the case wouldn't be worth much at all unless the party

responsible for the injuries had enough money, or enough insurance, to pay the damages. The most obvious defendant, admitted drunk driver Cindy Yerkes, wasn't going to help much: Her insurance limit was just a hundred thousand dollars. PepsiCo, on the other hand, the owner of the Pizza Hut restaurant where Yerkes had claimed she had been drinking beer before the accident, could clearly survive a multimillion-dollar verdict. The problem would be proving without witnesses that PepsiCo was responsible for Mrs. Yerkes's drunk driving.

At a focus group conducted by Patterson in June 1991 Cohen learned a great deal about the challenge before him. In typical fashion the focus group had been selected meticulously. Patterson had started with the lists the county used to call residents for jury duty, then factored in the no-show rate for different ethnic groups. In addition, he had accounted for the likelihood that individuals in certain professions, such as law office employees and journalists, would be eliminated in a real case through peremptory challenges. On the basis of these calculations, he had determined that the jury that would hear the case would probably include at most five white-collar workers, among them two professionals; four housewives; two unemployed people; and two to three retirees. Within this group at least three would be unmarried or divorced. Five, at most, would have college degrees. The pretrial focus group would reflect these calculations in the belief that it would presage the actual jury's attitudes and concerns. In voir dire, of course, Cohen would seek to use his peremptory challenges to control the shape of the jury that would hear his case.

Those members of the focus group who had been chosen through telephone interviews with Patterson's researchers arrived at a hotel in Allentown before 6:00 P.M. on June 18. They had been drawn by curiosity and the promise of a free dinner and a thirty-five-dollar fee—real incentives during the tough economic times that had hit the region. (In other times and places focus group members had received a hundred dollars or more for their labors.) Patterson, whose smooth manner and classy business attire suggested an advertising man more than an academic, had conducted hundreds of such groups and seemed fully in command as he breezily explained the ground rules. Lawyers would give opening statements for Bochini, for Yerkes, and for Pizza Hut. No witnesses would appear, but the lawyers would summarize what the witnesses would say at the trial. The focus group members, also known as mock jurors, weren't told which side was sponsoring the focus group so they wouldn't be tempted to tell the lawyers what they wanted to hear. Similarly, the mock jurors weren't informed that all the parts in the minidrama would be played by lawyers working for Marty Cohen's firm.

Dennis Feeley, a young partner in the firm, led off on behalf of Bruce Bochini. Feeley, a beefy former schoolboy football player with a bland speaking style, emphasized the seriousness of the injuries and then spent much of his time going over the details of the accident. Using a photo enlargement, he indicated the intersection where Bochini had been bicycling, the location at which Mrs. Yerkes had struck him, and the points at which witnesses had stood. Feeley left no doubt that Mrs. Yerkes had been drunk—her blood alcohol level of 0.16 had been well above the legal limit—and that a person that drunk was likely to have had difficulty seeing clearly or estimating distances and speeds. But he also acknowledged a weakness in the case against her: Though the accident had occurred almost twenty minutes after sunset, Bruce hadn't had a light on his bicycle, in violation of state law.

Feeley waited until the second half of his presentation to explore Pizza Hut's liability—the crucial issue as far as collecting big damages was concerned, but the weakest part of Bochini's case. The law in Pennsylvania, as in many other states, required that commercial servers of alcohol refuse to provide drinks to anyone who was visibly intoxicated. Under this statute, known as a dramshop law, if the plaintiff could prove that Mrs. Yerkes had been served while visibly drunk, Pizza Hut and parent company PepsiCo could be held responsible for any damage she caused after she left the restaurant. But where was that proof? Immediately after the accident Mrs. Yerkes had said she was drinking with someone at Pizza Hut but that she couldn't remember who it was, a story she had stuck to in later interviews with the lawyers. It seemed obvious that she was shielding someone's identity. Was she also lying about whether she had even been at Pizza Hut? Might she have been drinking somewhere else instead? If so, Pizza Hut would bear no liability at all. Appearing somewhat flummoxed, Feeley brushed past this extraordinary hole in the evidence to focus instead on Pizza Hut's apparent failure to instruct servers on how to handle intoxicated patrons.

Feeley summed up by describing Bruce's injuries in grim and graphic detail and tallying up the costs of treating him. Medical bills amounted to $145,000. A lifetime of lost wages would come to $1.2 million, based on the average in the region for a high school graduate. Residential nursing care would amount to $3 million. If Bochini were fully compensated, he would be set for life, and the plaintiff's lawyers, who would be paid one third of the award, would enjoy another big payday. But all this would depend on convincing the jury that Pizza Hut had been at fault.

After Feeley finished, Marty Cohen took the floor to launch a passionate defense of Pizza Hut. Trying to anticipate all the arguments that would be thrown at Bochini's lawyers at the trial, Cohen ridiculed his real-life client's case. What was Cindy Yerkes hiding? he asked the focus group. Whom had she been with? Where had she been drinking? Had she ever been at Pizza Hut?

Cohen accused the plaintiff's lawyers of blaming Pizza Hut simply because it was owned by a big company. And he ridiculed the plaintiffs' damage theories. "Do you think the three million dollars would be there [for residential nursing care] if he wasn't suing Pepsi?" Cohen asked acidly. Bochini didn't escape Cohen's attack either. Why had the boy cut across the intersection when it was filled with cars? Why had he ridden after sunset without a light? "We didn't put him on that highway, and we didn't take the light off that bike," Cohen said.

By the time the presentation was over, the outcome seemed obvious. Perhaps Cohen had done too good a job on behalf of his opponent. The focus group's initial vote, before any deliberations, only highlighted the weaknesses in the case. Nine of the twelve found that Cindy Yerkes had been negligent, and five thought Bruce Bochini was also partly at fault. But only one out of twelve believed Pizza Hut was also partially liable. Damage assessments went as high as four million dollars. But with Pizza Hut bearing no share of the fault and thus paying no part of the award, Bochini probably would collect only one hundred thousand dollars, the maximum Cindy Yerkes's insurance would cover. The rest of the damages would go unpaid and remain uncollectible.

The focus group's deliberations, following its initial private ballots, offered little encouragement to the Bochini legal team, which viewed them later on videotape. A brash thirty-three-year-old focus group member named Larry, a struggling actor, led off by questioning an element of the plaintiff's case that the lawyers had considered the least questionable: Mrs. Yerkes's responsibility for the accident itself. Larry held up the photo of the accident scene and pointed out shadows that appeared on the road and the apparently poor visibility at the intersection. His concerns about whether Bruce Bochini could have been seen even by a sober driver sparked a long and spirited discussion.

From there matters turned worse for the plaintiff's lawyers. Debbie, a thirty-six-year-old nurse, challenged Mrs. Yerkes's statement that she had been at Pizza Hut for lunch for two to three hours but had drunk nowhere else before the five-twenty accident. "What happened to the missing hours?" Debbie asked. Lori, a twenty-eight-year-old secretary, jumped in with the observation that Mrs. Yerkes had been estranged from her husband at the time. "She might have been at some guy's house having an affair," said Lori, "and she was never at Pizza Hut." The illicit-romance theory was widely accepted around the table.

Even if they believed Mrs. Yerkes's basic story, most of the group members agreed that they still wouldn't know whether a waitress at Pizza Hut had noticed that Mrs. Yerkes was drinking excessively. "What if her companion ordered the drinks?" one asked. "What if Mrs. Yerkes had been in the bathroom when the drinks arrived?" another chimed in. Then no one would have known she was drunk, and the restaurant wouldn't be liable.

The group's final vote, after deliberations, concluded overwhelmingly that Mrs. Yerkes and Bruce Bochini shared responsibility for the accident but that Pizza Hut did not. The mock jurors not only were certain of their votes but were angry at the suggestion that Pizza Hut and PepsiCo might be saddled with liability just because they had deep pockets. To an outside observer, it seemed a good time to drop the case or at least agree to a modest settlement.

But that was not what Cohen and Patterson had in mind when they met in Cohen's office on the rainy Thursday morning the following October to prepare for the trial. After a few minutes of sports banter Patterson turned to his sheaf of notes and began to pick apart the Bochini focus group results. The surprise, he said, was how strongly, even emotionally, the mock jurors had objected to placing blame on Pizza Hut. Ordinarily jurors were hostile to large companies and sympathetic to injured boys. But here the drunk driver's liability was more immediate and more obvious and had detracted from the case against the deep pockets. In addition, Patterson speculated, the emerging philosophy of the nineties seemed to be that people should take responsibility for their actions. The proposition that Cindy Yerkes should be responsible for her own drinking was related to the idea that a victim of date rape never should have gotten in the way of danger. The mock jurors' impulse "was the same impulse that led people to believe Anita Hill should have handled any harassment herself without complaining," he said, referring to that year's public hearings on Clarence Thomas's Supreme Court nomination.[5]

To address the jurors' concerns, Patterson devised an alternative opening statement. The new approach would acknowledge the issue of personal responsibility while shifting the blame to the restaurant. "No one can stop an of-age individual from drinking so much that they become drunk," Patterson read aloud from this statement. "No one poured those drinks into Mrs. Yerkes; she voluntarily drank what she did that day. But society, through the legislature and the law, does take steps to protect individuals from themselves and protect the public from drinking individuals, when that drinking takes place in commercial settings. Because don't forget, bars are commercial businesses; they operate to make money. And any time there's money to be made, the government has to set down regulations about what you can and can't do to make that money."

Cohen, who had been leaning back, edged forward in his chair. He liked what he was hearing. "What about agreeing up front that Cindy Yerkes and Pizza Hut are each partially responsible?" he asked.

"Good," said Patterson. "You get credibility that way. If you say, 'Forget Cindy Yerkes,' they'll see right through you. They know about the deep pockets.'' The key, he added, was to show that this wasn't merely an effort to shift blame, that Pizza Hut actually anticipated that some of its patrons would get drunk and cause accidents but—for financial reasons—chose not to reduce the risks. "We need to stress that the restaurant's profit margin on alcohol is higher than it is on food," Patterson said. "The restaurant is there to make money; they have a motive. Jurors love motives. Why did somebody do it?''

Just fifteen minutes into the discussion the direction was becoming clear: Combat the weaknesses of the case by convincing the jurors that Pizza Hut was far more than just a convenient target for a big-money lawsuit. Pizza Hut had done wrong by not teaching its servers how to detect drunkenness, and it had done wrong out of greed. Plant this idea early and often, and jurors might want to teach the company a lesson even if proof of liability in this particular case was flimsy.

Never mind that on the basis of any objective look at the merits of his case, Bruce Bochini didn't deserve to win damages from Pizza Hut. As Clarence Darrow had put it, "The lawyer's idea of justice" meant no more than "a verdict for his client." For Cohen, social science was a way to increase his chances of achieving that goal.

Cohen and his partners had accumulated a good deal of evidence to bolster their strategy of blaming Pizza Hut, including a pile of employee manuals that seemed to cover everything but how to deal with heavy drinkers. In a company that was so well managed, they would ask the jury, could this life-and-death matter have been a mere oversight on Pizza Hut's part? Further, Patterson suggested, the lawyers could try to turn against Pizza Hut the evidence that few people get drunk in its restaurants. Rather than let this fact make Pizza Hut seem virtuous, the lawyers could argue that profit-crazed

Pizza Hut didn't consider it cost-effective to train its servers for the few lunch-crowd beer guzzlers they might encounter. The argument would go like this, Cohen said: "Even if the risk is slight, for the one person hurt, it doesn't matter if it's just one in one thousand." Eagerly recasting Cohen's version to make it stronger, Patterson offered this: "They carry people like Bruce Bochini on their balance sheet as a small debit." Cohen nodded.

The key would be getting the jurors to believe that it was legitimate to make an issue of the lack of employee training. "In our mock trial and in other cases like this, jurors think they know all about how to tell if someone's drunk. We need to emphasize that this isn't true," Patterson said. "We need to show what other companies' training programs consist of. We need to make it legitimate to use all the dirt we have on Pizza Hut."

The session began to take on the feel of a sales meeting, with excitement running high. Far from dropping the case, the lawyers now seemed intoxicated with the challenge of learning enough from the focus group's reactions to win with a real jury. Returning to his notes, Patterson pointed out that the mock jurors had shown sympathy for the Pizza Hut waitresses, who might have been too busy and hassled to keep an eye on beer-drinking patrons. The solution Patterson suggested: "Aim the blame at managers. It's the executive, the people above. From the top, it's 'Sell, sell, sell.'"

"In voir dire, I'll ask whether they've ever been an employee of Pizza Hut, Pepsi, Taco Bell, Kentucky Fried Chicken [all divisions of PepsiCo]," said Cohen. "That will make it clear that it's a big corporation; its veins and corpuscles are money."

Sandwiches arrived. The four lawyers and their consultant continued working. At some point Feeley would have to deal in the opening with the factual weaknesses in the plaintiff's case. The first question was how to present Cindy Yerkes. They couldn't discredit her completely because they needed the jury to believe her testimony that she had, in fact, been drinking that day at Pizza Hut. It was the only evidence that linked the restaurant to the case. On the other hand, no jury would think too highly of a woman who was drunk as she drove to pick up her young son at a day care center. And everyone would have to doubt her credibility somewhat because no one would believe that she couldn't remember the identity of her companion.

Patterson's solution was twofold. The lawyers would have to depict her as a nice woman who had been having some temporary marital difficulties and may have been talking out her problems with a friend over a very long lunch. She was loyally shielding the identity of her lunch companion—not necessarily a lover—but otherwise her story held together. In the immediate aftermath of a traumatic accident she had told police that she'd been at Pizza Hut, that she'd eaten pizza. She'd said so on the accident report and had never wavered. Bochini's lawyers could argue that she would have been too distraught to make up the story initially and that she had had no motive to lie about where she had been. There was no reason to believe she had gone elsewhere to drink if she said she hadn't.

The long-emotional-lunch theory was tenable if told to the right jurors. Here Patterson's insights into jury behavior would be put to use. "Believing someone can sit and talk for three hours in a restaurant requires a certain type of person," he explained in the early afternoon. "You need someone who's had an affair, romantic types, housewives. Her husband said he was living in a trailer on the same property where she was living. They've since reconciled; maybe they were just having a fight. This is a soap opera. That's something we can work with."

Turning to the accident itself, Patterson said the lawyers would have to get the jury to dispose of the issues quickly and cleanly so they could concentrate on Pizza Hut's liability. That's what the mock jurors had failed to do. First, Patterson said, the lawyers had to toss out the photographs, the ones with the shadows that had spurred focus group questions about visibility, and replace them with simple diagrams of the accident site. Then they had to emphasize that drunkenness causes tunnel vision, which would have made it difficult for Cindy Yerkes to see Bochini coming from the side. "You've got to say she would have hit anyone who would have been crossing the road at that point," Patterson said. It also would be necessary to stress that though the sun had gone down, it was still light out when the accident occurred. A few minutes later Bochini would have been riding after dark without a light, but that had nothing to do with the cause of this accident.

Patterson had come equipped with ideas about every aspect of the case, even how to present Bochini's injuries to the jury. Here the plaintiff's team would have a big advantage that they didn't have in the focus group: Bochini himself would be present. Thus the injuries would become much more concrete to the jury, much more painful. "We need to give examples of why this guy isn't employable," Patterson said. Though Bochini's IQ had dropped from an average level down to 70 as a result of the accident, according to Cohen, IQ alone wouldn't be sufficient to make the point. "People with low IQ can work," Patterson said. "Thank *L.A. Law* for Benny for making that clear."

Instead, the lawyers would focus on Bochini's difficulties controlling his impulses and understanding the consequences of his actions. These problems would make it difficult for him to stay employed. Feeley pointed out that Bochini had worked odd jobs since the accident and had even lasted a year at one job. But, Patterson assured the lawyers coolly, "It's to his credit. Jurors love people who try. You want to get sympathy for this kid."

What type of person would respond best to Cohen's case as he and Patterson were redefining it? Social scientists had determined that race, ethnic group, and gender—the measures lawyers had traditionally relied on the most—provided only limited clues to how a juror was likely to vote. More important were individuals' actual attitudes. The trick was to learn about those attitudes during voir dire. Often, the research had shown, life circumstances provided clues to attitudes. Because most jurors wouldn't be candid about their attitudes, lawyers would have to rely heavily on such indirect information.[6]

To help the lawyers read the clues, Patterson had developed a handy two-page guide to the characteristics the plaintiff's counsel should seek and those they should avoid. The profile had been based on opinion research Patterson had conducted for Cohen's firm in previous cases, which Patterson had modified to reflect the special characteristics of this case. For the most part the list, called a jury profile, represented a leap in sophistication from the stereotypes plaintiffs' lawyers had traditionally used. Though Linn and Spence had called upon demographic classifications in the Marcos case, such categories were included on Patterson's list only when focus groups and polls had proved they were accurate predictors of jurors' attitudes. For example, the research for this case had shown that women would be more proplaintiff than men, older jurors would be more favorable than the middle-aged, the less educated better than the more educated, people with children more desirable than people without.

Patterson also advised the Bochini lawyers to find out whether prospective jurors owned or rented their homes and

102

to favor the renters. The research had shown that renters were more likely than homeowners to support the plaintiff in any personal injury suit. Renters, it seemed, were less concerned about liability insurance premiums and were less worried than homeowners about being sued.

Patterson also recommended jurors with so-called authoritarian personalities, meaning—in the corkscrew lingo of social science—that they readily accepted rules and obeyed authority. In ordinary personal injury suits, such people generally favored the defendant because they didn't let sympathy for the plaintiff get in the way of applying the law rigorously. But in a dramshop case such as this one, the plaintiff had to count on jurors' willingness to blame a waitress or a restaurant manager for an accident in which neither had played a direct part. Only "authoritarian" jurors could be relied on to enforce that law, even if it didn't seem entirely just to them.

The research also had shown that people who were active in community, school, or church activities would be more likely than not to blame a restaurant owner for a drunk-driving accident. Such people, whom sociologists describe as having "high social integration," wanted to keep the community safe and would be willing to send a message to anyone who might create a health or safety hazard.

In this case, of course, anyone who had been a victim of a drunk-driving accident, or was active in Mothers Against Drunk Driving or other such groups, would be ideal for the plaintiff. Similarly, nondrinkers or light drinkers would be much better plaintiff's jurors than would heavy drinkers. Also, people who served alcohol for a living would be bad plaintiff's jurors, as would business managers in general, because they would identify with the defense.

Patterson reviewed all these findings, adding nuances along the way. On the basis of his polling data, he'd found that bicycle riders would be good jurors because they would understand how defenseless a bicyclist could be with traffic bearing down on him. But drivers of sports cars should be rejected. "You don't want Ferrari or Porsche drivers," he explained. "They're risk takers. They think there are too many restrictions on drivers as it is."

It was approaching 3:00 P.M., and Patterson began summarizing the day's discussions. The most important thing to learn from the focus group, he said, was that the plaintiff's case had to concentrate on Pizza Hut's negligence and greed. Feeley had to start with it and end with it. He had to be merciless. "Right," Cohen said. "Scare the living shit out of Pizza Hut, and then see what happens."

After Patterson departed, Feeley and Cohen set to work redrafting their opening statement and planning the trial. Until then Cohen hadn't paid the case much attention; preparation had been Feeley's job. But over the weekend Cohen immersed himself in the material, as he always did just before a trial. By Monday morning he would be ready.

Although he had tried more than a hundred cases in his career, Cohen still had to fight back a wave of stage fright as he rose in a big modern courtroom in the new wing of the Northampton County Courthouse to address the panel of forty prospective jurors. The lawyer did his best to follow Patterson's guidelines on which jurors to favor or reject. In addition, he began in voir dire to plant seeds that he would water after the trial began.

In states, such as Pennsylvania, that allow attorneys, rather than the judge, to conduct the questioning of prospective jurors, clever lawyers have always seized the opportunity to start the process of persuasion immediately. Trial consultants have applied their research to this effort as well as to jury selection and have refined lawyers' techniques. One method is to confront the jury candidates with a proposition about which they might ordinarily have doubt and ask whether there is anyone who can't accept the proposition. The social pressure to go along will be great, and people might, in the process, persuade themselves that they do indeed agree. "The key to why this works and the reason why it is appropriate to voir dire is that jurors must not be aware that an attempt is being made to persuade them," Donald Vinson writes in his how-to book for lawyers. "They are convinced that they have changed their minds by themselves."[7]

The theory is that once a prospective juror agrees to a proposition, he will be more likely to defend it as his own. In one of the most successful applications of this approach, flamboyant Texas trial lawyer Joseph Jamail spent hours eliciting commitments from a Houston jury in 1985 about how companies should behave in contract negotiations. He persuaded the panel to agree that a businessman who shakes hands on a deal must be held to its terms, even in a multibillion-dollar transaction. The actual law on the issue was much more complex, but the jury remembered its commitment to the sanctity of the handshake and, in the biggest jury award ever, granted Jamail client Pennzoil more than ten billion dollars in damages against rival Texaco.[8]

On a smaller scale Cohen was seeking similar results. In their pretrial session the previous Thursday, Patterson had reminded Cohen to seek commitments from the jury panel. "The psychological research is very convincing that getting a promise does in fact work," Patterson had explained. "They believe that everyone in the courtroom will remember they made the pledge, plus they don't have positions yet. So if you give them positions, they adopt them." As Patterson had suggested, Cohen asked the jurors if everyone could accept and apply the state law that made a restaurant liable for serving alcohol to a visibly intoxicated patron, regardless of how he or she felt about the law personally. After getting general assent, Cohen added a touch of his own: He asked several jurors by name whether they could make that pledge. All said yes. He also tried something that the consultants call inoculation: getting jurors to consider and reject the opponent's argument before the opponent gets to make it. Pizza Hut's lawyer would challenge Cindy Yerkes's statement that she had drunk beer at the restaurant by suggesting that she lacked credibility. After all, anyone who claimed not to remember the identity of her companion either had a terrible memory or was lying. So Cohen asked the panel whether anyone would automatically disbelieve a witness who couldn't remember with whom she was drinking. They all affirmed that they wouldn't think of doing such a thing.

Voir dire gave Cohen the chance to advance his case in other, equally manipulative ways. In questioning the prospects, Cohen discovered that one had worked at a restaurant chain called Applebee's that sponsored a program to train employees on detecting the signs of intoxication. The existence of such programs at places other than Pizza Hut would help Bochini because it would suggest that Pizza Hut had been less concerned than other companies about preventing drunk-driving accidents. Cohen let the information about Applebee's sink in and then returned to the juror later in the questioning to emphasize the point. "You had that responsibility [for serving liquor]?" Cohen asked. "And you received training for it?" As Cohen and everyone in the room already knew, the answers were, of course, yes.

Cohen then introduced Bruce Bochini to the panel. Bochini had been sitting in the back of the room with his mother, and the tall, thin young man in a light blue suit stood up. With his crew cut and acne, he looked like an all-American teen; whatever pain and damage he had suffered wasn't immediately visible. Cohen thought this was good. Juries, he said, are usually more sympathetic to plaintiffs who don't look monstrous. "Bruce Bochini won't be in the courtroom during the trial," Cohen explained to the panel. "There will be testimony about his injuries and what will happen to him that's not appropriate for him to hear. Does everyone understand that?" Everyone did.

Cohen completed his voir dire questioning by extracting a pretty significant pledge: "Can you tell me that if we prove that Pizza Hut violated the law by serving liquor to Cindy Yerkes when she was visibly drunk or intoxicated, you can return a substantial verdict against Pepsi and Pizza Hut? Can you do that?" He called out several individuals' names. They all compliantly agreed to the pledge. Even before opening statements had begun, the case didn't look nearly as bad as it had once seemed.

Of course, two sides could play the same game, and Pizza Hut's lawyer, Stephen Kreglow, a savvy insurance defense attorney who had tried numerous personal injury cases, attempted to undo the damage when it was his turn to question the jurors. He elicited commitments from jurors to decide the case solely on the facts, not to rule against Pizza Hut just because it was a big corporation, and to send Bruce Bochini home without a penny if he deserved no damages under the law. But Kreglow miscalculated in his effort to neutralize Cohen's questioning of the Applebee juror. "You worked at Applebee's as a bartender, and Pizza Hut doesn't have a bar," Kreglow said. "Would you agree that the training you received might be different than what's appropriate in a Pizza Hut?" Rather than concur, the juror shot back: "Not necessarily. Whenever you sell alcohol, you must—" With that he was cut off by the judge, but Cohen's tight little smile was unmistakable.

Over lunch at a little sandwich shop across from the courthouse, Cohen was still cackling over his Applebee victory.

Nonetheless, because this was a civil case, state law entitled him to only four peremptory challenges. And the jury he would be able to seat would be far from ideal for his purposes. Though some social science consultants charge a small fortune for their dizzying array of services, they can't influence who happens to be called for jury duty on a particular day. And the forty from whom Cohen had to choose were an unsympathetic lot from a plaintiff's perspective.

Even after exercising his challenges along the lines Patterson had suggested, Cohen was left with a jury that included a company manager in a case in which Cohen would be bashing managers, a grocery store owner who might identify more with restaurant owners than with an injured plaintiff, a majority of males in a case in which Patterson recommended females, and several people who were too young or drank too heavily to fit the plaintiff's ideal juror profile. Luck being, in this sense, the enemy of science, it was fortunate that Patterson's advice the previous week had also focused on how to win the case even if the jury turned out to be as skeptical as the focus group had seemed.

By nine-fifteen on Tuesday everyone was in place, and it was Feeley's time to pitch the client's cause. Given the money and effort that had gone into trying to shape the jury along partisan lines, his opening line seemed particularly disingenuous: that those now in the jury box were "the twelve best people to decide the case." Then he launched directly into an assault on Pizza Hut. The case was no longer about an irresponsibly drunk driver who wouldn't even explain with whom she had been drinking, nor was it about a boy who had ridden at dusk without a light on his bicycle. Instead, it was about a large corporation that, Feeley declared, "was more concerned about profit than about the safety of the people they serve."

To illustrate the new theme of the case, Feeley marched the full length of the jury box to pick up a stack of reports he had strategically left at the other end, then marched back to the counsel's table with the documents and threw them down. These, he said, were Pizza Hut training manuals. "They teach and test them on every aspect of management and service," he declared, keeping to the script. "They teach them what to do when a vacuum cleaner doesn't work. They have a whole section called 'Troubleshooting Beer,' how to serve beer, how to hold the glass, how cold, how much foam to put on top. Yet if you look through all their manuals, there's nothing in there that tells them the effect of alcohol or the safety associated with the service of alcohol."

To strengthen the point, Feeley emphasized that many other companies, including Anheuser-Busch, sponsored training programs on detecting the subtle signs of visible intoxication. But, he said with apparent disgust, Pizza Hut was more interested in making a profit on alcohol than in guarding against its dangers. Feeley also concentrated on both the large size of the company and the large size of the pitcher in which the beer was served (sixty-four ounces). And he took considerable time outlining the effects of alcohol on a drinker's perceptions, particularly its tendency to reduce peripheral vision by as much as 90 percent.

By the time Feeley got to the accident itself, the case had a moral force that hadn't seemed possible the night of the focus group. The jurors had indeed been "shown the dirt" on Pizza Hut. Now Feeley could put the accident in the context of Pizza Hut's well-established negligence: Cindy Yerkes was driving drunk because Pizza Hut had let her drink too much.

According to Patterson's theory, a jury predisposed to punish Pizza Hut would be less picky about some of the evidentiary gaps in the case. And Feeley now sidled up to the weaknesses in the story, in an effort to confront them and minimize their significance. He pointed to each place on the police report, which had been blown up on a chart, where Mrs. Yerkes described her activities on the day of the accident. She had eaten lunch, she had written in one place. She had eaten pizza, she had explained further. She had been at Pizza Hut, she had elaborated. These statements were consistent and had come right after the accident, Feeley stressed, and only then did he note that she hadn't remembered with whom she had been that day. But he immediately provided a possible explanation: that her marriage had been troubled and that she had met some unnamed person with whom she could commiserate. The hint of an extramarital affair caused several jurors to sit up in their seats. "You'll have to decide," Feeley suggested, "whether it's reasonable that she might have been sitting there talking to someone, commiserating, for a couple of hours."

It was an artful finessing of the missing person issue, and Pizza Hut lawyer Stephen Kreglow knew it. He leaped to his feet to object that Feeley was making inappropriate inferences rather than summing up the factual basis for his case. But the damage had been done. So far Pizza Hut looked like a villain, Cindy Yerkes like a vulnerable woman who should have been protected from herself. The Art Patterson approach seemed to be working.

But this jury wouldn't be allowed to decide. As Feeley continued, he turned to the anticipated testimony of a scientific witness. The expert would testify, Feeley said, that, on the basis of medical evidence, Cindy Yerkes had been visibly intoxicated. Although Feeley didn't explain the details, he was referring obliquely to a method under which one determined whether a person was visibly intoxicated at any given time on the basis of the person's blood alcohol level many hours later. The method, called the relation-back theory, wasn't universally accepted, and because the judge had not yet decided if he would let the jury consider it, the lawyers had been told not to discuss it during their opening statements. Kreglow shot to his feet and asked that a mistrial be granted because Feeley had introduced the subject. Judge Robert E. Simpson, Jr., boyish-looking and slight despite his high perch and judicial robes, took only a few minutes to decide. At five minutes after ten he granted the mistrial motion. The case would have to be tried before a new jury. In most jurisdictions that would mean delaying the new trial for weeks or months, until everyone's schedule permitted them to reconvene. But not in the efficient Northampton County courts. "We'll select another jury in one half hour. Please tell the jury clerk we need forty more jurors," Judge Simpson said sharply, before walking off the bench.

Cohen was desolate and embarrassed. "This is the first time this has happened to me in twenty-three years," he muttered, while defending Feeley and maintaining that the opening statement had stopped short of discussing the forbidden theory. Beads of sweat formed on Cohen's nose as he contemplated preparing to question a second jury panel immediately. It would be difficult to approach the task with the same level of interest and intensity he had summoned the day before. "It's like going to the same movie right after seeing it," he said.

Cohen ducked into the judge's chambers to seek a delay in the trial, but the judge refused. By five minutes after eleven, forty new prospects were in their seats, and Cohen, seeming a little flatter than the day before, began the task of praising, analyzing, and persuading this fresh panel. It didn't take long, though, for Cohen to realize that the mistrial might have been a blessing in disguise. Five of the panelists were connected in some way to anti–drunk-driving organizations. One announced through tears that her father had been killed by a drunk driver and that the defendant had been tried in this courtroom. That juror was dismissed by the judge, but not before the rest of the prospects had gotten a firsthand lesson in the tragedy of drunk driving. Another panelist had a close friend who had been injured by a drunk driver. Another was a professor of special education who dealt with the teaching of handicapped individuals such as Bruce Bochini.

Even after Kreglow had exercised his peremptory challenges, the jury remained decidedly proplaintiff. "The second jury scared me," Kreglow said later. "I couldn't strike everyone I wanted to." Kreglow still believed Bochini had a very tenuous case against Pizza Hut, but now he was worried. Feeley's opening statement in the first trial had been powerful. With this new jury it might be even more effective.

Before the trial Pizza Hut had offered $150,000 to settle the case. This reflected an evaluation that the plaintiff probably wouldn't win but that it would be worth spending the money to eliminate the small risk of a much larger jury verdict. When Cohen had rejected the sum, Pizza Hut had dispatched one of its in-house company lawyers to Easton to watch the start of the trial and evaluate for himself whether the plaintiff might win. "One reason I did an extensive voir dire was because the Pizza Hut lawyer was there," Cohen said later.

After the second jury had been picked, Pizza Hut authorized Kreglow to offer a bigger settlement. Judge Simpson adjourned court early on Tuesday afternoon to let the lawyers haggle. Pizza Hut suggested $325,000. Cohen asked for $375,000. They settled on $350,000. Cindy Yerkes's insurer would pitch in the full amount of her insurance: $100,000. Cohen's firm would get a third of the $450,000 total, which seemed a pretty tidy sum in such a farfetched case. But, explained Kreglow, "You may assess your liability side at a ninety percent chance of winning, but you now have a ten percent chance of a two- to three-million-dollar verdict. So I knew we would have to settle."

Art Patterson's behind-the-scenes advice to Cohen had proved crucial in forcing Pizza Hut's hand. Thanks to Patterson's work, the plaintiff's lawyers had discovered that their original approach to the case had bombed before a focus group. Patterson had helped them recast their opening statement, which had taken the attack directly to the company, while the company's lawyer watched and worried. The consultant also had helped prepare Cohen for his voir dire, which the lawyer had used to begin the process of persuading the jurors. Patterson's experience and perspective also had helped the lawyers remain optimistic about their own case and eliminated any temptation to drop the suit. "Although the case looked very weak based on the results of the focus group," Patterson said after the trial, "they didn't drop the case because they saw why they had lost, and they learned ways to correct the problem." If the stakes in the case had been higher, Patterson would have tested the new approach as well and probably refined it even further.

In a justice system structured to seek the truth by letting opposing parties clash, what's wrong with strengthening the weapons at the adversaries' disposal? That's all the social scientists say they're doing: replacing stereotypes and myths with scientific data.

But one obvious consequence is that the jury system loses much of its moral authority. Why should we defer to the decision of a group of individuals who have been selected for their likely partisanship and then persuaded by many of the same techniques that sell soap and breakfast cereal? When verdicts come to seem more manipulated than majestic, one thinks of *Brave New World* more readily than *12 Angry Men.*

Even high-priced lawyer David Boies, whose career skyrocketed with the help of Donald Vinson in the IBM case, has begun to wonder whether jury consultants are good for the system. The reasons to use juries, according to Boies, "are not enhanced by turning the process into a psychological analysis of particular jurors and how they are likely to respond."

A further consequence is that clients who can't afford social science consultants are placed at a practical disadvantage, exacerbating the disadvantage they already face because they can't afford the best lawyers. "The affluent people and the corporations can buy it, the poor radicals get it free, and everybody in between is at a disadvantage," sociologist Amitai Etzioni has said. "And that's not the kind of system we want."[9]

A third, even more dire consequence is that jurors who might once have served proudly and well are being excluded in voir dire, not just on a hunch but on the analysis of a data-driven scientist. Ironically, just as jury service laws have been changed to allow a broader cross section of people into the jury room, technology has evolved to exclude new groups on the basis of their demographic characteristics, values, and psyches. Juries are thus rendered less representative of their communities. And many well-qualified individuals become disappointed in a system that, despite its promise of inclusion, rejects them as jurors precisely because they would be fair and thoughtful decision makers.

Numerous rules already exist to temper the adversary process in the interests of fairness. Opposing parties can't intimidate witnesses, steal documents from each other, destroy evidence, or bribe jurors. There's an elaborate law of evidence, and there are clear rules of the road for examining and cross-examining witnesses. Jury consultants have evaded restrictions so far. But their work relies heavily on the continued existence of peremptory challenges, the elimination of which would have a Kryptonite-like effect on these new super-men of the legal world. More direct restrictions on particular practices, such as paying shadow jurors to sit in a courtroom, could also be imposed. The goal would be to move back toward what de Tocqueville described, and what we still struggle to envision, as the American jury: "a political institution [that is] . . . as direct and as extreme a consequence of the sovereignty of the people as universal suffrage."[10]

4

WHAT'S A BLIVET?

—

A N hour before dawn on June 1, 1989, Rocky Phillips launched a plastic worm into a patch of shivering reeds and waited calmly for a bass to hit. In the hilly green countryside around Thomasville, North Carolina, Rocky was renowned for his skill. One time half the fishermen in town had set their sights on a particular overgrown lunker in a particular pond, and Rocky had finally been called in to bring the fish to justice. After his inevitable success Rocky had tossed it back. His trophy wall had already been full; besides, he liked a fair fight and wasn't prone to being vindictive.

These days Rocky was wearing his hair long in the back and working nights for a furniture manufacturer; as an assistant supervisor he was pulling down twenty thousand dollars a year and was proud of his unit's top-of-the-line six-thousand-dollar bed. At twenty-five, though, he was locked into a troubled marriage that didn't seem likely to survive. He worried about providing for his baby girl, fantasized about joining the police force, drove a pickup with the model name Rocky, and, whenever he could, just fished for bass. This early morning, as usual, he got his fish.

On the same day, several hundred miles to the northeast, in

116

the posh Georgetown section of Washington, D.C., Garret Rasmussen also had risen before dawn to get a four-thirty jump on a busy morning. Garret, long-necked and awkwardly handsome, pulled on his sweats and headed for a boathouse on the Potomac, where he slid into a shell and hit the river hard. After an hour of fast rowing and a cold shower, he bicycled the few blocks to his office, more eager than seemed reasonable for a forty-year-old lawyer preparing for a day of antitrust practice at a giant firm.

Later that day a summons arrived at Rocky's home. He had been called for jury duty in a civil case in federal court in Greensboro, twenty-seven miles east of Thomasville. The trial, he was informed, would take eight to ten weeks. Secretly Rocky was thrilled. Summer was approaching, and his unair-conditioned apartment would be stifling. Besides, he was happy to get away for a while from his wife and his job, happy to take stock. He didn't know what the trial was about, but friends had told him great jury stories, and the process had always sounded like fun.

Garret, too, was anxious for the trial to begin. For nearly five years he had been preparing for this case, taking depositions, writing briefs, practicing his cross-examinations. Mostly, though, he had been perfecting a novel antitrust theory that he was about to try out in the nasty price war that had landed two giant tobacco companies in court. The theory involved one of the most complicated commercial laws in America, called the Robinson-Patman Act, the interpretation of which lawyers and judges had been debating in scholarly articles and abstruse court opinions for years. Rasmussen's take on the law was even more difficult to comprehend than just about anyone else's. But he had tried out his theory on lots of very patient friends and colleagues in Washington and New York, and they had found it persuasive. Now he was eager to see how a jury would respond.

The scene, then, was set for a shattering collision between a

North Carolina jury in which Rocky Phillips would be foreman and a small army of high-priced commercial lawyers in
which Garret Rasmussen would be the guiding intellectual
force. Caught in the middle were two big tobacco companies
—Liggett & Myers and Brown & Williamson—that were betting tens of millions of dollars on the outcome. And unavoidable along the way was the issue of jury competence: whether
juries have outlived their usefulness in complicated civil cases
such as this one and whether they should be replaced by professional judges or business experts who, at the very least, understand the problems they are asked to resolve. For this trial
was to transform the Greensboro federal courtroom into a
theater of the absurd.

The chief argument for juries in civil cases, which involve
personal and commercial disputes as opposed to criminal
prosecutions, is that juries are more likely than individual
judges to be incorruptible and impartial. In addition, civil
cases often involve questions of how the community wants
people to behave toward one another, and it has often been
said that the jury, as the voice of the community, is in the best
position to serve as both constable and referee. As John Adams put it in his florid eighteenth-century prose, trial by jury
in civil cases meant that he could "lose none of my Property,
or the Necessaries, conveniences or Ornaments of Life which
indulgent Providence has showered around me, but by the
Judgment of my Peers, my equals, my Neighbours, men who
know me and to whom I am known . . . men who are indif-
frent on which side the Truth lies, if I dispute with my Neigh-
bour."[1]

This was the kind of thinking that led to the ratification of
the Seventh Amendment to the Constitution, guaranteeing
jury trial in civil cases. But what if the jury doesn't have any
idea what the lawyers are talking about? What good is a system
in which jurors reach their verdicts through favoritism, preju-

dice, or even guesswork because they don't understand the issues? That's what many lawyers and judges, particularly those with close ties to the business community, have been wondering for the past thirty years or more. In 1963 Harvard Law School Dean Erwin Griswold stirred up the legal world by asking, "Why should anyone think that 12 persons brought in from the street, selected in various ways, for their lack of general ability, should have any special capacity for deciding controversies between persons?"[2] Two decades later former Supreme Court Chief Justice Warren Burger observed that "even Jefferson would be appalled at the prospect of a dozen of his stout yeomen and artisans trying to cope with some of today's complex litigation."[3]

The argument against the jury in such cases was made most powerfully by jurors themselves in a 1978 California trial in which IBM had been accused of monopolizing various markets in the computer industry. After five months of trial and more than three weeks of deliberation in the financially and technologically complicated case, the jury couldn't reach a verdict. Before allowing a mistrial, Judge Samuel Conti called the jurors into his chambers to find out how much they had understood about the case. "Mr. Vasilev, what is software?" the judge asked when the jurors were gathered around him.

"That's the paper software," the juror responded.

The judge continued: "Do you know what an interface is?" He was referring to the connection between a computer and an auxiliary piece of equipment, a concept that had been discussed at length during the trial.

Vasilev answered: "Well, if you take a blivet, turn it off one thing and drop it down, it's an interface change, right?"

Other jurors didn't fare much better. "Do you know what demand substitutability is?" juror Bratovich was asked.

"Well, I would like to kind of look into that," he replied.

"And how about barriers to entry, Ms. Keller?"

"I would have to read about it."

After the mistrial was granted, Judge Conti questioned the jurors further, and most said frankly that they hadn't understood key elements of the suit. Asked whether a jury could ever be qualified to hear a case of such complexity, the foreman replied: "If you could find a jury that's both a computer technician, a lawyer, an economist, knows all about that stuff, yes, I think you could have a qualified jury. But we don't know anything about that."[4]

The case in which Rocky Phillips and Garret Rasmussen were to meet was easily as perplexing as the IBM dispute. The facts, in simpler terms than the jury ever heard them, were these: Until recently all of the Big Six cigarette companies had charged a standard price for all brands of cigarettes and had raised prices virtually in unison. Though the scheme sounded a good deal like illegal price-fixing, it hadn't violated antitrust laws because company executives had never agreed explicitly to the arrangement. It was more like price tag than price-fixing, though the effect was much the same: high prices for consumers and extraordinary profits for all the cigarette manufacturers.

Liggett, however, with only 2.3 percent of the market, had been on a long, slow slide since the 1950s and was selling too few cigarettes to make the game worth playing any longer. New smokers seemed an unlikely source of business, as young people were finally heeding years of surgeon generals' reports. The only path to rejuvenated profits seemed to be to break the unwritten industry rule, slash prices, and build sales among budget-conscious smokers.

The Liggett plan worked. The company's new supercheap cigarettes, selling at 35 percent discounts in nondescript black and white packs, hit the Piggly Wigglys and Winn-Dixies of

America in 1980. By early 1984 the company was spewing out twenty billion so-called generic cigarettes a year, 65 percent of its entire volume.

Liggett's good fortune, however, didn't escape the notice of competitor Brown & Williamson, a distant third among cigarette makers behind Philip Morris and R. J. Reynolds. Customers had deserted all the major cigarette makers to take advantage of the Liggett bargain, but smokers' loyalty to B&W brands such as Viceroy and Kool appeared to be particularly weak, and the company was especially hard hit. In self-defense B&W executives decided to market a cheap cigarette of their own and charge some big wholesalers even less than they had been paying for Liggett's version. The B&W counterattack quickly cut into Liggett's sales. Liggett cried foul and filed suit.

B&W's executives claimed that they were merely competing aggressively, and lawfully, in the new low-priced market that Liggett itself had created. Liggett and its lawyer, Rasmussen, saw it differently. Under the Robinson-Patman Act, companies were barred from charging some customers more than others for the same product if the price difference was aimed at interfering with free competition. The law was supposed to prevent a big supermarket chain, for instance, from slashing prices temporarily in a particular store (in order to wipe out a competing grocer) while keeping prices higher in its other stores. Unless such behavior was prohibited, lawmakers had reasoned, the chain would be able to eliminate each mom-and-pop competitor and then raise its prices even higher.

Rasmussen seemed to have found a way—a complicated, even serpentine way, but still a way—to apply this law to Liggett's situation. As he had excitedly explained it to colleagues, B&W was offering larger price rebates to bigger wholesalers than to smaller wholesalers and therefore was running afoul of the prohibition on charging some customers more than others for the same product. B&W was doing so, it seemed, to encourage the biggest wholesalers to distribute B&W's product exclusively rather than Liggett's.

For B&W's actions to be anticompetitive under the Robinson-Patman Act, Liggett would have to prove that B&W's aim was to keep prices high in the long run. So Liggett would have to argue that B&W sought to enter the generic cigarette business only to drive Liggett out of it. Once competition from Liggett was reduced or eliminated, the theory went, B&W intended to drop its line of low-priced cigarettes and go back to selling even more of its expensive, full-priced brands. In that way, following the supermarket analogy, short-term price cuts would have resulted in the eventual sale of more cigarettes at a higher price.

But even if B&W had intended to damage its competitor, Liggett's argument seemed to make sense economically only if none of the other, bigger cigarette makers were capable of adding low-priced brands of their own. If they could, then they, too, could compete with B&W at the lower price, and B&W would gain nothing in particular by driving Liggett away. B&W sold only 11 percent of the nation's cigarettes, so it didn't seem to have the market power to keep others from entering the low-price niche. In fact, by the time of the trial nearly the entire cigarette industry had turned to low-priced cigarettes as a profitable supplement to such expensive brands as Marlboro, Camel, and Winston.

Would the jury view B&W's price-cutting as healthy competition or dirty pool? That would depend on how artfully the case was presented to Rocky Phillips and his fellow jurors, on what they understood of it, and on how they dealt with the multitude of issues they would discover they couldn't possibly comprehend.

*   *   *

Rocky rolled into Greensboro on Monday morning, July 10, and found his way to the federal courthouse, a modest four-story building that doubled as the city's main post office. Greensboro, population 155,000, was a very big city to Rocky, and he didn't get there often. He was neatly dressed in a blue short-sleeved work shirt and gray-green safari pants with giant pockets. He felt a little jittery as he entered the high-ceilinged courtroom lined with portraits of judges and packed with serious-looking people.

As in the Marcos case, many of the better-educated people in the jury pool had already removed themselves before voir dire. Of the hundred jurors called for the case, fifty-four had sent in written excuses, and four more who had shown up had convinced officials that they should be released. As usual, most of the excuses had involved work-related conflicts; in a case about business conduct, it was notable that many of the work-related excuses came from people who ran their own businesses. Frank Bullock, the elegant, bald judge, greeted the prospective jurors who remained and ran through a brisk voir dire. Lawyers exercised their challenges, rejected jurors were replaced, and by day's end a jury of six, plus three alternates, had been picked. (In the early 1970s, many courts began to use juries of fewer than twelve in an effort to save money. The practice, while condoned by the Supreme Court, remains controversial because of the belief that smaller juries are less likely to be representative of the community.)[5]

Rocky Phillips's colleagues in this strange venture looked as if they had been seated for a Norman Rockwell painting. They had much in common with him—and less with Garret Rasmussen. Most were active in church affairs; many worked with their hands. Not one had proceeded beyond high school; not one had any significant business experience; not one read a national newspaper; few read books. Among the nine who were to hear the case were Henry Barnhardt, a sixty-four-year-old retired groundskeeper; Dianne Goodman, forty-three, a housewife and part-time tobacco farm worker; Cicero Beatty, thirty-five, a school custodian and the only black juror; and fifty-two-year-old Darlene Hall, a textile factory supervisor. The only one who had traveled much outside the state was Cleo Stanley, fifty-three, a postmaster living in the small town of Mount Airy, reputed to be the model for the TV village of Mayberry. Rocky was placed in seat number five. The next day opening statements would begin.

Try to imagine settling in as a juror in *Liggett & Myers* v. *Brown & Williamson*. The judge has informed you that you must decide the facts of the case and apply the law to those facts. You're told that millions of dollars are at stake. You look out at the courtroom from your sideways view and see about twenty intense men in business suits on the left side and another twenty dressed just the same on the right. You'd need a scorecard to tell who's on which team if they strayed far from their benches. They seem to be surrounded by stacks of file boxes, and about half the men, plus a handful of women in tailored suits not often seen in Greensboro come summer, are doing nothing but staring at you. Many people have recurrent nightmares in which they are hunched over a final exam in a subject they've never taken or a language they've never seen. For the Greensboro jurors, the test booklets were about to be handed out.

Rasmussen's partner, Greensboro trial attorney Allen Foster, gave the opening statement for Liggett. Foster seemed to have none of Rasmussen's preppy intellectualism, although in truth Foster was a summa cum laude graduate of Princeton, drove a Ferrari, and belonged to an elite wine connoisseurs' club that met at a château in Burgundy. For purposes of this

124

trial, though, he was just a local country boy who hunted game, grew tobacco, and cussed colorfully.

But while the outlines of the Liggett argument could be explained relatively simply, the mechanics of proving a so-called predatory price discrimination case demanded the use of terms—such as *predatory price discrimination*—that were awfully difficult for Foster to disguise, regardless of his familiar local speech cadences. He had to show, among other things, that B&W had charged some customers more than others for the same product, that it had been pricing below "average variable cost," that the "price-value" submarket affected cigarette pricing as a whole; and that consumer demand was a function of the "price-value relationship." He had to discuss oligopolies, market share, market analyses, and market power.

Within minutes Rocky was dumbfounded. This wasn't exactly what his friends had been talking about when they discussed sitting on juries and tossing one criminal or another into prison. But this was the substance of the commercial law at issue in the case, and the language of this sort of law wasn't the language of the streets or the bass ponds. A jury didn't have to be uneducated or ill informed to get lost in such an arcane world. Nearly any group of people without specialized economic or legal training would have been gasping for air after Foster's wind sprint through the terrain. Nonetheless, the idea that these simple country jurors, with their glazed looks and increasingly slumping shoulders, were thoughtfully measuring the lawyer's argument was particularly fanciful and grew even more so as the weeks went by.

The estimated length of trial, which had seemed so long to the jurors at first, became something of a joke as the trial ran through the hot, wet summer, spanned the fall, and threatened to outlast the winter as well. There were ever more intricate legal points for the lawyers to brief and argue, breaks for holidays and illnesses, and more witnesses and longer cross-examinations than anyone had expected. By the tenth week Judge Bullock seemed increasingly beaten down by the delays and often held his head in his hands or puffed out his cheeks in nervousness or impatience. But he set no time limits for the witnesses, although he could have, and let the case drift forward. Eventually it filled more than seven months and became the longest trial in North Carolina history. In this sense alone it strayed from the ideal of the brief, efficient American jury trial; the legendary Zenger case had taken only a single day to resolve.

For nine memorable days in October 1989 Martin London, a tall, spitfire antitrust lawyer from New York, cross-examined an economics expert from Boston who had been paid more than a million dollars by Liggett to study the matter and offer his thoughts. The jurors heard from him about cross elasticity of demand, the tax consequences of last-in, first-out accounting, and oligopolistic collusion. Garret Rasmussen said at the time that he thought the case was going well for Liggett. The jurors seemed to be in good spirits, he whispered during one recess. And that seemed to mean they liked the plaintiff's case.

But in truth, the most substantive testimony was drifting like morning mist over their heads. And though they tried to concentrate, Rocky and the others often found themselves focusing on more concrete matters. Foster wore his suits too tight; another lawyer picked his nose. A young paralegal on Liggett's side of the courtroom was a vision of blond hair and delicate pastel dresses, and Rocky kept catching her eye and imagining her in his arms. One day the ogling got so obvious that a B&W lawyer tried to make a legal issue of it. From then on the Liggett lawyers joked among themselves about Rocky's penchant for ocular sex.

126

Another time Darlene Hall, whose years in the textile mills and tobacco fields had turned her hair prematurely gray and her face weary and hard, suggested that they all dress in black and white to mimic the cigarette packs that were the center of the case. They did it; everyone laughed, and for all of them it was the most memorable moment of the trial. Meanwhile, Rasmussen and the other lawyers earnestly tried to analyze what it meant: Did the jurors' mirth signal that they were pleased with Liggett's case or with B&W's? But this time— and again and again during the trial—the lawyers were appraising the clothes of an emperor who simply didn't have any. The only deeper meaning was that the jury was fiercely bored.

Cicero Beatty regularly threw his head back and appeared to be sleeping as the lawyers made their various points. Rocky kept nudging Cicero, who had become a drinking buddy after hours, but Cicero invariably drifted off again. Beth Chapman, a thirty-four-year-old office clerk, daydreamed about home or rated the witnesses and lawyers on their looks and demeanor. B&W president Thomas Sandefur, she thought, was cute as a button, while the company's chief trial lawyer, Norwood Robinson, would look better in a pair of overalls.

Rasmussen seemed awfully nervous for a lawyer in a big case like this, Beth observed, but he also seemed sincere and was a whole lot more polite than some of the other northern lawyers. He said good morning to the jury before he started each day's cross-examination, and he finally seemed to relax in late January as he eagerly engaged a witness on the merits of the Robinson-Patman Act. But that still didn't mean he was getting through to Beth. One day at lunch he and his cohorts pored over their notes and expressed confidence that he had scored important points during that morning's cross-examination. Looking out the jury room window at an imposing new office building that had risen since the trial began,

Beth asked no one in particular, "What's the Robinson-Patman Act?"

Beth was not a highly educated woman, but she was alert and lively and by no means stupid. She knew the stakes were high for the companies involved, and she wanted to do the right thing. Her attitude was typical of most jurors in all kinds of cases. Whatever their capabilities, they take their jury responsibilities seriously. She and the others had quietly assessed one another's abilities during the first months of the trial and had decided that Rocky, though the youngest, was the savviest of the group. They had informally designated him as foreman months before it was time to deliberate.

Rocky knew this and was concentrating particularly hard. But it was a tumultuous period for him personally. In November, five months into the trial, he separated from his wife and moved in with his mother. After that he spent weeknights in the Ramada Inn in Greensboro, where most of the jurors from out of town had gravitated—at court expense—as the trial progressed. By the standards of a business traveler, the hotel was tacky and drab. But few of the jurors had stayed in a hotel before, and Rocky and the others marveled at the little luxuries: the basket of sundries in the bathroom, daily maid service, free shoehorns. Rocky quickly romanced a girl who worked at the hotel, to much hooting and encouragement from some fellow jurors. He drank and caroused with Cicero and soaked in everything he could understand during the long days of the trial.

But month after month Rasmussen's theory continued to elude Rocky Phillips. How could it hurt competition if B&W was charging less for its cigarettes? He thought about brands of beer. You buy Coors for a dollar a bottle. Amstel Light wants your business. If it charges seventy-five cents, you might try it. At a dollar, why should you bother? Anyway, what was illegal about trying to drive your competitor out of business? Every company wants to do that.

Closing statements in late February, more than seven months after the trial had begun, promised to help clarify things a bit. The lawyers displayed colorful charts and drew connections between the testimony of various witnesses in a way nobody had done during the trial. Liggett's Allen Foster was particularly articulate and folksy, nearly bursting the buttons on his snug suits as he made his points. By now all the jurors were connoisseurs of courtroom oratory, and they nodded in admiration when Foster squinted through his glasses and declared with apparent disgust that "B&W drafted their scheme, and then they executed it, and Liggett bled buckets, and cigarette prices climbed, and B&W saw what they had and sat back and gloated over it."

But the closings ultimately were as confusing as the trial itself. When Foster spoke, bristling with righteous indignation and exhorting the jury to avenge a horrible wrong, Rocky thought maybe he had a point. But then Norwood Robinson, whose country lawyer oratory battled Foster's to a draw, spoke for B&W, and all of a sudden Liggett was the bully, sneakily filing a lawsuit to prevent B&W from engaging in good old-fashioned robust competition. Which, Rocky still wondered as the arguments ended, was it?

In any lawsuit the judge's instructions to the jury are the final and only word on what the law requires. All trial long the lawyers have presented their versions of the facts and have implied that the other side's actions were unspeakably sleazy. But no one has told the jury along the way precisely which actions are illegal and what tests they must apply to decide the question. One federal judge likes to compare the odd practice with "telling jurors to watch a baseball game and decide who won without telling them what the rules are until the end of the game."[6]

It's a process that virtually guarantees that in any complicated matter the jury will fail to comprehend the significance of various pieces of testimony until the end of the case, if at all. The ostensible reason that jurors aren't told the law at the start of trial is that the law itself is complicated and often controversial, and the judge wants to wait until he himself has heard all the testimony and arguments before deciding precisely how to word his legal instructions to the jury. That seemed particularly important for Judge Bullock, who had admitted to the lawyers before testimony began that he knew little about antitrust and that the trial would have to serve as his crash course on the subject.

Nonetheless, in the hands of an artful communicator, instructions, when they finally come, can be a revelation. Suddenly all becomes clear, and the jury's mission is established. If the defendant did x in combination with y with an intent to produce z, he has broken the law. But even the best judge is limited in the language he can use to describe the law. With complicated laws such as Robinson-Patman, appeals court judges have parsed and interpreted and refined the statute so intricately that many trial judges think they must use the appellate courts' exact words in explaining the law to the jury. Otherwise, they fear, their instructions will be found faulty on appeal and the case will have to be retried.

The most confident and creative judges still try to find a way to communicate clearly. As one judge put it, "the object of a charge to a jury is not to satisfy an appellate court that you have repeated the right rigamarole of words, but to try to make jurors who are laymen understand what you are talking about."[7] More timid or less experienced judges stick to the recipe, however. Judge Bullock seemed to fall in the latter category.

For the jury, the judge's instructions dashed any lingering hope that the case would come together for them. Judge Bullock began reading at the start of the morning session and didn't finish until midafternoon. In an address that was to fill eighty-one pages of the trial transcript, he gave the jury its dizzying marching orders. It wasn't that some of what he said didn't make sense to them; it was that none of it did. The words rained down:

> The outer boundaries of a product market are determined by the reasonable interchangeability of use or the cross-elasticity of supply and demand between the product itself and substitutes for it. . . .
>
> The average variable cost test is a double inference test because if you find that Brown & Williamson priced below its reasonably anticipated average variable cost, you may infer that Brown & Williamson had predatory intent, and from predatory intent, you may infer that Brown & Williamson's conduct had a reasonable possibility of injuring competition in the cigarette market. . . .
>
> You may wish to reject an inference of predatory intent, if you find that a substantial motivation for Brown & Williamson's entry into black and white cigarettes was LIFO decrement avoidance tax benefits.

When the instructions were completed, the shell-shocked jurors were dispatched to the jury room to begin deliberating. With the approval of both companies, the three alternates had been allowed to become part of the actual jury, so there were now nine of them seated at the four wooden tables that had been pushed together in the center of the room. Dianne Goodman, a shy, sweet-tempered woman who made porcelain dolls during her long days at home and seldom questioned authority, wasn't just confused; she was angry. Dianne had felt overwhelmed throughout the trial but had clung to the belief that the jury would end up with the task of making a single, clean choice. Like a vote for a candidate, it would be yea or nay for Liggett's accusations, and then they'd all go home.

But now they were faced with a jury form that required them to answer eleven separate questions, each unanimously. Even number one was a killer: "Did Brown & Williamson engage in price discrimination that had a reasonable possibility of injuring competition in the cigarette market as a whole in the United States?" Dianne knew she didn't have a clue, and she didn't think it was fair to make her decide.

Pauline "Polly" Hurley, a strong-willed woman of fifty-nine who had made it to court each day even though her husband had just had spinal surgery and she was caring for a hundred-year-old father-in-law, seemed near despair. She had considered jury service an unavoidable duty, but now she lashed out at the system. When Rocky asked her whether she favored Liggett or B&W, she responded, "How should I know? I don't know what this means, and I don't know what that means, and I don't know how we're going to figure it out." Rocky said that the instructions hadn't sunk in for him either but that the jurors would have plenty of time to make sense of them.

Judge Bullock had made one concession to aid the jury in understanding the case: Although he usually didn't let jurors see a written transcript of his instructions, in this case he sent them copies. And now the jurors pored through them, seeking guidance. Cleo Stanley, the postmaster, set out to mark key passages with an orange highlighter, but it didn't help; unsure of what was important, he ended up highlighting virtually every word. Cicero Beatty figured he could make sense of one sentence in every two paragraphs. The instructions were giving him headaches.

Vocabulary was a particular problem, as it had been throughout the trial. What does *ambiguous* mean? Polly Hurley demanded. How about *oligopoly?* How about *LIFO* and *FIFO?* Nobody could say for sure. (*LIFO* stands for "last-in, first-out" accounting; *FIFO,* "first-in, first-out.") The judge's definition of *market power* was so confusing that Polly decided she could get a better definition from a resource she was more familiar with: a dictionary. But in Garret Rasmussen and Judge Bullock's world, *market power* had to be defined precisely as the most relevant appeals court decision had most recently defined it. That version wouldn't appear in any dictionary. When Polly requested one, she was told to go back to the instructions for guidance. She wasn't told why.

For a time the jurors wallowed in their inability to make progress and channeled their considerable anger into wry jokes about one another's incompetence. Beth Chapman handed Cicero Beatty a calculator and solemnly told him it was his job to compute whether B&W had, in fact, priced below average variable cost. Cicero just laughed. Another time, the pro-Liggett jurors secretly agreed to vote no on a question that they had previously answered yes. The plan was to fool Henry Barnhardt, the pear-shaped groundskeeper who seemed to understand even less of the case than they did. When they went around the table, the man they affectionately called Papa fell right into the trap. "I reckon I'll vote no, too," he said. The group exploded in laughter; Papa, ever good-natured, joined in.

Deliberations began as a joint inquiry—the kind of evidence-driven process that jury experts advocate as the best way to analyze a case—but quickly evolved into a partisan debate, with Rocky leading the forces for Brown & Williamson and Cleo Stanley taking up the Liggett cause.

B&W's internal records, which had been aired at trial and seemed to reveal evil intent, had convinced Cleo of the company's bad faith the moment they were introduced. Now he argued it was nasty, underhanded, and just plain wrong for B&W to seek to "put a lid on Liggett," as the company's planners had themselves phrased it. Liggett was harmed, he said, and should be compensated. The reasoning was crisper than that prescribed by the jury instructions and had the special virtue of sidestepping LIFO, FIFO, double inference tests, and the like.

Darlene Hall had wavered in her view of B&W's behavior throughout the case. Though she had labored for twenty-four years at a mill owned by a big textile firm, she felt she had no idea how big businesses operated. She suspected that all businesses tried to obliterate their competitors, but she didn't know that for sure. However, when Cleo took a strong position, she gratefully adopted it. "Cleo was a leader, a fellow who could really make it understandable," she said after the trial. Her switch left only three jurors in the B&W camp.

Rocky had accepted the foreman's role reluctantly, feeling that he was too young and too insecure to lead the group. He was particularly cowed by Cleo, the round-faced, graying postmaster. Compared with Rocky, Cleo was a man of the world, having lived longer, traveled more extensively (as far as Chicago and St. Louis), and achieved a higher status in his community. But Rocky had his own ethical compass, and it was pointing in a different direction. Free-spirited himself (and a child of the Reagan years), he couldn't shake the view that unfettered competition was normal and good. Both companies had tried to undermine each other's business, he said, but that was okay. Neither company was angelic, but neither was supposed to be.

The debate wandered back through the trial record, stopping at one witness or another but frequently backsliding into an assessment of an expert witness's personality rather than the substance of his testimony. Each company had presented a high-paid economist as its chief expert, and each had stayed on the stand for days, weaving incomprehensible theories. Choosing between the companies meant, in part, picking one economist over the other, an easier task than understanding their theories. Dianne Goodman said she liked Liggett's man, William Burnett, because he spoke beautifully and never became flustered, even when Martin London, B&W's New York lawyer, tried to twist his words. Besides, Burnett had studied the facts closely and had done what Rasmussen had reverently called a "market analysis." If a man this brilliant favored Liggett, she suggested, so should they. Not everyone shared her taste in economics experts, however, complicating this approach to decision making. Polly, for example, was so enamored of Kenneth Elzinga, the B&W expert, that the other jurors called her Mrs. Elzinga. Polly blushed at the nickname but kept insisting that she liked the way he put things; he was more down-to-earth than Burnett, less academic.

Skip Eads was another witness the jurors discussed. He was a tobacco wholesaler whom Liggett had called to discuss B&W's pricing policies, and Martin London had sharply confronted him over a small misstatement he had made about his educational background. London's cross-examination had been aimed at undermining Eads's credibility as a witness, but the jurors unanimously saw it as an elitist attack by an overeducated lawyer against one of their own. "That was uncalled for," Dianne said months later, still steaming over the incident. "That man worked for what he got."

For a while the jurors let loose their rage at London—"typical Yankee lawyer," Cicero muttered—and compared notes on the time London angrily tossed a pencil across the room and then unconvincingly claimed it had slipped out of his hand. They also noted testily that some of the B&W lawyers in the second row had pointed at certain jurors during the trial and seemed to be laughing at them as they sat, defenseless, in the box.

*   *   *

While the jurors were deliberating, Rasmussen was growing increasingly concerned. Although he had little prior experience with juries, he thought he had become quite adept during seven months at reading jurors' minds. Beth Chapman had smiled at him many times; Henry Barnhardt had given a thumbs-up when Rasmussen had rehabilitated Skip Eads's reputation after London had tried to skewer it. During closing statements the jurors had seemed solidly pro-Liggett. They had leaned slightly forward when Foster spoke, had nodded at the Liggett charts. Rocky, in particular, had seemed a sure bet to all the Liggett lawyers. Rasmussen had predicted a short deliberation and a favorable verdict.

But as the deliberations continued, the jurors' behavior began to seem ominous. They sought a great deal of testimony and asked the judge many questions that suggested their grasp of the case was shakier than he had imagined. Rasmussen wondered why the jurors were asking to read Skip Eads's testimony. Had London's punishing cross-examination damaged Eads's credibility? And he couldn't figure out why the jury had started going for walks late each afternoon. The first day it appeared to signal that they had reached a verdict and wanted to clear their heads before delivering it. The following afternoon it seemed as if two jurors were walking together to try to resolve their differences. When the practice continued, its meaning no longer seemed clear.

In fact, the jury had remembered the London cross-examination of Eads without the aid of a transcript but had sought to review Eads's testimony largely because they liked and admired Eads. They remembered that he had been both sincere and amusing, and they needed a break from the pressure of deliberations. As for the walks, they, too, were just tension breakers. The drab little jury room, with its green vinyl chairs and tired green rug, had begun to feel like a jail cell.

*   *   *

Although it might have alarmed the lawyers, what seemed to matter most to the jurors by the second week of deliberations were the personal alliances that had developed among them. In the search for a verdict that would leave the jurors believing they had done the right thing, was Rocky a better guide or was Cleo?

Cleo's prestige within the jury as a whole was unquestioned. No one ever became angry with him. Certainly he was one of them, yet in an inoffensive way he seemed somehow better. Even if his arguments were based on misconceptions, as many of them were, none of the other jurors seemed to think so. To them, Cleo was strong, avuncular, smart, and understanding. There had been a side issue in the case, a question of whether B&W had infringed Liggett's trademark, and only one juror, Beatrice Jenkins, had believed a violation had occurred. Cleo took her aside one day, and when the two returned to the table sometime later, Bea had changed her mind. The others were impressed; none of them could have budged Bea, a loner on the jury who had strong opinions and didn't like to be pushed.

Rocky had fewer fans, but those he had seemed loyal. He had spent many nights for months playing guitar, singing songs, and drinking beer with Cicero. They were a rambunctious pair, flirting with women, clowning in the hotel pool, telling racy jokes. Jurors considered Cicero a sure vote for whatever position Rocky held. Indeed, at one point during the deliberations Rocky had privately admonished his buddy not to rely on him too much. "The blind leads the blind," Rocky told him, "and you both fall in a ditch." But by the second week of deliberations Cicero had declared his independence and switched to Cleo's side. Rocky was his pal, but Cleo seemed to make more sense.

In the final days of the eleven-day deliberation, only Rocky and Polly—tight friends and now a coalition of two—remained unconvinced. Polly still didn't have any idea what *mar-*

ket power meant, and she wasn't about to say B&W had it if she didn't know what it was. She also seemed to be letting her warm feelings for Rocky become a major factor in the deliberations. In the evenings she and Rocky would return to the hotel together after a tense day in the jury room, and Rocky would confide in her about his quandary. On the one hand, he was embarrassed about becoming a holdout. He liked to go along, to be popular. He liked to be patted on the back and told what a fine fisherman he was, what a regular guy. He respected Cleo and didn't want to cross him. On the other hand, he was still quite sure that B&W had competed aggressively but fairly.

If one bought Garret Rasmussen's theory, of course, B&W's underpricing wasn't a standard effort to compete aggressively in the same market but an illegal plan to drive Liggett away and then increase the prices again. But nobody, and certainly not Cleo, understood the law well enough to explain this to Rocky. In turn, Rocky didn't understand economics well enough to question whether Rasmussen's theory could possibly make sense in a market in which other cigarette makers were also free to compete for cost-conscious customers.

Breaking the deadlock, therefore, wouldn't be a matter of leading Rocky or Cleo to some richer understanding of Liggett's or B&W's legal position. If consensus came at all, it would have to emerge from misconceptions that both jurors could share. Or Rocky would simply have to give way to the will of the majority and drop his opposition to a pro-Liggett verdict. Polly told Rocky she would stick with him until he made up his mind. Nonetheless, he couldn't help feeling lonely as he went back to his room each night.

It was Cleo who finally found a way to offer Rocky and Polly enough concessions to drive them, reluctantly, into the Liggett camp. Cleo's breakthrough was to arrive at an acceptable damage figure even before Rocky and Polly had agreed that B&W should be held liable at all. Liggett had asked for $89.6 million, the amount it had spent to match B&W's price cuts. Through a series of complicated and entirely faulty calculations, Cleo had decided that $49.6 million was more appropriate. Mainly he had trimmed $35 million because the jury believed B&W hadn't violated Liggett's trademark, as Liggett had alleged in an additional claim for damages. The $35 million had nothing to do with the Robinson-Patman claim, but out it went nonetheless. Another $5 million hit the cutting room floor because Cleo remembered some testimony—again irrelevant to Liggett's claim in this case—that the company had spent this amount to compete with R. J. Reynolds's new Doral brand. These cuts took a big bite out of Liggett's damages, and thus, he thought, might make a Liggett verdict palatable to the others.

On Tuesday, February 27, Cleo finished his calculations and motioned for Beth to come over and look at them. She then read the amount—and the fanciful explanation for it— to the others. "What do y'all think about this?" she asked. "We're giving," she added, referring to Cleo and the pro-Liggett jurors. Turning to Rocky and Polly, she said, "You'll give, too." Polly was ready to relent, and Rocky too felt he had little ground left to stand on. By Wednesday night he had tentatively agreed to go along.

But walking back to the Ramada with Polly, Rocky had second thoughts. He told her how he had been taught to respect his elders and how painful it had been to stand up to Cleo the past nine days. He also felt guilty about keeping the others there so long: Cleo's wife had had an operation for cancer and had grown depressed; she needed him at home. Beth had a three-year-old she wasn't seeing enough because of the trial; Polly herself was strained to the limit because her husband and father-in-law both were disabled. "But my daddy taught me to stand up for what I believe in and to back down and

139

apologize only if you're proven wrong," he said. "And nobody has proved me wrong." As they crossed a little railroad
bridge behind the hotel, he was close to tears. "Polly, what
am I supposed to do?" he asked.

Polly said fervently that he should listen to his heart, and
she'd be with him. So the next morning he withdrew his Liggett vote and insisted on being convinced anew. Cleo went
back to work, concentrating this time on the fairness of the
damage award and the need to avert a mistrial that would put
all their work to waste and require another jury to grapple
with the case. On Thursday afternoon Rocky decided once
again that he would go along. But the jury didn't announce
its verdict then. For seven and a half months men in suits had
been keeping secrets from them. Now the jury would keep a
secret from the men in suits, at least overnight.

At 10:00 A.M. on Friday, March 2, Rocky asked the court clerk,
Anne Vaughen, to come into the jury room. He then pulled
out his notebook and began reading a remarkable letter he
had composed the night before.

> In the beginning God created the heaven and the earth and
> the sea and the stars. He also created the animals and the
> birds and the fish. He created all the other beauty that sur-
> rounds us everyday of our lives. But on July 10, 1989, he again
> created something very special, nine very special people from
> all walks of life destined to meet and not only became the
> world famous "Generic Jury" but more importantly became a
> family.

Most of the jurors were already in tears. Darlene was weep-
ing. Rocky continued:

> This "Generic Jury" consist of 9 of the most wonderful people
> to ever have served on Jury Duty together. We've had our

share of hard times but then what family hasn't. We've gotten angry with each other at some time or another but what family hasn't.

But through it all we have had a lot of good times and the good times out-weigh the bad times by 1,000 to 1. But the most important thing is that through all the good times and the bad times, the fun times and the sad times we are still able to do what some families can't do. We can still look at one another in the face and say to each other, "you are like a brother to me" or "you are like a sister to me."

When Rocky was done, the jurors all gathered around him, hugging him and one another. Then, just before noon, Rocky handed the verdict form to Anne Vaughen. As she read off the jury's answers to the eleven questions, Rasmussen's face turned beet red, and he flashed a smile to the jurors. Then he raced to a phone and called his wife.

Rasmussen's victory was short-lived. Bullock himself overturned the verdict, Liggett appealed, and in June 1993 the Supreme Court issued the final word on the case. The High Court first noted that "a reasonable jury is presumed to know and understand the law, the facts of the case, and the realities of the market." Then the Court concluded that "a reasonable jury" could not have found that B&W's actions had been illegal. Since Rocky and his colleagues had, in their ignorance of the law, the facts, and the market, acted unreasonably, their verdict wouldn't stand. Common sense had suggested, as Rocky had suspected all along, that B&W had engaged in rough but lawful competition. But ironically, it took a panel of erudite justices who could cut through the complexity of antitrust law, rather than a lay jury from the community, to write a commonsense ending to the story.[8]

As in the IBM case, many of the jurors themselves hadn't really believed they had understood what they were deciding. Back home in her living room after the trial Dianne Goodman wasn't ready to say she had been competent to reach such a verdict. "I think they should have had nine economists on the case," she suggested. More than seven months of trial had left her with great curiosity, but huge gaps in knowledge, about the court system. "Is the Supreme Court made up of judges or of jurors like me?" she wanted to know.

Polly Hurley, too, remained confused about the case yet eager to learn more about a trial that court officials had deemed so important that she'd had to leave her ailing family. She still viewed market power as the key to some mysterious world from which she had been shut out. "Do you know what it means?" she asked during an interview in her backyard.

Rocky talked about the case shortly after the trial in the lobby bar of the Greensboro Sheraton, a cool, shiny place across town from the Ramada. It was where the lawyers from New York had stayed during the long winter, and it could have been Hartford, Connecticut, or Sydney, Australia, for all the local color it let in the door. Rocky brought with him a scrapbook that included every piece of paper that the case had generated for him: his summons from the previous June, his paper badge stamped JUROR, photographs of the jury dressed in black and white, the letter he had read them on the final day, newspaper clippings, the certificate of appreciation he had received from the judge, a note asking for his participation in this book.

Rocky said he continued to doubt that B&W had done anything wrong. Attempting to explain why he ultimately voted for Liggett, he ended up making an impassioned argument for B&W. Of his jury experience, he said, "I enjoyed it, had a good time, and would do it again. But as for my opinion of the justice system, I don't believe you can leave law and justice to people who don't know laws and business management."

Put into legal terms, Rocky's complaint amounted to an

argument in favor of a "complexity exception" to the Seventh Amendment right to jury trial in civil cases. In other words, if a judge doesn't think the jury will understand a particular civil case, he decides it without a jury. This isn't allowed in most jurisdictions, but one federal appeals court permitted it in one case on the theory that "due process precludes trial by jury when a jury is unable to perform this task with a reasonable understanding of the evidence and the legal rules."[9] In former Chief Justice Warren Burger's words, "The common sense of the common man, which is, of course, very important—cannot work without comprehension of the facts and the law."[10]

There's no doubt that the Liggett case gives ammunition to those who want the complexity exception adopted nationwide. Federal Judge Jerome Frank might have been talking about the Liggett jury when he observed in a 1949 opinion that the jury has "infinite capacity for mischief, for twelve men can easily misunderstand more law in a minute than a judge can explain in an hour."[11]

The Liggett case resulted in an illogical verdict, it wasted the taxpayers' money and the jurors' time, and it soured some of them on jury service. But barring juries from big commercial cases isn't the only possible alternative. As will be discussed in the book's final section, even the most complex case can be made more comprehensible if managed more intelligently by the judge.

Indeed, it's often the trial judge who deserves the biggest share of the blame for the disappointing work of juries. In the Liggett case, nine patient, self-sacrificing jurors devoted a collective five years of their lives to the trial, yet they were given next to no help in their effort to decide the case sensibly. Instead of waiting until the case was over to issue his jury charge, for example, the judge could have provided terse, plain English instructions at the start of the trial. That might have helped the jurors put the testimony in context and listen more closely for material that was relevant.

The judge also could have placed time limits on witnesses to combat repetition, boredom, and confusion; a trial that had been estimated to last eight to ten weeks didn't have to fill seven months. In addition, he could have permitted the jurors to present questions to the witnesses in writing; at the very least this would have signaled the lawyers that the jurors weren't understanding the case. He could have let the jurors take notes to aid their recollection. He could have allowed the lawyers to give brief, periodic minisummations throughout the trial to keep the key issues in the jurors' minds. He could have written his final jury instructions with the aim of clarifying the case rather than with the apparent intent of avoiding being overturned on appeal.

It remains an open question whether even these techniques could render cases such as Liggett comprehensible enough to realize our vision of the civil jury as the fair, reasoned voice of the community. But jury scholar Richard Lempert suggests why, even in the face of decisions such as Liggett, it's worth trying. "Complex cases—such as large-scale antitrust litigation—are some of the most 'political' cases that the system hears," he writes. "Vast sums of money are involved, and the structure of the nation's largest companies may be at issue." In a democracy, he argues persuasively, the community should exercise this power—not through judges whom public officials select but through juries that the community itself sends into court.[12]

144

5

BLOOD MONEY

—

S USIE Quintana, a pious, fifty-five-year-old Catholic mother of four, became infected with the AIDS virus in May 1983 during a blood transfusion. Nearly a decade later her case against the company that had supplied the blood from a homosexual donor finally came to trial in a Denver courtroom. By then Mrs. Quintana was seriously ill, her husband was depressed and distant, and her conservative little community of Dolores, Colorado, wanted as little as possible to do with either of them. On the other hand, the Quintanas' lawsuit had the potential to make them rich. In it they sought a jury verdict ordering the blood bank to pay for their medical costs, as well as for much less tangible losses: Susie's pain and suffering, her diminished enjoyment of life's pleasures, and the tragic disruption of their lifelong love story.

Like the Liggett case, the Quintana lawsuit triggered a civil, rather than a criminal, trial. But in pitting an individual against a company, rather than a company against another company, it was to offer different opportunities—and pose different and even greater risks—for the jury system.

Ideally, the jury in such a case functions as an equalizer.

Though the company is typically richer and more powerful than the individual, its wealth provides it no particular advantage before a jury that is randomly picked from the community. The company can't buy the jury's protection, as it conceivably might buy the loyalty of an elected state judge who's dependent on campaign contributions. And it can't benefit from social connections at the top tier of society that's shared by corporate and judicial officials but not by the average juror.

The playing field is level. Or is it? In recent years the business community has claimed—vociferously, in fact—that it's the party at a disadvantage, that juries reflexively favor injured individuals over faceless corporations, that jurors function as angry avengers of the powerless rather than as sober arbiters of disputes. Critics complain that juries are too quick to find companies liable when evidence of alleged wrongdoing is weak and then are far too extravagant with the damage awards they deliver.

The perception that jury awards in such cases are excessively high and are sapping the strength of the private economy is frequently referred to as the tort crisis. It was a major target of Vice President Dan Quayle in the 1992 presidential race, apparently the first such campaign in which public disappointment with juries became a prominent political issue. Drawing on the research of conservative legal scholars, Quayle and his staff maintained that the full cost of our jury-based civil liability system—including damage awards, lawyers' fees, increased insurance rates, and any otherwise unproductive efforts to avoid liability—approached three hundred billion dollars a year. This huge burden, Quayle insisted, was putting the United States, the only major nation that allows juries to determine liability and damages in civil cases, at a competitive disadvantage internationally.[1]

The jury's sanctified role in our national mythology is so

146

great that the Quayle effort was carefully packaged as an attack on greedy trial lawyers who sought huge damages, rather than on the juries of average Americans who actually doled out six-, seven-, and eight-figure awards. But the remedies proposed, if ever put into effect, would strike at the heart of the jury's power. The Bush administration sought to impose a $250,000 limit on what juries could award individuals for pain and suffering in medical malpractice suits, one category of tort cases. And it sought to deny juries the power to set the amount of punitive damages, which are awarded in civil cases to punish particularly harmful behavior. Though such proposals died on the vine in 1992, similar curtailments of the jury's discretion have been proposed in most state legislatures and approved, to varying degrees, in at least twenty states.

Is such an attack on the jury warranted? Should it be encouraged or combated? Evidence backing or refuting Quayle's critique has been frustratingly inadequate. On the one hand, academic studies indicate that juries give bigger awards when the defendant is a company than when the defendant is an individual. A Rand Institute for Civil Justice study of nine thousand jury trials in Chicago between 1959 and 1979, for example, found that losing corporate defendants were ordered by juries to pay 4.4 times more than individuals to compensate plaintiffs for serious injuries.[2] In another study two pools of experimental jurors were given the same facts of a case, one against a defendant called Mr. Jones, the other against the Jones Corporation. The Mr. Jones jurors awarded the plaintiff an average of $82,178 for pain and suffering; the Jones Corporation jurors, $170,700. This would surely seem to suggest that an anticorporate, or at least a pro–little guy, bias is at work.[3]

On the other hand, recent research shows that plaintiffs win personal injury cases against corporate defendants only about half the time; in contrast, when an individual sues another individual, the plaintiff succeeds 61 percent of the time.[4] This suggests a probusiness leaning or at least a significant degree of receptivity to corporate lawyers' arguments. Moreover, the conservatives' $300 billion figure for the overall cost of the liability system has been sharply attacked by other legal scholars, who suggest figures as low as $130 billion.[5] When plaintiffs do prevail in personal injury suits, damages are usually much lower than critics imply when they cite only the most extreme awards. In the county courts in Chicago between 1981 and 1985, for example, the median—or midpoint of all the verdicts, including those against corporations—was just $19,382. A later study of twenty-seven state courts set the figure at under $30,000. Hardly a number that Dan Quayle would want to use as the cornerstone of a legal revolution.[6]

Though the Quintana case would do nothing to put the debate to rest, it would appear, at least, to support Quayle's bleak view of how the American civil jury actually performs. Once again the case would underline the contradiction between the enduring ideal of the jury in America and the reality of its often disappointing performance. In theory, Susie Quintana seemed to deserve the individual attention and the high level of concentration that only a jury—immersed in "the awful court of judgment"—can provide. Perhaps, too, she deserved the measure of extralegal sympathy that a jury might insist on factoring into a damage award, even as a jury in the case of Maude's horse and Benny's hay ignored legal instructions that made no sense under the circumstances. In reality the Quintana jury nearly matched the Marcos jury for one-sidedness and the Liggett jury for inadequate comprehension.

Deciding whether Susie Quintana should win her lawsuit should not have been easy. Though there was no doubt that the defendant, United Blood Services, had supplied the lethal blood, there was lots of doubt about whether it had been technically at fault for doing so. The legal question was whether the blood bank had exercised "reasonable care under the circumstances" in its acquisition and handling of blood. If it had, it wasn't liable for accidental errors; the jury instructions explained that UBS was not required to provide "absolute safety in the product it delivers."

But though the jurors were told this, it was a difficult concept for them to accept wholeheartedly. For the most part, they were consumers, not business managers, and if there was anything they agreed on, it was that companies should do everything possible and spend whatever was necessary to provide safe products. In this sense, at least, they fitted snugly into the anticorporate stereotype.

In reality, most policy making by private companies and governments entails some degree of cost-benefit analysis. Every time a building is erected or a bridge is built, the planners know that a certain number of workers will die on the project. To reduce that number to zero would make the project too expensive to pursue. Similarly, many lives might be saved if a cop stood on every corner of every street in America, but Americans can't afford so much security. As voters and consumers, citizens seem to accept such limits; otherwise, they would have to support even greater tax increases than they already face and to pay higher prices for products.

But studies show that jurors tend to hold defendants to a standard of safety that's considerably higher than the law requires. In one survey involving eighteen personal injury cases, two thirds of the jurors agreed that safety standards could never be too high. And three quarters rejected the idea that it could ever be too expensive to make products 100 percent safe.[7]

The Quintana jury was no different. Gary Dahl, a thirty-seven-year-old meat inspector who usually spent his days amid the stench of packinghouses, poking at the entrails of cattle, chickens, and hogs, was decidedly pro-Quintana from the beginning. He imagined that the homosexual blood donor must have seemed to the blood bank the way a questionable piece of meat seemed to him. Personally he never took a chance on safety; he just pulled that carcass right out of line so it wouldn't end up on someone's table. "In my job," he explained after the trial, "if you have a suspicion of something and it's right in front of you, you have to follow through as if it's fact until it's proven otherwise."

Juror Rose Bowles, fifty-eight, lived in one of the nicer sections of Denver and managed the finances of a suburb that had an annual budget of three million dollars. She didn't seem to have much in common with Dahl. But she, too, wanted the blood bank to focus on saving lives, whatever the financial cost. What was wrong with the nation's entire health care system, she believed, was that people worried more about money than about health. She'd even said so in voir dire. Other members of the jury shared these absolutist ideas. If it turned out the blood bank could have prevented Susie's illness, it should have—regardless of other considerations and particularly regardless of cost.

Adding to the Quintanas' lawyers' advantage in the case was the presence in the courtroom of Susie Quintana herself. The eight jurors only had to look at her to recognize that she was in terrible pain. Her large tinted glasses, shielding eyes that were rapidly going blind, seemed to swamp her worn, bony face. Her clothes floated on a stick figure frame. She wore pants to hide how thin her legs had become and a blazer to conceal the device that pumped morphine into her body. She propped herself on a pillow because the courtroom's wooden chairs were too hard for her. Many days her chair was empty because she was at the hospital receiving treatment.

The task of introducing the case to the jury on July 15,

1992, fell to the Quintanas' young lawyer, Bruce Jones. Square-faced as Al Gore, and nearly as earnest, Jones did everything he could to convince the jury that UBS had failed to make sure its blood was 100 percent safe. Even as early as 1983, he emphasized, the link between homosexuality and AIDS had been well known to doctors, researchers, and blood bank officials, and donated blood had already been linked to several AIDS cases. What blood banks should have done to protect the blood supply, Jones said, was to question all donors confidentially, asking men directly if they had had sex with other men and excluding anyone who said yes. Jones also said that though there hadn't been a direct blood test for AIDS at the time, blood banks should have administered various indirect tests that would have removed about nine out of ten gay men with AIDS. "UBS didn't do these things, and most blood banks didn't do these things," Jones lamented. "Didn't do the things that would have protected the public health."

As a result, he said, Susie Quintana had become ill two years after the transfusion, first developing swollen glands, then severe throat problems. When a direct blood test for AIDS had become available in 1985, she'd tested positive. And as the years had passed, she'd developed ulcers down her throat and into her esophagus, yeast infections in her mouth, a virus that clouded her vision and was leading to blindness and dementia. She'd lost seventy pounds just in the six months before trial.

In addition, she'd been ostracized by many in the insular southwest Colorado community of Dolores, population 860, where she and her family lived. Residents, mostly farmers, ranchers, and commuters to jobs in nearby Cortez, worked hard, went to church, and amused themselves by hunting, fishing, picnicking, and square dancing under the broad shadow of the San Juan Mountains. It had seemed as likely to them that a quiet, dutiful homemaker would get the alien disease as that she'd discover a cure for it.

Turning to the question of how much the Quintanas should be compensated, Jones said he didn't know precisely how much Susie had suffered, but he assured the jury that, translated into dollars, her losses couldn't be calculated in fewer than seven figures. "She's survived for a long time, but she could go any time or she could keep going on," Jones lamented, "suffering in a way that will be hard for you to imagine until you hear the testimony about just how terrible it is."

Jones's line was a classic bit of plaintiff's lawyering: Show that the defendant caused the injury and that the plaintiff had suffered horribly, and downplay the legal nuances, such as whether the defendant truly acted in a manner that the law prohibited. Such nuances, however, were all UBS lawyer Arthur Downey had going for him. As silver-haired and silver-tongued a lawyer as ever delivered by central casting, Downey insisted again and again in his opening statement that UBS had been extremely prudent, given what was known in 1983.

It hadn't truly been proved yet that AIDS could be contracted through transfusions, Downey explained. As for asking people if they were gay, the blood bank had decided that the question could antagonize the homosexual community and thus imperil a valuable source of blood. And as far as indirect blood tests went, Downey continued, they might have caught some AIDS carriers, but they would also have eliminated a lot of safe blood, screening out as much as 5 percent of the nation's already scarce supply and thereby threatening other lives.

As of April 1983, Downey declared, UBS was providing donors with factual information about AIDS and encouraging anyone who believed he was at high risk to remove himself from any blood drive. UBS was also taking complete medical histories from donors, asking about everything from their drug use to their travel itineraries to try to identify possible AIDS carriers. Downey insisted that not a single industry group or regulatory agency had asked UBS to do more than it had done. Only now, a decade later, after AIDS had emerged as a mass killer and its characteristics had come to be understood better, could anyone presume to doubt UBS's standard of care. "Susie's infection did not come from negligence," Downey concluded solemnly. "It came because medicine is an inexact science, and man does not have the ability to be perfect."

The actual testimony in the Quintana trial lasted nearly three weeks, and it mirrored the opening statements. Helping the Quintanas' cause was the fact that their main witnesses were the doctors who had noticed AIDS first and fought it the hardest. These people had taken AIDS patients into their homes, battled bureaucracies to make them take the disease seriously, goaded blood banks into taking stronger precautions. Unlike the blood bank officials who would testify for UBS, they hadn't had to weigh other interests—such as holding down costs or maintaining an adequate blood supply— against patient care. The plaintiff's witnesses also had passed the test of hindsight: It turned out that in 1983 they'd been right, rather than alarmist, about AIDS. They'd shouted that the sky was falling, and for once it truly had been.

Dr. Donald Francis was typical of these witnesses. To the blood bankers in 1983, he had been the ultimate alarmist. Then a forty-one-year-old hepatitis researcher for the Centers for Disease Control, he had attended a memorable January 4, 1983, conference the CDC had organized to discuss the emerging threat of AIDS. Francis, testifying on videotape because he was attending an international AIDS conference in Amsterdam, described how the meeting had turned contentious as the doctors and scientists had debated what, if anything, should be done to protect the blood supply from the little-understood disease. The CDC doctors had recommended fast and radical action, including direct questioning of donors about their sexuality and mandatory surrogate blood tests. But blood bank officials had raised objection after objection to such measures, including how much they'd cost, whether they'd be effective, and whether they would reduce the supply of good blood along with bad. Some gay leaders at the meeting had warned against stigmatizing all gays by excluding them from blood drives. And some of the federal health officials, particularly those from the research-oriented National Institutes of Health, had wanted blood testing to await further studies of its effectiveness.

Francis, blond, clean-cut, and, at fifty, a remarkably baby-faced presence on the courtroom television screen, testified that he'd listened to all the equivocations and excuses and had finally lost his temper. He'd banged his fist on the table and had demanded to know how many people would have to develop AIDS before the blood bank officials would take action. "It was frustration I had in their inability to accept the reality," he testified. "It was something like having a bend in the train track and sitting there, and you hear the whistles, and the signals are blinking, and the tracks are beginning to shake, and they're saying, 'There's no train coming.'"

Francis weathered a powerful cross-examination by Downey, in which the blood bank's lawyer attempted to depict Francis as a low-level government doctor whose views had been shot down by wiser and more experienced officials. The charge didn't stick, and as Jones and his law partner, Maureen Witt, had hoped, the witness turned out to be an overwhelming sensation with the jury.

David Gesink was particularly impressed. A twenty-one-year-old in search of a calling, Gesink had tried art school, caring for office plants, bagel making, and housecleaning. He lived in an apartment in his grandmother's basement on a pleasant enough block in Denver and was taking a few classes at a community college. He wore a gold hoop in each ear and had a mane of fine blond hair that fell well past his shoulders. He was polite, engaging, and very anonymous. But to a corporate defendant who encountered him in the jury box in a personal injury case, he seemed to embody a recurring corporate nightmare. Would he, a relative nobody, shed his gentility behind the closed doors of the jury room and, suddenly powerful, become Robin Hood? In fact, Francis's testimony was all it took to convince Gesink that UBS had been negligent. Thereafter he never wavered.

The issue in this case, of course, was whether UBS had been "reasonably careful" in 1983, not whether its judgments had proved wrong in hindsight. And the subsequent testimony by UBS's executives and others in the industry generally supported the blood bank's contention that it had complied with most of the safety standards in general use at the time of the Quintana transfusion. But the jurors were virtually deaf to such testimony, except to recognize it as reinforcing their belief that the blood bank hadn't made its product 100 percent safe. In addition, the defense witnesses fitted the jurors' most negative images of the medical establishment—just a bunch of corporate executives in lab coats. These were the bureaucrats who pushed paper, went by the books, promulgated rules, passed the buck.

To the jurors, a case in point was Ernest Simon, the medical director of UBS's parent company, Blood Systems, Inc. Jones had been responsible for the cautious language used in the informational materials that UBS had provided to potential blood donors in 1983. His idea, he said, had been to encourage applicants to exclude themselves if they fit into any of the high-risk categories while not offending, embarrassing, or excluding anyone who might be a healthy and valuable donor. But on cross-examination Jones ridiculed the notice as tepid and insufficiently explicit on the risks of AIDS, and he lambasted Simon for failing to consult anyone other than people who worked for him about the wording of the warning.

Gary Dahl, the meat inspector, immediately saw parallels to situations he'd had to deal with in his own job. Simon, he thought, was the supervisor who did a shoddy piece of work and then showed it to his subordinates—rather than to someone more independent—to get their comments. Invariably the subordinates said, "Sure, boss, it's great. Now where's my promotion? Where's my raise?" Everyone kissed up to the boss; in Dahl's view, a boss who didn't understand that wasn't worth very much. Linda Woods, a medical notes transcriber, also thought Simon could have avoided much of the problem with the warning notice if he'd asked "some regular people, laymen, for advice" on how it should be worded. David Gesink, the twenty-one-year-old, attributed part of the problem to an age gap: Simon had gotten his degree long before and had become stuck, Gesink decided, in an older frame of mind.

The other UBS witnesses fared little better. Dr. Harvey Klein, the chief of transfusion medicine at the National Institutes of Health, had the task of explaining why indirect blood testing for possible AIDS carriers would have been premature in the spring of 1983. Relying on an antibody test before scientists had studied it properly might have removed many more healthy people from the supply of blood donors than it would have eliminated AIDS carriers, Klein explained, and this might have created a severe blood shortage and cost many lives. "That's acceptable if you know the test is going to improve the safety of the blood supply. If you don't know that, it's irresponsible," he insisted.

David Gesink was hostile in the extreme. Waiting a year to

validate the tests, as Klein suggested, was simply callous, he thought. It suggested a lack of concern for human life. "He was ready to let it slide and just watch them," Gesink said after the trial. "That to me is like genocide. It's a scary thing to do." As usual, Gary Dahl was in sync with his fellow male juror. He considered Klein "the final dagger in UBS's side." Said Dahl: "He wanted to see some casualties and use actual numbers before they wanted to react, which is sad."

The trial testimony suggested that if UBS was liable, a substantial award was in order. Michael Mead, a psychologist who had been treating Susie Quintana since 1988, told the jury that in addition to her physical symptoms, she was suffering from post-traumatic stress disorder, most commonly diagnosed among war veterans and crime victims. She was experiencing flashbacks to the time when she'd first learned she had the disease and was having nightmares about her plight. "We are talking about something really frightening," Mead told the jury. "This is not a normal disease. . . . She never expected it to happen to her, and it should never have happened to her."

Mead related how Susie had become obsessed with the idea that someone might catch the disease from her and had gotten into the habit of scrubbing her hands until they were raw. She had worn rubber gloves when working in the kitchen, used a bathroom set aside just for her, and slept in a separate bed from Chris, her husband of thirty-nine years. The psychologist also said that Chris had developed a major depressive disorder as a result of her illness. Chris kept thinking, Mead said, that Susie would "snap out of it," that the doctors had somehow been wrong in their diagnosis. He believed that he could take her to Las Vegas for a vacation and she'd suddenly feel better.

Quintana family members, too, took the witness stand. Ron Quintana testified that AIDS had robbed his parents of their future. He also explained, reluctantly, that his ex-wife had barred their daughter from visiting her grandmother, a prohibition that had pained Susie terribly. Susie's sister, Eleanor, lamented that Susie had been shunned by her neighbors, that she couldn't go into a grocery store without people whispering to each other not to touch any produce that she had handled. "She's not living," Eleanor said. "She's not alive; she just exists. She is continually in pain; she is continually sick; she can't eat."

On Wednesday, July 22, Chris Quintana, a short, balding fifty-eight-year-old man with downcast eyes, took the stand. A serviceman for a local gas company who came to court in his dress-up outfit of neat blue jeans, open-collar shirt, and cotton baseball jacket, Chris seemed out of place and very nervous in the formal courtroom environment. He haltingly told the jury about how he'd learned of his wife's illness. After she'd been diagnosed, she and their son had driven out to Cortez, where he had been answering service calls from gas company customers. They'd cruised the streets until they had found him with his truck, and Susie had rolled down her car window and said, "Short," as she called him, "I've got AIDS." He said it had felt as if his whole world had fallen out from under him. He'd relied on Susie to take charge of their shared activities, their family get-togethers, camping trips, evenings of dancing, and afternoons of firewood gathering. But now Susie was always sick and had become a recluse. She couldn't sew, cook, clean house, play bingo. He began to fear her, to worry that he, too, would get the disease. Their sex lives, indeed physical intimacy of any sort, were over. They barely even spoke.

Susie testified the following day. Her son, Ron, led her to the stand. She had had her hair and makeup done beautifully and, in her white blouse, cherry red blazer, and blue slacks, looked about as well as she had in some weeks. But her frailty was astonishing. "She looked all bone," juror Karen Dwyer later recalled. "When they put her on the stand, I was just devastated."

Susie's expression was pained but proud, and she didn't shed a single tear as she described her physical distress and her loneliness in inhospitable Dolores. Now, she said, "I stay away from people, I just keep to my family. That's about it." She said she'd burned her extensive doll collection, which had always been special to her, because she didn't think anyone would want to touch dolls that had belonged to an AIDS patient. She spoke of how the disease had distanced her from her husband. Barely audibly she added, "All I can say is that it's terrible. I wouldn't wish it on my worst enemy." After roughly forty minutes, the length of her endurance, she stepped down.

This wasn't a tearful jury; some members, in fact, had promised themselves not to betray emotion and not to be guided by it. David Gesink reminded himself several times not to become too involved in Susie's and Chris's suffering. "You're working as a machine, computing information. You have to stay detached," he kept telling himself. But the part-time community college student shuddered with recognition at the descriptions of a small town's cruelty. Gesink had spent his early teens in a Nebraska village of about three hundred. Football and heavy metal music had dominated the lives of the kids. David had been interested in art. The adults had spent an inordinate amount of time gossiping about one another's comings and goings. Nonconformity, or even individuality, hadn't been high on anyone's list of virtues. Gesink figured that Susie deserved some extra measure of damages just for doing her suffering in such a place.

As the Quintanas testified, juror Margaret Fleming reflected that she truly liked them. Though the well-educated retired school library supervisor wouldn't have been in the

Quintanas' working-class social circle, she admired their close-ness as a family. And she believed that their loss of family cohesion was among the toughest consequences Susie had had to face. Susie, who'd complained that she no longer had a wide enough lap for her grandchildren to sit on, had to be especially distraught, Margaret figured, that her daughter-in-law wouldn't let her see her own granddaughter.

Juror Juanita Underwood had been particularly poker-faced until the Quintanas' testimony. But the family-focused housewife, the only black on the jury, seemed absolutely dev-astated by the destruction of fellow homemaker Susie Quintana's life. Meanwhile, after watching Chris and Susie testify, medical secretary Linda Woods, a thirty-nine-year-old single mother, suddenly wanted to give Susie as much money as she legitimately could.

Throughout the trial the jurors had waited with increasing eagerness for the lawyers or the judge to tell them how to decide on damages. They'd become particularly fond of Jones's law partner, Maureen Witt, whose concern for her client appeared to many of the jurors to transcend her role as an advocate. But in an impassioned closing statement on Friday morning, July 31, Witt disappointed them. She merely asked in passing whether Susie's suffering might have been worth a million dollars a year or even more. She didn't give any rationale for the amount she'd thrown out so casually, and she moved quickly on to another subject.

In the defense's closing statement, which followed, Downey said that if his client were found to be negligent, a result that he counseled against, a sum in the neighborhood of five hun-dred thousand dollars would be appropriate. He suggested that the Quintanas could invest that amount at 10 percent a year and end up with more annual income than they'd ever earned in their lives.

Next, Judge Nancy Rice instructed the jury that if they

found UBS liable, they must award the Quintanas enough to "reasonably compensate" them for each of the categories of noneconomic damages, which she merely listed. They included Susie's past and future physical pain and mental suffering, her loss of enjoyment of life's pleasures, and Chris's emotional distress and so-called loss of consortium. This the judge defined as Chris's loss of his spouse's affection, society, companionship, and aid and comfort, as well as the loss of any household services that Susie had performed. Like the Liggett jurors, many on the panel had expected more guidance. In this case they had hoped to be told how much plaintiffs had won in previous lawsuits involving similar circumstances. Some had anticipated that they would be shown a chart, as they had been for Susie's medical expenses, that would rationalize the proposed damage award for emotional and psychological losses. But as the judge's instructions ended, Gesink realized with growing anxiety, "We would be blind in the dark."

At about 6:00 P.M. the jurors were dispatched to the jury room, where they tossed a coin to pick David Gesink as foreman over rival candidate Margaret Fleming. Gesink immediately called for a vote on whether the blood bank was liable for the Quintanas' damages. The jurors had no trouble agreeing that UBS could have—and therefore should have—done more educating, screening, and testing of blood donors than it had done. In particular, the jurors thought, the blood bank should have asked potential donors directly if they were gay and excluded those who were. The vote was unanimous, a slam dunk—as the Quintanas' lawyer Bruce Jones later put it —for the plaintiffs. There was no need, these jurors believed, for further discussion on this question.

Having dispensed so quickly with the liability issue, the jurors broke for the evening and were shuttled by paddy wagon to a nearby hotel to spend the night, sequestered, as it turned out, to keep them from hearing that Susie Quintana had died that morning, just eight days after testifying.

On Saturday they arrived at the courthouse early and launched immediately into a discussion of damages. The first thing they did was vent their anger at UBS attorney Downey for proposing the paltry sum of five hundred thousand dollars in his closing argument. "That's not even a good amount for a car accident," Rose Bowles said afterward. "That made me angry. I felt it was a put-down to the Quintanas for their lifestyle and the kind of money they had been used to living on." Downey's optimistic prediction of future interest rates also annoyed some of the jurors. "Where's he banking?" wondered juror Karen Dwyer, a nineteen-year-old college sophomore who had been working during her summer break as a receptionist for a moving company before jury service had interfered.

They knew they'd give more than half a million, but how much more? No one had a particularly clear idea of how to begin. "We were flying by the seat of our pants," recalled Linda Woods, the medical notes transcriber. "There's no objective way to come up with a number." In the absence of other ideas, foreman David Gesink decided to steer the jurors away from their anti-Downey invective and ask everyone to provide an overall figure that each thought would be appropriate.

Woods seemed to know the most about the range of other verdicts in personal injury cases. She remembered hearing talk in the office about medical malpractice verdicts against individual doctors in the three- to four-million-dollar range. The defendant here was a company; ten million dollars, she told the others, might make sense.

When others protested that the figure was too high, Woods

revealed herself as exactly the sort of juror that giant corporations fear. She argued straight out that the damages should be inflated precisely because the defendant had big pockets. "To me the size of the corporation made a big difference," she admitted later, not even acknowledging the inherent bias in that view. "This is a conglomerate," she said. "I'd give less to a smaller company." Part of the reason was ability to pay. "If an individual can be sued in the millions, this big company could support paying out more money," she said. In addition, she saw big companies as capable of doing greater harm than smaller outfits and thus more in need of a slap on the wrist. "This was one little case in one little town," she reflected after the trial, "but it could have an impact in other places." What she was talking about was punishment, and though only some of the other jurors agreed, her insistence on adding a punitive component to the damages helped define the range within which the discussion took place.

Though she didn't know it, Woods's approach was a clear deviation from the law. Compensatory damages are meant, in a word, to compensate. Punitive damages are supposed to be reserved for cases in which a defendant has engaged in willful wrongdoing, which hadn't been alleged in this case. Yet when damage measures are as vague as those involving pain and suffering or loss of a spouse's companionship, extraneous considerations have a tendency to enter. In the Quintana case, as in many, it was indeed the oft-cited anticorporate bias that waltzed in.

Rose Bowles, who'd spent thirty years immersed in the books of the town of Fort Lupton, Colorado, sensed that Woods's number was on the high side, regardless of the identity of the defendant. "I think I might be a little more conservative because of my government background," she explained later. Also, she added, "A lot of times when people come into a lot of money, it does more harm than good."

Four million might make more sense, she now offered. Gary Dahl aimed for the low side: He figured a few million dollars would go a long way in Dolores. Everyone else picked a number between Woods's ten million and Dahl's "few." Juanita Underwood was up near Linda Woods's range. Now what? There didn't seem to be a sensible way to proceed. "You can't really translate pain into money. There's no way to price that," foreman Gesink complained.

Then Karen Dwyer remembered the jury instructions: The jurors weren't supposed to name a single figure. They were supposed to work their way through a verdict form and give a certain amount for each of the categories of damages that had been listed. They quickly turned to the instructions and confronted the first such category: past and future physical pain and mental suffering. The terms were not defined. And, as usual, the jury wasn't provided with any historical context that might have helped them make sense of their puzzling task.

The history of damages for pain and suffering might not have provided much guidance, though, except to establish that the notion of easing a person's pain by paying him money is an ancient one. Indeed, as far back as 450 B.C. in Rome, laws provided specific sums to compensate for broken limbs and other bodily injuries. These figures were constant for a particular injury, whatever a person did for a living, suggesting that some element of the payment was for inconvenience or pain rather than just for lost wages. How the amounts were decided on, however, is impossible to reconstruct.[8]

Similarly, in medieval England a victim could receive a set payment, known as a *bōt*, for injured feelings if, for example, someone called him a bad name. In the jury system that evolved in England after the Norman invasion, however, the extent of an injury and the damage that it caused had to be proved in court. No statutes existed to dictate an amount to be awarded for any particular harm. This may be why damages for pain and suffering were slow to reemerge. Yet sometimes the circumstances seemed to dictate that suffering be compensated, and sometimes it was, even if the rationale for such an award was left unclear. One early example is *Ash* v. *Lady Ash,* a 1696 case in which a jury assessed the extraordinary sum of two thousand pounds against a mother who had pretended her daughter was mentally ill, forced her to take certain medicines, and confined her against her will. The amount was far too high to cover any costs the daughter had incurred; it must have been intended to punish the mother and soothe the daughter.

This case and others like it must have inspired lawyers. Soon they were openly requesting and winning payments for painful injuries. Money might not actually ease the pain, they argued, but it might more generally allay the suffering. Pain and suffering emerged in the nineteenth century as a common element of personal injury suits. In turn, lawyers, judges, and juries sought logical ways to measure such losses in monetary terms. To the detriment of the Quintana jury and others like it, they never quite succeeded.

Some lawyers have suggested that jurors try to imagine how much they'd want to receive if they were the victims. But most courts have barred this golden rule approach because it encourages jurors to identify with the plaintiff rather than remain neutral. Other lawyers have recommended that juries break down the assignment by deciding how much a victim should be compensated for a single day of suffering and then multiply that sum by the number of days the person is in pain. But the per diem method, which some courts allow, still begs the question of how the jurors should decide the value of even one day's pain.[9]

As one state appeals court has put it, "No market place

exists at which such malaise is bought and sold. . . . It has never been suggested that a standard of value can be found and applied. The varieties and degrees of pain are almost infinite; the only standard for evaluation is the amount that reasonable persons estimate to be fair compensation."[10]

The jury in the Quintana case, offered no guidelines at all, agreed that Susie would suffer more in the future than she had in the past. They agreed, on the basis of doctors' estimates, that she'd probably live another eighteen months. Beyond that they were stumped. David Gesink suggested, without having heard of the golden rule theory, that the jurors try to put themselves in Susie's place in setting an amount. But this method collapsed when jurors started focusing on their own lives rather than the Quintanas'. After a few minutes Gesink suggested they try something else. Someone recommended that they award Susie a hundred thousand dollars a year for past suffering, a hundred thousand a month for what was still to come. No one could remember afterward who had proposed the formula; it just seemed to have drifted into their minds. Yet the numbers sounded sensible and reflected their belief that Susie's suffering would only intensify. The jurors adopted it and rounded up: three million dollars for pain and suffering. They moved on: damages for medical expenses. These were easy. The Quintanas' costs had been outlined in a chart, and even Downey hadn't contested them. The jury decided to provide five hundred thousand dollars in this category.

Then came the real brainteaser: loss of enjoyment of life. This was even stranger than pain and suffering. How much were a person's pleasures worth? And how much pleasure was lost when pain set in? The questions had a certain philosophical, not to say metaphysical, cast to them. And the Quintana jurors realized that some weird math was involved as well. They'd have to value both Susie's past and present levels of pleasure and then subtract one from another to decide how much she'd lost. Arguing for the blood bank, Downey had suggested in his opening and closing statements that Susie had already been living with pain before the 1983 transfusion and had already lost some of the ability to enjoy her life. Starting in the 1970s, she'd undergone a number of abdominal operations. She'd had ulcers, gallbladder problems, almost constant diarrhea. She'd had to stop working as a medical assistant in 1977 because of her discomfort. Then there had been the direct effects of the accidental gunshot wound she'd received in 1983, for which she'd needed the transfusion. These effects would have slowed her down regardless of the later complication from the tainted blood, he'd suggested. The jurors had found Downey's reference to these earlier disabilities uncharitable, if not unpalatable. But now they found themselves flinching less and less as the hours went by and the need to find a figure intensified.

One obvious question included whether the Quintanas, who'd slept separately after the AIDS diagnosis, had engaged in sex in the years before that. Gary Dahl wondered if Susie's prior ailments had already curtailed their sex lives. David Gesink asked whether people their age, regardless of health, still engaged in sex. Gesink was popular with the other jurors, so the laughter that followed was affectionate, and some of the older jurors quickly set the twenty-one-year-old straight. But to many of them the path they were pursuing seemed undignified. "I feel like we're playing God here," Karen Dwyer remembered saying at one point. Who were they to say whether or not Susie had enjoyed life before AIDS? Besides, said Gesink, whatever ailments she'd suffered from prior to the transfusions surely had been made worse by AIDS. The jurors decided to drop the inquiry—to forget about Susie's past life—and assume that she'd experienced all the pleasures of a healthy married woman. They started to toss numbers

167

around again. One and a half million dollars sounded about right to most of them. Add that to the damages for medical care and pain and suffering, and Susie would collect five million dollars in all.

By now reconciled to the guesswork involved in their decision making, the jurors turned to Chris Quintana's loss of his wife's companionship and household services. In her summation, Witt hadn't even hazarded a suggestion for loss of consortium.[11] This remarkable area of damages had its origins in the thirteenth century, when British law first permitted a master to sue for the diminished value of an injured servant. At the time a wife was legally her husband's servant. A court in the case of *Guy* v. *Livesey,* in 1618, put the two ideas together and allowed a husband to collect damages from someone who deprived him of his wife's services.[12] As the law evolved, a man was permitted to collect for a wife's impaired ability to maintain the home, care for family members, show affection, procreate, and engage in sexual activities. A woman, though, had no claim if her husband was injured because women, as servants, were deemed to have no legal right to men's services. It wasn't until 1950 that a U.S. federal appeals court concluded that both spouses in a marriage contract were entitled to material services and to "companionship, felicity, and sexual relations."[13] But it wasn't until the 1970s that a majority of courts adopted this reasoning and allowed loss of companionship lawsuits to flow both ways.

The Quintana lawsuit was traditional in that it sought, among other things, economic damages for Chris's loss of his wife's household services. There had been much testimony about how dependent Chris had been on his wife to cook, clean, shop, and manage the household. And such services surely could be priced; one needed only to estimate how much it would cost Chris to pay someone to do the same work Susie had performed throughout the marriage. But a nineties jury that included six women, five of whom had established careers outside the home, wasn't prepared to make the kind of calculation that male juries had been making for more than three centuries. Karen Dwyer, Linda Woods, and Nancy Uebelhoer, the three youngest women in the jury, immediately raised the alarm when the jury instruction was read. "This was tragic, but he can make his own dinners," Dwyer said later. The others agreed. Some also noted that the Quintanas' daughter had been coming to the house to help with cooking and chores and that Chris hadn't appeared to be paying her.

The jury was, however, prepared to consider giving Chris a substantial sum for the less quantifiable loss of Susie's affection, society, companionship, aid, and comfort. The marriage had been unusually close. And Chris had fallen to pieces after Susie had become ill. A figure of $1.15 million materialized, again for no apparent reason. This time Gary Dahl balked. That seemed like an awful lot of money for a man who had suffered only secondarily from AIDS, he said. He could understand giving Susie and Chris enough money to pay her medical bills and live in comfort for her few remaining months. But Chris had testified that he might like to take Susie on vacation to Las Vegas. If the jurors gave him so much money, wouldn't he gamble it away? "We were talking about serious damages in the millions of dollars; it didn't seem right to me," Dahl said later. "I wanted them to use the money to get their life back together." But, he added, "the other jurors told me to go take a hike. So I left it at that. I didn't want to bring on any adversities like that." Other jurors remembered the incident, too. Said David Gesink: "We all thought it was stupid. I figured if [gambling] will help the man drown his sorrows, I think it's his privilege. I didn't care what he did with the money as long as it helped him out."

The $1.15 million figure was not challenged any further.

"At the time we were all in agreement, and it all made sense," Linda Woods said later by way of explanation. For the last category of damages, the jurors tossed another $130,000 Chris's way to compensate him for emotional distress, based largely on his fear of contracting AIDS after Susie was diagnosed.

It was close to noon on Saturday, August 1. The jurors had been deliberating for more than five hours. Karen Dwyer was concerned. Though it appeared that the jury had given the Quintanas enough money, she told the others, the family wouldn't end up with nearly so much because their lawyers would probably get about a third. Dwyer, who was self-possessed and assertive, said she knew this because her father was a lawyer. The other jurors took her word for it and shared her concern. They decided that the Quintanas should get the full amount that was intended for them, not just two thirds of it. They agreed to add 30 percent to the award. That brought Susie's damages up to $6.5 million and Chris's to $1.65 million. Total award: $8.15 million. The jury instructions hadn't authorized the jurors to make this adjustment. Indeed, lawyers are barred from suggesting that jurors tack on more money for fees, and some judges expressly warn jurors not to do so. But it is the kind of ad hoc calculation that juries make every day.

Because jury awards for noneconomic damages are subject to so much discretion anyway, and because juries' specific considerations during deliberations ordinarily aren't reviewable by the court, extra damages for legal fees often become part of the ultimate award in personal injury suits. In one experiment involving mock jurors, 20 percent said they had considered legal fees in setting the damage award, even though the jury instructions had said nothing about the issue.[14] And in a 1984 asbestos case in which researchers had studied the actual jury's deliberations, the jury had added 40 percent for legal fees for each plaintiff. One of the jurors explained afterward that if the plaintiff had received only the intended amount of damages "and had to give the lawyer half of it, then he wouldn't have the money that maybe he needs for his medical expenses for the rest of the time he's going to be alive, and I didn't think, personally, that he should have to pay out of his pocket for hiring a lawyer to take the company to court."[15]

Was justice done in the Quintana case? Was the $8.15 million award excessive? Would society benefit if UBS had to reduce the money it spent for blood collections to cover the cost of one couple's misfortune? These questions go to the heart of the debate about the direction and purpose of personal injury law. They are difficult to answer.[16]

It's clear that the Quintana jury wasn't a responsible arbiter when it came to the central issue of UBS's legal responsibility. The question of negligence was a close call. The trial judge initially had ruled that if UBS had complied with the professional standards of the blood banking community at the time, it couldn't have been negligent. But the appeals court had required that the issue be explored more fully by a jury. The idea had been that a jury might legitimately decide that UBS officials knew a good deal about AIDS transmission by 1983 and that they couldn't avoid liability for negligence simply by showing that they had met the industry's standard of care. But by imposing an impossibly high, absolute safety standard of its own, the Quintana jury had avoided the more nuanced questions on which the case truly turned.

Having found the company liable, the jury then issued an award that was undeniably high compared with similar Colorado cases. The average medical malpractice award in Colorado over the previous six years had been eight hundred thousand dollars. Loss of consortium claims in those cases had averaged eighty thousand dollars. All jury awards thus far in AIDS transmission cases had averaged two million dollars. As Linda Woods's comments suggest, the Quintana award certainly appeared to reflect a middle-class jury's animus against rich and powerful corporations and its failure to countenance any cost-benefit analyses.[17]

The jury's casual prejudices seemed disappointingly familiar. Within twelve months of the Quintana verdict, a Texaco worker had coaxed more than $17 million from a Los Angeles jury when she claimed she had been passed over for a promotion and harassed because she was a woman. A man had won $18.5 million from an Illinois hospital that a jury believed had failed to prevent his suffering a stroke. Even in conservative Iowa City a jury had doled out $4.3 million to a couple who merely complained that someone might have been watching them make love through a false mirror on their motel room wall.[18]

The magnitude of these awards had been impossible for the defendants to predict and reflected juries' well-known inconsistencies. One study of personal injury damage awards between 1972 and 1987 found that verdicts in cases involving comparable injuries varied crazily from one trial to another. In this two-state sample, awards for equivalently severe personal injuries ranged from $147,000 to $18.1 million.[19]

The inability of potential defendants to anticipate how much they might have to pay for causing an injury has significant costs. It may make it difficult for a drug company, for example, to determine whether it can afford to market a new drug because it can't determine how much a jury might make it pay for the occasional, unanticipated failure of the product. Additionally insurers claim that if they can't calculate their potential risks with some degree of certainty, they have to charge more or offer less coverage, or both. Beyond such practical considerations lies the question of whether it's simply unfair for the civil justice system to charge so much more in damages to one defendant, such as United Blood Services, than to another under similar circumstances.

The Quintana case adds up to another disappointing jury story and seems to offer more ammunition for anyone's brief against using juries in civil cases. But choosing to support the jury in the face of cases such as Quintana isn't just an act of faith; it's a recognition of the vitality with which our original vision of the American jury survives even such disappointments.

Only in a jury trial can each person's case be treated as unique, as worthy of a fresh look and an independent calculation of its value, based on the best judgment of people unburdened by either expertise or direct self-interest. Despite the jury's deficiencies, Susie Quintana's damage award reflected such factors as her entrapment in a small town that had judged her harshly and the particularly painful course her illness had taken. Chris Quintana's damages had been enhanced by the closeness of his marriage and his dependent role in that relationship. Community values, rather than mere formulas, had been brought to bear on the outcome.

The considerable challenge for the jury system is to preserve these virtues while tempering the jury's tendency to rough up corporate defendants and assuring a greater degree of consistency in verdicts.

The approach that Quayle had hoped to impose nationally, and that corporate lobbyists have convinced many state legislatures to try, was to place precise dollar limits on how much money a jury can give a plaintiff for pain and suffering, sort of like the *bōt* prescribed by Anglo-Saxon law. Another more radical solution that has been suggested involves handling such cases administratively, much the way workers' on-the-job injury claims are now decided through the workers' compensation system. In such a system Susie's injuries would simply have been cataloged and assigned standard monetary values based on formulas set by legislators or other officials. Both approaches are long on promoting consistency and short on preserving the jury's positive role as a democratic decision maker in civil disputes. And they reflect a dispiriting trend toward making jurors less harmful by limiting their power to go wrong rather than making them more useful and effective by giving them the tools to do right. In the process legislators who purport to believe in the jury system are speeding its erosion.[20]

A more promising direction involves helping jurors make wiser decisions by providing them with more education, information, and guidance about how to do so. That jurors change their behavior on the basis of new information is apparent in some of the most recent studies of how juries treat corporations. For one thing, the Quayle message concerning the tort crisis seems to have gotten through to jurors: While in 1988 plaintiffs won 63 percent of personal injury cases against companies, by 1992 that figure had decreased to 52 percent, according to one prominent study. Meanwhile, average damage awards have been holding roughly steady, after earlier periods of big increases. Polls indicate that such data reflect jurors' growing awareness of, and agreement with, the business community's complaints.[21]

More important than such media-related messages to the general population are specific efforts to guide actual jurors toward more sensible methods of considering evidence and deciding both liability and damages. Some of these methods, such as providing earlier, clearer jury instructions, permitting lawyers to offer periodic minisummations during the trial, and letting jurors ask questions and take notes, have been noted in preceding chapters. In addition, in cases involving such difficult-to-assess categories of damages as pain and suffering, juries might benefit from being told the range of verdicts in previous cases involving similar facts, information that the lawyers and the judge have but that jurors are never provided. Another approach might be for legislatures to set a range of awards permissible for different injuries. Such a system might resemble the sentencing guidelines that judges look to in criminal cases.

Perhaps the most creative approach has been suggested by Robert Satter, a state court judge in Connecticut. He recommends that the liability portion of each civil case be tried first. Then, if the defendant is found liable, each side could propose an appropriate damage amount. The jury would be instructed to pick either the plaintiff's figure or the defendant's, not some number in between. By treating damages like a baseball salary arbitration, Judge Satter figures, courts would guarantee that each side chose a figure that had a reasonable chance of success. The procedure would encourage moderation by the lawyers and would give jurors a more clearly defined task.[22]

The Quintana jurors would have appreciated the assistance. "It was ridiculous to determine damages without any guidelines," Linda Woods reflected weeks after the trial. "We did muddle through it, but we had no clue."

6

LOVE AND DEATH IN
NEW JERSEY

—

O N Friday, March 15, 1991, police answering a call at 36
Sunnyslope Road in Millington, New Jersey, found
Fabio Hernandez, bloodied and groaning in pain, on the
floor of the master bedroom. He had been shot in the chest
and was also bleeding from a laceration near his left eye. He
was dressed only in a pair of khaki pants, open at the belt,
with the zipper down. Police officers found a 9mm shell casing under his body. He was rushed to Morristown Memorial
Hospital, where he died the next day during surgery.

Other than Hernandez, who gave no statement before he
died, there had been two witnesses to the shooting. One had
been Kevin Schneider, a Newark narcotics detective who had
lived in the house before his divorce from Marisol Schneider
a few months earlier and who owned the gun that had shot
Hernandez. The other witness had been Marisol, who still
lived in the house and had been Hernandez's lover both before and after the divorce. Kevin's and Marisol's versions of
events contradicted each other on most important details.
Physical evidence was inconclusive. It would be up to a jury,

after Kevin was charged with murder, to decide who was telling the truth about this triangle of love and death.

This is the kind of case in which juries are supposed to excel. There's no legal gobbledygook to parse, no complicated finances to follow, and little apparent room for prejudice to squeeze out reason. Here the common sense of the common man, the jury system's most treasured asset, can take over. And jurors do bring a lifetime of experience to judging whether other people's words square with their deeds. In their daily lives jurors make hundreds of such calculations: whether the used-car dealer is telling the truth about the mileage; whether the job applicant is lying about his experience; whether the child is concocting a tall tale about the missing homework; whether the spouse is working late or playing around. A knack for knowing whom to trust, whom to believe, whom to shun is the essence of common sense. Collectively twelve jurors would seem likely to have a great deal more of it than any single judge, no matter how well versed in law or experienced in life.

Yet for the most part the Schneider deliberations do not support this upbeat hypothesis. The jury in this case was a good deal more alert, sophisticated, and well educated than most. Nonetheless, more than in any other trial in this book, the jurors' various lapses, oversights, and unsupported assumptions raise questions about whether juries do anything well enough to justify our continuing reliance on them. Moreover, academic studies suggest that the traps the Schneider jurors fell into as they assessed the witnesses' credibility are, depressingly, all too common.

Indeed, in the last decade or so a startling consensus has emerged among researchers that observers without special training, such as jurors, are egregiously bad at determining when someone is telling the truth, inadvertently giving false testimony, or lying. This, of course, contradicts the cherished folklore about jurors' common sense and powers of observation. It also helps explain why it's so difficult to find ways to help jurors such as those in the Schneider case do a more effective job.

Marisol Schneider described Friday, March 15, 1991, as a typical weekday morning. She rose early, as usual, to get her children ready for school. Eleven-year-old Jennifer raced through her morning rituals and was out the door by seven-thirty, right on schedule. By eight Marisol had her six-year-old, Kevin, Jr., dressed and seated at the kitchen table for breakfast. But the boy was more interested in the snow falling outside than he was in his cereal, and Marisol told him he could stand by the window and watch for a few minutes before catching his bus to school.

Almost immediately Kevin shouted that his father was outside. That was odd, Marisol thought. Kevin, Sr., whom she had divorced the previous November, wasn't supposed to be here because she had decided he was too dangerous and had convinced a judge to bar him from the house. Marisol told her son not to open the door. She went to the window and scanned the street but saw no one. Maybe her son, who missed his father, was just pretending. She opened the door to check further, and Kevin, Sr., suddenly materialized and pushed his way in. He seemed to be looking for someone: He poked his head into the living room, then the dining room. He walked back toward the door, grabbed Marisol, and kissed her on the cheek. He just wouldn't give up, it seemed to her; she pulled away. Kevin said he was here to pick up some banking records, but he didn't walk over to the file cabinet in the first-floor den where all their financial files were kept. Instead, he said he wanted to use the second-floor bathroom and began to climb the stairs.

Marisol followed. She knew something he couldn't know

for certain but seemed to suspect: Her lover, Fabio, the "other man" who had precipitated the Schneiders' divorce, was asleep in the big bed she'd once shared with Kevin. A few paces behind Kevin, Marisol reached the landing, where the stairs turned 180 degrees, and lost sight of him for a couple of seconds. After she turned, she realized he wasn't on his way to the bathroom, which was straight ahead. He had veered to the right and entered the master bedroom. Terrified, she charged after him. Kevin, who was thirty-three, was a black belt in karate, a brown belt in judo, a fitness fanatic. More than once, even since the divorce, he had erupted in jealous rages and had threatened to harm Fabio if Marisol didn't stop seeing him. And Kevin was carrying his standard-issue semiautomatic pistol in a holster at his belt.

She heard groaning even before she entered the room. Fabio was lying naked and facedown on the bed, and Kevin was standing over him, pounding him with the butt of his gun. Fabio was screaming now as he tried to pull his big, flabby body out of harm's way. An El Salvadoran restaurateur who had come to America to escape the violence back home, Fabio was a man who avoided confrontations. Although Marisol was now a single woman, Fabio had taken the precaution of parking his white Mercedes out of sight of the house, just in case hotheaded Kevin should come around. Now Marisol hurled herself against Kevin and tried to pull him away. This gave Fabio the chance to roll off the bed, grab a comforter to wrap around his exposed body, and stagger, bleeding from several head wounds, into the sunroom, where he had left his clothes the night before.

Marisol, though strong and lithe, was no match for Kevin. He quickly brushed her away and, his gun drawn, ran after Fabio. She pursued them both and jumped between them in the sunroom, but Kevin was steely. "Honey, you know I have to defend myself. He's a burglar. I have to defend myself," he said. She realized that the line sounded chillingly familiar:

Kevin had always had a habit of offering explanations in advance for behavior he knew was wrong. She begged him not to shoot. Calmly reaching around her, he aimed and fired. Fabio, who had dropped the comforter and had been leaning over to pull on his pants, fell to the floor. Blood was everywhere. When the local police arrived, Kevin was arrested, hauled off to jail, and indicted for murder and a host of lesser crimes.

But there wasn't a murder, or even a crime, to be found in Kevin's version of the same day's events. According to his rendition, he drove up to his former residence at eight that Friday morning, parked right in front, and waved to his son through the window. He walked over to a fenced-in area to greet his big husky, Hercules. Then he approached the front door, knocked, and waited. Marisol called out, "Who is it?" and Kevin answered, "It's me." There was a surprisingly long pause, about fifteen seconds, and then she opened the door and let him in. Although Kevin hadn't called, it should have been no surprise that he had dropped by; despite the divorce and a restraining order restricting his visits, he and Marisol, whom he called Dolly, had remained on good terms. They'd been sharing custody of the children, including Jennifer, Marisol's daughter from a prior relationship, and he was paying $625 a month in child support. Kevin often drove his son to the bus stop in the morning. Despite the court order, Kevin had also been at the house on Sunnyslope Road for Jennifer's big birthday party and even to pick up presents from Marisol and the kids on his own birthday, just a week earlier. In addition, with Marisol's approval, Kevin had been helping a great deal around the house, putting up Christmas lights, fixing the persistently cranky boiler, painting the shed, moving a picnic table into the yard.

He was at the house that morning because a week earlier he'd received troubling news from his banker. It seemed that the bank thought Kevin was seventeen hundred dollars behind on a checking account that he believed he had closed out a year earlier. Kevin kept his old checking records back at the house—not in a filing cabinet in the downstairs den, as Marisol claimed, but in a desk upstairs in the sunroom, just off the master bedroom. He had a meeting planned with the banker later in the morning, he told Marisol, and he was here to pick up the old checkbook so he could bring it with him. But first, nature called. Kevin walked into the closet of a bathroom off the kitchen, closed the flimsy plastic louver door, then realized he wanted more privacy and decided to use the upstairs john. He headed up the steps, figuring that he'd pick up the banking records in the sunroom, then bring them into the upstairs bathroom to read on the toilet. He had to go through the bedroom to get to the sunroom, but the bedroom door was closed. He reached to open it and was met with a fist in the face. Fabio was hardly asleep in the bed; he was on the attack.

The blow to his right eye stunned Kevin, and he fell against Marisol's dresser to the right of the door. As Kevin tried to regain his balance, Fabio, who was wearing khaki trousers and nothing else, got him in a bear hug and grabbed for his gun, undoing the buckle on his holster. Forty-two-year-old Fabio, at about five feet, seven inches tall and 220 pounds, outweighed his younger, fitter, karate-trained adversary by 50 pounds. The weight difference and the element of surprise had turned this into an even match. They struggled for the gun. At one point Kevin got control and managed a couple of glancing blows with the gun to the front and top of Fabio's head as Fabio continued to charge him. That explained the head wounds. Marisol entered the chaos, screaming, and Kevin yelled for her to call the cops. Instead, she jumped on

Kevin, and the three of them ended up on the bed. By the time Kevin shrugged her off his neck, Fabio had gotten both hands on the gun. Kevin put one hand on it, too, and they fell onto the bed, then stumbled the few feet into the sunroom and crashed into the desk where Kevin kept his checking records.

Kevin was still shouting for Marisol to call the police. Instead, she raced in and again grabbed Kevin around the neck. Both Fabio and Kevin had hands on the gun when it accidentally discharged. The barrel happened to be facing Fabio. The recoil sent Kevin and Dolly flying back into the door. Fabio fell as the bullet crashed through his chest, lung, and diaphragm and lodged in his liver. He landed on a comforter lying on the floor and soaked it with his blood. Kevin was panicked. In eleven years of exemplary police work of the riskiest sort, nothing like this had ever happened. He hadn't committed any crime, though, and had nothing to hide. That was why he immediately called the local police.

When they arrived, he nervously jumbled the story. Trying to explain about the banker and the checkbook and the sucker punch to his eye, he blurted out instead that he had been attacked by a banker and had had to shoot him in self-defense. Later he explained that his assailant wasn't a banker but that the shooting had, indeed, been an act of self-defense. The same day, at his arraignment, his lawyer used the self-defense argument to buttress a plea for low bail: "We do have a defense of self-defense and we do have a police officer entitled to carry the weapon. I think that minimizes [the seriousness] somewhat," the lawyer, Anthony Pope, said. Much later Schneider changed his story again. By the time of the trial his version was that the gun had discharged not in anyone's self-defense but entirely by accident, during his fierce struggle with Fabio.

* * *

Two witnesses, two versions of the truth. If Marisol's was entirely accurate, Kevin was guilty of murder. But if Kevin's story was completely true and the shooting had been an accident, he was guilty of no crime at all. He had a right to carry his police gun, and if he hadn't fired it intentionally, he hadn't used it for any unlawful purpose. If Kevin had stuck to a self-defense theory, he'd have had to convince the jury that he hadn't used more force than was necessary to protect himself, and he'd have had to show that Fabio had placed him in mortal danger. Legally, an accidental shooting offered a far cleaner defense. If the truth lay someplace in between—say, that Fabio had started the fight but that Kevin had shot him to end the skirmish—a conviction on a lesser charge such as manslaughter or aggravated assault might be appropriate.

Each side would be able to harness ballistics evidence and other expert and character testimony to back one version or the other. But each side's story was internally consistent and couldn't be conclusively proved false by any independent means. The only way the jury would be able to decide would be to put its years of collective experience, wisdom, and common sense to work and determine who was lying.

The Morristown courtroom was beautiful and old, with elaborate woodwork, brass railings, maroon leather benches for the spectators, red curtains on tall windows, and a high ceiling with two concentric circles of decorative carving. At the back there was a balcony that appeared not to be in use. On the morning of the first day of the trial, Tuesday, February 18, 1992, the jurors filed in, admired their surroundings, then listened to the powerful harangues of the prosecutor and the defense attorney as they outlined the two versions of the killing.

Prosecutor John O'Reilly, beefy, broad-shouldered, and wholesome-looking, with a pale, round face that tended to flush when excited, cast Kevin Schneider in the ugliest light. A picture emerged of a jealous, violence-prone bully who had stalked Fabio Hernandez, threatened him, and then savagely followed through. Defense lawyer Michael Critchley, a product of tough Newark streets who had worked his way through night law school and resembled Robert De Niro's Al Capone in *The Untouchables,* was coarser and blunter than O'Reilly; he praised Kevin and depicted Marisol as a suburban gold digger and a liar. The jurors found both lawyers persuasive, just as the advocates were on the TV courtroom dramas some of them liked to watch.

O'Reilly had planned to bring Marisol's daughter, Jennifer, to the stand first. But when her turn came, the pretty sixth grader in the gray dress sobbed uncontrollably, and the judge allowed her not to testify. O'Reilly was doubly disappointed. Though Jennifer hadn't seen the shooting, she would have backed her mother on other details—such as the fact that Kevin had threatened to harm Fabio in the past—and would have generated sympathy for the prosecution side. Now O'Reilly would have to lead off with Marisol herself. He and investigator Matt Brady had spent a week with her in preparation for the trial, and they were anything but confident about her testimony. Though she'd stuck to her basic story about the shooting, she'd changed her mind about certain specifics. In addition, O'Reilly wasn't sure he knew everything he needed to know about her, and he hated surprises.

This was the jurors' first chance to get a good look at Marisol Schneider, and some of the men were clearly disappointed with how the leading lady had been cast. Marisol was a plain, almost mousy young woman with big teeth and long, kinky hair. She wore a blazer, slacks, and a white silk blouse, standard demure-witness attire. Juror Bill Westerfield, a sixty-one-year-old retired telephone company engineer, didn't think she was someone who'd be able to bewitch *him.* "Why would Kevin be so obsessed with her that he'd want to kill someone?'' he wondered. Juror Rick Smith, forty-five, a truck mechanic and national guardsman with a military crew cut, also was surprised. "I expected she would be a foxy-looking lady that Kevin couldn't resist," Smith recalled after the trial. "But she wasn't so foxy; she didn't have a great body; she was an average-looking girl. I figured, why make such a fuss about her?'' Doreen Morgan, a meticulously well-dressed and carefully groomed woman of thirty, whose long nails were painted in two pale shades, also noticed immediately that Marisol was plainly dressed and not very good-looking. In addition, Marisol had a don't-mess-with-me demeanor that suggested an unpleasant toughness. Wendy Meadows, a nineteen-year-old bank teller who was the youngest of the jurors, thought the witness seemed kind of snobby. Marisol had already made a strong and negative impression on both the men and the women, and she hadn't even begun to speak. Could the jurors disregard their personal impressions of her in assessing her testimony? Or were their personal impressions of value? The academic research was unequivocal on the subject: Though a witness's likability bears no relation to whether he or she is telling the truth, jurors overwhelmingly believe that an unappealing witness is more likely to be dishonest.

As O'Reilly had feared, Marisol turned out to be a disastrous spokeswoman for the prosecution. Initially, when he took her slowly through her testimony, she told the story of the shooting clearly and well and almost exactly as she had told it to the police within minutes of the incident. She seemed to remember everything and to respond readily to O'Reilly's many questions. Factually her most important contribution was that the naked Fabio had run away from Kevin after being attacked in bed, had found his pants in the sunroom, and had been leaning over to put them on when he had been shot by Kevin, who had pointed the gun downward.

Her version seemed to account neatly for two crucial facts: that Fabio had been shot at a downward angle, even though the two men were the same height, and that the police had found him with nothing on except his unbuckled, unzipped pants. Why would either of these things be true if Fabio had attacked Kevin and the gun had discharged accidentally, as the defense claimed?

Yet the logical power of Marisol's testimony on this point escaped nearly all of the jurors. Instead, they focused primarily on side issues. It jarred some of them, for example, that Marisol appeared so unemotional, even when she described the death of her lover and then identified various blood-splattered articles of his clothing. "Latins are emotional," thought computer specialist Doreen Morgan, herself part Italian, "and here she shows no emotion. She's cold." For Mike Poremba, a hard-charging forty-eight-year-old Dean Witter Trust vice president, the cool demeanor also created suspicion, in his case not because of his preconceptions about Latins but because of his view that women typically are highly emotional, demonstrative beings. Yet here was Marisol, with not a tear in her eye or a crack in her voice, giving almost sterile descriptions of the most tragic, traumatic events.

Poremba also suspected that her apparently sharp memory had been enhanced by coaching. "She remembered a half turn of the doorknob, the precise number of steps she was behind Kevin. It was just too detailed to be believable," he said later. In a jury of twelve, though, what sounds coached to one juror may sound credible to another: Ed Zawada, forty-five, a mild, deeply religious AT&T manager, listened approvingly to Marisol's meticulously detailed recounting and figured her level of specificity probably meant she was telling the truth.

On cross-examination, though, whatever was left of Marisol's credibility was shredded. An excellent cross-examiner,

Critchley was relentless but civil. Only once did he berate Marisol; mostly he let her destroy herself. Part of her problem was one of attitude. While Marisol had been cooperative with O'Reilly, she was impatient and sharp with Critchley. Even when caught in small inconsistencies, she contested every suggestion that she might have made a mistake. She seemed too defensive, several of the jurors thought.

Critchley was at his best as he took Marisol through the months prior to the shooting and thoroughly dismantled her version of that period. O'Reilly had tried to show in his opening statement and in his direct examination of Marisol that the shooting had been just the last in a series of violent episodes. The previous May Marisol had been forced to get the restraining order barring Kevin from the house because of his outbursts, she had said. She'd wanted nothing to do with him; a couple of weeks later he'd returned to the house and been arrested for violating the court order. Two days later he had tracked Marisol to the restaurant owned by Fabio. Hearing voices in a courtyard there, he had climbed the roof and leaped down onto a picnic table, shouting that he was Agent 007 and scattering people and food. Again he had been arrested. Several other times that summer and fall Marisol had had to call the police, she had told O'Reilly. Twice more Kevin had been arrested. This was a man with a short fuse who couldn't accept that his wife had taken up with someone else, O'Reilly had said.

But Critchley confronted Marisol with evidence that she'd had one voluntary encounter with Kevin after another even while the restraining order had been in effect. The purpose was to show that Marisol hadn't been afraid of Kevin, that they'd been on good terms and in regular contact. The court order was presented by Critchley as a cynical weapon of convenience for Marisol, to be invoked whenever she wanted Kevin out of the way, to be ignored whenever she needed him. Yes, she admitted, with the restraining order still in effect she'd let Kevin come to the house to hang the Christmas lights; yes, Kevin had gone with her in January to get her Alfa-Romeo repaired; yes, they had gone to Dunkin' Donuts for coffee; yes, they'd gone to the town pool together; yes, they'd been out to dinner; yes, they'd been to the shopping mall. Wendy Meadows, the youngest juror, frowned. She was the daughter of parents who had divorced when she was three. She knew from her own experience that divorced people could remain on cordial terms and that they needed to deal with each other a good deal in relation to the children. Marisol's initial denials that she'd voluntarily spent time with Kevin seemed pointless and unbelievable. If she was lying about this, how could anyone believe what she had to say about the shooting?

Critchley further undermined Marisol's character credentials by exploring her personal background. She'd met Kevin at a go-go bar when she was twenty. Her sister, known as Cookie, had been a dancer there. Before that Marisol had lived with the man who had fathered Jennifer, when Marisol had been just seventeen. Before that, still in her mid-teens, she'd lived with another man. Critchley's purpose was clearly to suggest that Marisol marched through life from man to man, that Kevin knew this and had stopped pursuing her or worrying about whom she was dating. "It would be absurd, based on what he knew, to expect her to come back to him," Critchley said. If the jury knew this, he expected, they would be less likely to believe Kevin had come to the house on March 15 seeking revenge against Fabio.

Critchley had the jury pegged perfectly. As Doreen Morgan learned more and more about Marisol, she liked her less and less. "What a shit, bitch, whore," Morgan began muttering to herself, and sometimes to her fellow jurors, as the trial proceeded. As in many trials, some of the jurors disregarded the admonition that they not discuss the case with one another until deliberations. And Marisol's moral deficiencies became a popular lunchtime topic among some of the panelists.

Juror Lilly Tai, a scientist who had come to the United States from the Far East and still spoke English hesitantly, was particularly intolerant of Marisol and unwilling to give any credence to her testimony. Just a couple of hours into Marisol's first day on the stand, she'd made up her mind that Kevin was not guilty, and she'd never looked back. Critchley had been questioning Marisol about some work she had undertaken in January and February 1991, while she was still relying on the court's help in protecting her from her supposedly violent ex-husband. Marisol had been selling knives for five hundred dollars a set, and part of the job had involved giving demonstrations. Concerned that she wasn't performing them correctly, she had gone to Kevin's apartment to practice. In addition, she'd called virtually all of Kevin's friends, including one as far away as Rochester, New York, to try to sell them knives, often dropping Kevin's name as if they were still together. Learning this had been the moment of truth for Tai. "I figured whatever that lady said is not reliable," she revealed later. From that point on Tai didn't much care what had transpired in the bedroom and the sunroom on March 15. To her, Kevin had been Marisol's dupe, and whatever had happened, she said later, "A year of turmoil was enough punishment. He deserved to get back to a normal life."

Critchley's lengthy explorations of events such as these took the jury far away from the scene of the shooting—and from a defense theory that required the jury to believe that a half-dressed, unarmed, out-of-shape man who had been too scared to park his car in Marisol's driveway had struck the first blow against an armed martial arts expert, whose gun had then discharged accidentally at a downward angle. And Critchley's microscopic focus on the events of May 10, 1990, proved even more significant than the knife-selling incident in guiding many jurors away from the logical weaknesses in the defense case.

That day, according to Marisol's testimony, she'd arranged to spend the evening with Fabio, while telling Kevin (then still her husband) that she was with her friend Roberta. Kevin didn't know of the affair with Fabio at the time. Marisol stayed out until 5:00 A.M. When she got home, Kevin confronted her. Later she called the police, claiming that Kevin had broken a plate, shattered the Plexiglas door, and run around the yard in his underwear, shooting a toy dart gun at her. The next day she got the court order barring him from the house. Marisol had presented the incident as evidence of Kevin's violent nature. Critchley was intent on creating a different impression: of Marisol as villain rather than victim:

Critchley: You called the cops?
Marisol: Yes.
Critchley: He didn't strike you that day?
Marisol: No, he didn't.
Critchley: He never struck you, did he?
Marisol: He didn't get a chance.
Critchley: Ever in life?
Marisol: No.
Critchley: You call the cops. . . . Did you think it was a good time to get him out of the house because now, if he's out of the house, you have a little bit more freedom with your new affair, Mr. Hernandez? You don't need a cover with Roberta?
Marisol: No.

Critchley followed with an interrogation regarding the tubal ligation Marisol had undergone that spring to prevent her from having any more children. He also asked her about her false statement to Kevin that they couldn't have sex for twenty days after the procedure and her trip during this period to Cancún with Fabio, when she'd pretended to be with her sister in North Carolina. Despite the surgery, the Cancún trip had produced a pregnancy and then a miscarriage.

Critchley: That child that was miscarried on May 11 was Mr.
   Hernandez's child, wasn't it?
Marisol: Yes.
Critchley: I'm sorry?
Marisol: Yes.

The courtroom was dead silent. Doreen Morgan once again was struck by Marisol's matter-of-fact tone, by the fact that she seemed to have no shame about all this. "In the garbage," juror Mike Poremba remembered thinking. "Her credibility is in the garbage."

Nonetheless, it was one thing for the jurors to conclude that Marisol was a manipulative person who had a tendency to lie. It was quite another to conclude that as a result, her story of the actual shooting should be disregarded entirely. And Critchley wasn't counting on the jurors to do so. Instead, he was hoping that he could find internal inconsistencies in her account of the morning of March 15. He did succeed in convincing most of the jurors that Kevin hadn't barged into the house, as she had claimed, but had been ushered in by Marisol. And he caught her in clear, if minor, errors concerning how long it had taken for the various events to transpire that morning. Similarly, Critchley made much of such details as whether Kevin had asked Marisol to call the police before or as the shooting occurred, exactly how much of the pistol-whipping she had seen, and whether one comforter or another had been on the bed the previous night.

191

Of course, none of these avenues undermined the logic of Marisol's basic story of the shooting or lessened the improbability of the defense's accident theory. But they were powerfully important in making the jurors more skeptical of anything the government's chief witness said. More important, in demonizing Marisol, Critchley made it much more difficult for the jurors to focus on the two most relevant questions. First, though Marisol had lied about other things, how probable, under the circumstances, was it that she had devised a fictitious version of the shooting just moments after it had occurred?

To bother inventing the story that Fabio had been leaning over to put his pants on when he'd been shot, she would have had to know in advance that the issue would emerge in the criminal case against Kevin. To know that, she would have had to know that the bullet had entered Fabio at a downward angle, something she wasn't likely to have realized or even considered in the minutes after the shooting. In addition, for the issue to be relevant at all, she would have had to know that Kevin was going to claim that Fabio had attacked him and had grabbed the gun, which had then discharged accidentally. Kevin hadn't given this story to Marisol, or to anyone, at the time. None of the jurors gave serious thought to the question of whether Marisol would have had the motive or the wit to invent this particular falsehood. Instead, they lumped all of Marisol's statements into one pile and then discarded the entire heap.

The second highly relevant question all but lost in Critchley's powerfully diversionary defense was, simply, which version of the shooting was probable on the basis of what was known for certain? Kevin's scenario not only involved his peculiar failure to deck Fabio or gain full control of the gun while tumbling on and bouncing off a bed and moving from one room to another but also involved the failure of the highly sensitive semiautomatic weapon to go off during the bedroom phase of the struggle, only to discharge once they were in the sunroom, after all the acrobatics, and to create an entry wound that also happened to be fully consistent with Marisol's impromptu story. If an accident was going to happen, why hadn't it happened earlier? If Fabio had been holding the gun when it discharged, why hadn't he had trace metals and gunpowder burns on his hands? As Robert Ingersoll, a famous trial lawyer of his time, advised a jury in 1891, "Thousands of people imagine that detail in memory is evidence of truth. I don't think it; if there is something in the details that is striking, then there is; but naturalness, and, above all, probability, is the test of truth. Probability is the torch that every juryman should hold, and by the light of that torch he should march to his verdict. Probability!"[1]

On Wednesday, February 26, Critchley called his client to the stand. And once again Critchley got the jurors to focus less on probability than on likability. Unlike Marisol, Kevin looked right at the jurors when he talked, as if he were speaking with them in their living rooms, Mike Poremba thought. It was such a simple thing, yet jurors always seemed to notice it. To them it signified trustworthiness. It also was a sign of good coaching. The best lawyers and trial consultants always drill their witnesses to make eye contact with jurors, and Critchley, of course, had done so with Kevin as they had prepared for trial together in the basement conference room of Critchley's office in an old clapboard house in West Orange. In any event, as a narcotics detective Kevin had had substantial experience testifying at trials and appealing to jurors.

The defendant also had the good fortune of being clean-cut and pleasant-looking, with a certain air of sadness. Numerous academic studies, usually involving trial simulations rather than actual cases, confirm that appearance counts in the courtroom. According to the researchers, good-looking defendants are convicted at lower rates and, when convicted, given shorter sentences, than unattractive ones. Additionally, one study of criminal cases involving juvenile defendants found that defendants who look sad or distressed are less likely to be convicted than those who look happy or angry. Other research indicates that convicted criminals who appear to be suffering, whether from remorse or physical injury, receive shorter sentences than those who don't seem to be in pain.

While Kevin looked appropriately pained, Critchley, whom some of the jurors had resented earlier because of his aggressive cross-examinations of the prosecution's expert witnesses, also was suddenly softer and apparently more genuine. He let Kevin speak at length, without leading him. And Kevin seemed eager to explain, as if he had nothing to hide. Was it that he was telling the truth, or was it that he was the most experienced testifier in the room, a man who had learned to gain a jury's trust through what O'Reilly in an interview later estimated to be some two hundred court appearances in narcotics cases? One's interpretation depended in large part on what one wanted to believe.

The early part of his testimony made Doreen Morgan want to believe the rest, even more than she had anticipated she would. She noticed, with approval, that Kevin didn't seem at all polished, despite the fact that Critchley had had plenty of time to shape him any way the lawyer had wanted. Kevin wasn't wearing a great suit; his shoes weren't particularly new or especially nice. His grammar was lazy; this wasn't a man who was putting on airs. Marisol, in contrast, had seemed a bit more stilted in her speech patterns. Morgan's reaction to these grammatical differences reflected not only her lifelong respect for honest blue-collar workers in the mold of her own grandparents but also a broader pattern of how jurors assess credibility. One study has found that many modestly educated witnesses tend to use what the researchers call hypercorrect speech because these witnesses are nervous and seek to speak appropriately in an unfamiliar and intensely formal setting. The hypercorrect speech reflects no less honesty or accuracy, yet observers consistently rate witnesses who use such a style much lower for truthfulness and competence.[2]

Steered gently by Critchley, Kevin described his life before Fabio; becoming a cop, falling in love with the nineteen-year-old Dolly, getting married, bringing young Jennifer into his home, and treating her as his own. "I thought we had a good marriage," he told the jury. "I loved [Dolly] and believed she loved me. When I married her, I planned to raise children and be her husband. I never planned for divorce."

Kevin had seen financial security as a key to their future, and he had eagerly set out to make money, buying real estate in what seemed to be an ever-rising market, with the intention of renovating the properties and selling them at a profit. But the venture had been ill fated. What might have worked brilliantly in the early eighties had proved a flop in the late eighties, as real estate prices had tumbled and Kevin had found himself stuck with four thousand dollars in mortgage payments and three properties he hadn't been able to unload. Kevin had exercised poor business judgment, perhaps, but the likes of Donald Trump had made much the same mistake and were now struggling, as was Kevin, to raise cash to stay afloat. Kevin had started taking odd jobs in addition to his police work. "It was nonstop work," he remembered. "Our bills were paid, but it was always work. The bills were always paid, but they were late."

The long hours might signify to the jurors that Kevin had abided by a virtuous work ethic or that he had neglected his spouse by staying away from home most of the days and evenings. That, again, depended on the jurors' own attitudes toward work and family. Lilly Tai, part of an eighties wave of ambitious Asian immigrants to the United States, had no hesitation. "Kevin worked hard to make them have a good life, to make a better life for the family," she concluded, while Marisol just went looking for pleasure.

As Kevin told it, while he had been working his increasingly long hours, Marisol had begun to stay out late. But Kevin said he hadn't suspected at first that she was having an affair. He said he believed now that it must have started in 1989, when Marisol had begun serving him Mexican takeout food that she'd said had been made "special" by a restaurant owner she knew. "I didn't think anything of it at the time," Kevin added ruefully.

Kevin was sheepish about his escapade on the roof of Fabio's restaurant on May 28, 1990, but he said he hadn't been there to hurt anyone. He'd been angry and wounded by Marisol's deceptions and had gone out that day to find her. When the door to the restaurant had proved to be locked, he had climbed a ladder to the roof to see the courtyard on the other side. He admitted he'd made a fool of himself when he'd jumped onto the picnic table below after seeing his wife there. "It was the silliest thing I ever did," he said, looking over at the jury regretfully.

In addition to Kevin's believable demeanor, the jurors' own life experiences were influencing their view that he was probably telling the truth. The ability of jurors to pool such experiences and draw wisdom from them is supposed to be one of the system's strengths. The danger is that jurors who have never committed a serious crime may decide from their own experience that there must be an innocent explanation for what appears to be terribly troubling behavior.

To the jurors in the Schneider case, Kevin's actions before the shooting weren't those of a dangerous man building up to a murderous rage. They were, thought Mike Poremba, mere "trivial marital burps," understandable reactions of a man who was just getting the message that his wife was cheating on him. Poremba figured Kevin had probably had a few beers before he climbed the roof and had decided to hassle Marisol a little because she was causing him so much trouble. Rick Smith, the truck mechanic, also thought that he had Kevin figured out. Kevin was like a lot of truck drivers Rick knew. They lived in a violent world and sometimes used coarse language and even threatened to do harm, but most were just ordinary people with families, and most threats and bluster came to nothing. Kevin had been mad at his wife, but he wasn't a cold-blooded killer.

Ed Zawada also saw the roof incident as an understandable lashing out, no worse than when Ed had once punched a hole in a wall after his girlfriend had jilted him. Bill Westerfield, the oldest juror, also was inclined to be indulgent on this one. Maybe Kevin had seen too many James Bond movies, he thought. Then his mind flashed to *Naked Gun 2½*, a slapstick cop movie that was playing in 1991; Kevin was the bumbling detective, Westerfield thought, chuckling to himself.

Prosecutor O'Reilly had presented the 007 incident as one of his most compelling proofs that Kevin was prone to acts of jealous rage, but the jury was giving Kevin every benefit of the doubt. Wendy Meadows, who had remained receptive to the prosecution case long after others had tuned it out, found Kevin's explanation totally disarming. O'Reilly, she thought, had presented the 007 incident far more ominously than the facts turned out to merit. And he became less credible to her because he had exaggerated.

The next day, Thursday, February 27, Kevin was back on the stand, this time to tell the story of the fight and the shooting. The sucker punch, the struggle, the intervention by Marisol, the accidental shooting: They were all straight out of

West Side Story. Would the dramatic also be believable? Spectators jammed the grand old courtroom to find out. Kevin told the story. Then Critchley asked Kevin to act out his version of the struggle. Critchley played Kevin, Kevin was Fabio, and another defense lawyer, Ellen Marshall, took Marisol's role. At the dramatic high point Ellen Marshall's Marisol grabbed Critchley's Kevin around the neck to restrain him, Kevin's Fabio pulled down on the gun, and the hammer clicked. Several jurors gasped. Critchley and Ellen Marshall jumped backward, as if reeling from the recoil. If the gun had been loaded, it was clear, Kevin's Fabio would have been shot, roughly where, in real life, the bullet had in fact entered Fabio. To Ed Zawada, this was a key moment in the trial. The story was now something physical, and it certainly looked real.

O'Reilly's cross-examination of Kevin was a disaster. The prosecutor tried to get Kevin to explain how a man in Fabio's poor physical condition could have fought Kevin to a stalemate, given Kevin's martial arts training. But Kevin effectively parried that he'd been dazed by Fabio's surprise punch. This was good enough for most of the jurors. Besides, thought juror Bill Westerfield, judo wasn't everything it was cracked up to be. Westerfield suddenly remembered an Ernie Kovacs TV show, perhaps thirty years earlier, in which a judo expert who'd claimed to be able to take on five burly club boxers at once was humiliated when the boxers easily subdued him. Size mattered in a fight, he reasoned in one of those quirks of jury reasoning that can rarely be anticipated, and Fabio was bigger than Kevin. Mike Poremba recalled that he had once been hit by a fat man and had felt as if his head were about to come off. A good punch could have changed the whole equation, he figured. O'Reilly had been certain that the jurors would laugh at the notion that Fabio could have outfought Kevin—so certain that he had declined to present experts on the efficacy of martial arts. But what O'Reilly had considered patently improbable, the jury, after hearing from a witness as appealing as Kevin Schneider, had accepted as distinctly possible.

Critchley was a torrent of emotion during his three-hour closing argument. He pleaded with the jury to compare the two witnesses' core values. Marisol, he said, "deals in shadows, and she wallows in lies and deception." Would they want Marisol in their social circles? How would they feel if a relative brought her home and said they were engaged? Kevin, on the other hand, was a hardworking, honest man whose many friends had rallied to his side during his time of trouble. Drawing a straight line in Magic Marker on a flip chart, Critchley said that this was Kevin's lifeline before Marisol threw him out on May 11, 1990. He drew a squiggly line to depict the time of turmoil during which Kevin had done some foolish things. Then he straightened out the line again to represent all the time since the divorce in November 1990 that Kevin had sought to lead a peaceful life and let bygones be bygones. Finally Critchley told the jurors that Kevin had been in his care until now, but soon he would be in theirs. "But when I let him go," Critchley said, "when I pass him to you, you take care of him the way he's entitled to. You don't abuse him the way Mrs. Schneider did. Don't let it happen again. Please take care of him." Critchley choked up when he said this, and Wendy Meadows's eyes also filled with tears.

O'Reilly, who seemed to the jurors to be somewhat beaten down by now, was briefer but still meticulous and insistent: Fabio was dead, Kevin had had the motive and the opportunity to kill him, and the evidence showed beyond a reasonable doubt that he had done so. There was simply no other credible explanation, he said, for the combination of incontestable facts: Kevin's past threats and his long-running antipathy toward Fabio, Kevin's advantage in terms of fighting skills and physique, the downward angle of the bullet, and the fact that Fabio's pants hadn't been buckled or zipped, suggesting he had been in the process of putting them on. You may not like Marisol, O'Reilly told the jurors. You may think that Kevin shot the wrong person. But that can't interfere with your obligation to convict him of murder.

Decision time for the jurors had arrived. Each of them had had two weeks in which to absorb the testimony, observe the key players, reflect on their behavior and on their demeanor now.

Doreen Morgan, even more than some of the others, had structured her analysis of the case around the question of which players she liked, trusted, and respected and which she didn't. This calculus included the lawyers, and she strongly preferred prosecutor O'Reilly to defense counsel Critchley. Indeed, O'Reilly's apparently sincere, apparently deeply held belief that Kevin was guilty was the best thing the prosecution had going for it, as far as she was concerned. But because she thought Kevin was a decent man and Marisol was "a sleaze," she was quick to pick up on the various holes in her story.

Without subjecting Kevin's story to the same level of scrutiny, she forgot that he had first claimed self-defense, then asserted the factually different—and legally cleaner—defense that the gun had gone off accidentally. She didn't consider at all why Marisol would have fabricated a story that Fabio had been leaning over to put his pants on when he'd been shot. It was enough that Marisol had been shown, in general, to be a liar. She gave only passing thought to whether it was plausible that Kevin would be unable to use his street-fighting skills, including karate and judo, to overcome any assault by Fabio. "I don't know karate," she later explained that she had reasoned. "Would I throw down my gun if I was a Newark cop and use karate? I don't know." She fell back, finally, on her affinity for Kevin, the hardworking man who had been wronged. "I was relieved he had a good excuse for what happened," she admitted later. "I liked him. I felt bad for him and all he'd been through. I didn't want to believe that he did it in cold blood." She also liked his friends, many of whom had testified on his behalf and many others of whom had sat in the spectator seats each day and offered him moral support. Marisol's cheering section had been decidedly smaller. Doreen Morgan had noted the disparity.

A professional judge, who had observed hundreds of witnesses and lawyers perform, might not have paid so much attention to appearances. And he or she might have tried harder to sweep aside irrelevant or peripheral testimony to home in on proof directly related to the crime scene.

For better and for worse, a professional judge also wouldn't have had access to twelve people's separate caches of diverse information. For while Doreen Morgan was focusing on the moral chasm between Kevin and Marisol, Ed Zawada was chewing over a much different concern that stemmed from his own life: specifically his intimate knowledge of guns. After Fabio had been shot in the sunroom, he had staggered back into the bedroom. The police officer who'd arrived first on the scene had testified that the shell casing from the fired bullet had been found under Fabio's body when he'd been lifted off the floor. Zawada knew from his own experience as a hunter and gun owner that shell casings fly back and to the right when a bullet is fired from a semiautomatic pistol. Therefore, he figured, if it hadn't met an obstacle, the shell casing would have landed somewhere in the sunroom. If it was in the bedroom instead, that could only mean that the casing had gotten caught in Fabio's clothing and then fallen to the floor when he collapsed in the bedroom. If so, Zawada thought, then Kevin and Fabio had to have been close enough together when the shot was fired for the casing to fail to clear their bodies. It must have bounced off Kevin and onto Fabio. Kevin's story of the hand-to-hand struggle and accidental shooting was probably accurate, Zawada concluded. Marisol's assertion that Kevin had shot the gun at a distance of three to four feet from Fabio could not be true. (Another possibility, which Zawada didn't ponder, was that the casing might have been picked up or kicked by someone after the shooting or might have bounced off a sunroom wall and rolled out the door to the bedroom.) Zawada wasn't sure that Kevin's entire story held up, but the shell casing evidence helped convince him that he couldn't find guilt beyond a reasonable doubt.

While Morgan was weighing morality and Zawada was contemplating ricochets, Wendy Meadows was falling back on raw emotion. Jurors in posttrial interviews almost never admit that they reached their decision out of sympathy or hate; even unsophisticated jurors know that this isn't an answer that reflects well on them. But jurors' sound bite responses to quick interviews often obscure, rather than illuminate, what goes on in the jury room. In longer or repeated conversations and in the comments of other jurors on the same panel, one often uncovers the messier, less logical dimension to people's decision making.[3]

In Meadows's case, the anti-Marisol rhetoric she'd heard inside the courtroom—and outside, during the jurors' lunchtime tirades—hadn't made much of an impact. "Maybe because I'm so young, I didn't mind that she was cheating," Wendy reflected later. "I told them that she's not on trial." She'd listened to Marisol with some sympathy and receptivity. She couldn't understand why Marisol had bothered to deny staying in contact with Kevin after the divorce, but overall she'd found Marisol's story of the shooting credible. Kevin was the final witness, though, and his three days of impassioned testimony had won her heart. He'd looked and sounded gentle, as if he "couldn't hurt a fly," as she put it later. She also remembered eleven-year-old Jennifer, who had cried so hard the first day of trial, and imagined that having a stepfather in jail would create hardships for the girl. Protecting Jennifer made emotional sense to Wendy, and the lottery of jury duty had dealt her the splendid power to wipe away the girl's tears. When Critchley cried during his closing argument, Meadows melted. Kevin's lawyer never would have let a client get so close to him if the client wasn't innocent, she figured. To her, tears signified sincerity—a supposition for which the academic research, not surprisingly, offers no support. She wanted to hug Kevin. She certainly had no intention of sending him away.

For separate and largely personal reasons, each of the other jurors had reached the same verdict even before the end of the trial. (Although all the great jury dramas of fact and fiction turn on a hard-fought jury room struggle, research has shown that the outcome of many cases is predetermined the moment the jurors enter the jury room after trial.)[4] But the jurors didn't tell one another their conclusions at first. Instead, they began their deliberations by looking through the exhibits, handling the weapon, and reenacting the shooting in little groups of their own to see whether both scenarios seemed physically possible. They did.

When, after an hour, forewoman Morgan assembled them all around the table and asked for their views, she encountered no significant disagreements. Everyone was confident that the murder charge couldn't stand. Everyone agreed that Marisol was a liar. Several jurors, including Rick Smith, Wendy Meadows, and Bill Westerfield, wondered whether Kevin might be guilty of one of the lesser crimes listed in the jury charge. One possibility was "passion/provocation manslaughter": an intentional killing committed in the heat of passion resulting from a reasonable provocation. Another, even easier to prove, was aggravated assault: that he had knowingly or recklessly caused serious bodily injuries by his own actions. After all, some jurors thought, shouldn't some price be paid for the loss of Fabio's life? But Mike Poremba argued forcefully that the jury charge was clear: Each of the lesser crimes required that the shooting be intentional. If it had been an accident, as they all were willing to believe, it couldn't be a crime.

The jury had been out for less than two hours. The room was small, and the heat was on full blast, making everyone uncomfortable. The jurors were anxious to vote. But one juror, church secretary Sue McNamara, suggested that it would look unseemly if the jury came back too quickly. So the jurors dutifully read each charge, discussed it, and voted—just to slow down the process a bit. After deliberating, if that was the right word, for barely three hours, they returned with their not-guilty verdict.

Kevin Schneider and Michael Critchley cried and hugged. Kevin's friends celebrated and sought out the jurors to pump their hands or exchange embraces. Wendy Meadows looked longingly at Kevin, but reporters were watching, and she decided a hug wouldn't look right. She'd forgo it. Instead, she yelled to him, "Good luck!" Doreen Morgan cried quietly. Meanwhile, Fabio Hernandez's brothers, who said they had been nearly certain of a conviction, strode from the courthouse without saying a word.

Only when the jurors listened to the news that night and read the papers the next morning would they realize that some commentators thought a terrible mistake had been made. "With a black belt in karate, a brown belt in judo and training as a narcotics officer working the streets, why Kevin never used these skills to better control the situation is a mystery," wrote one local columnist. "Too bad so many cases can turn on how well witnesses are portrayed during the trial. . . . Too bad for Marisol and Hernandez's relatives if she was telling the truth this time."[5] After the verdict another local paper wrote a sympathetic story in which Marisol was quoted as saying: "Dead people don't speak. I think it all boils down to Kevin looks pretty nice in a suit."[6]

After his acquittal Kevin Schneider was reinstated to the Newark police force, where he was welcomed back enthusiastically and later promoted to the rank of lieutenant. The verdict also enabled him to continue fighting for, and ultimately to win, joint custody of Kevin, Jr. The jury's version of the truth, whether accurate or not, was the only one that would survive.

More than a year after the Schneider jury had spoken, a federal judge in Newark, ruling in an unrelated case, ordered reporters not to interview jurors about the votes or statements of any other juror during deliberations that had recently been concluded. Judge Nicholas H. Politan declared that the smooth operation of the jury system depends on the confidentiality of jury decision making. When reporters are allowed to reconstruct what goes on in the jury room, he said, they end up annoying the jurors and discouraging jurors in future cases from taking unpopular positions that might later subject them to public criticism.[7] A further concern that others have articulated is that public confidence in jury decision making is damaged when press reports reveal a deliberation process as messy as sausage making—hardly the elegant ballet of *12 Angry Men.*

Judge Politan might well find the Schneider trial a good case in point. The jurors' obsessions with Kevin's likability, Marisol's adultery, and a series of minimally relevant events long before the shooting had turned out to shape their decision as much as any evidence directly related to the murder charge. And their off-the-point concerns had obscured the vital question of how Marisol, if lying, could have foreseen minutes after the shooting what was the right lie to tell in order to get Kevin convicted.

Barring interviews with these jurors would have left their deliberations a mystery and perhaps lent the verdict more credibility. But it also would have obscured a problem with juries that must be confronted in order to be overcome: If mystery is all that jury verdicts have going for them, the jury system is surely in deep trouble.

The truth is, cases such as Schneider bolster, rather than undermine, the argument for a strong, effective system of trial by jury. He-said, she-said cases such as this one pose a problem for any decision maker, whether professional or amateur, because the truth about what happened can never truly be known. In science, history, and even biography, truth can be provisional, and new truths can rise and fall in turn. We shift easily from diets high in iron to those low in cholesterol, from the celebration of the discovery of America to the repudiation of conquest and slavery, from adulation of a slain ex-president to revulsion and back again. But in order for any system of justice to attach consequences to wrongful acts, it has to rely on some official version of events. The question isn't who knows the truth (because no one does) but whose version of the truth we should prefer.

Having a judge or panel of judges decide what's true, as most countries do, wouldn't guarantee a better result than a jury, and these professional decision makers would bring their own different limitations and prejudices to the table. A judge might not have cared that Critchley had cried during his closing statement; indeed, such showboating might have been held against him. But a judge also might not have had

Doreen Morgan's useful insights into working-class life, or Ed Zawada's possibly helpful knowledge of guns, or Mike Poremba's distinctive experience with taking a hard punch from an overweight man.

A judge, hardened by his many past experiences with mendacious defendants, also might not have made an honest effort to consider whether Kevin's defense might possibly be truthful. Judges have heard every phony alibi dozens of times; they are certainly correct in assuming that it's usually not true that the dog ate the homework, or that the murder defendant was with his parents the entire night, or that the deadly mix of chemicals was intended to create a miracle drug rather than a bomb. But sometimes the excuse is true. And a judge may miss the clues because he has heard it all before and has lost sight of the awful court of judgment, something a jury, for all its faults, almost never does.

Another reason to prefer a jury over a judge in cases of great public concern is that if the jury system is working properly, a jury's verdict should be more acceptable to the community. This is a logical assumption when one considers that juries spring from the community and then return to it. Indeed, assuring the community that justice has been done is a core function of the jury system. Juries, rather than judges, became the primary triers of factual disputes in medieval England in part because they offered a credible and civilized alternative to vigilante justice and trial by combat.[8]

If a judge had found Schneider not guilty, people could have speculated that it was just a matter of a cop getting a sweetheart deal from a fellow government employee. Ideally, the jury system protects against the accumulation of such corrosive conclusions. At least, with the jury, in the absence of certainty, we have democracy.[9] The fact that this comforting thought didn't prevent the rioting that followed the first Rodney King verdict may partly reflect our declining faith in the quality of jurors' decisions. More than this, though, it reflects particular problems with that case, including its location along the nation's most volatile racial fault line, the jury's apparent disregard of videotaped proof, and the unfortunate choice of a suburban venue far from the scene of the crime.

Despite the King case, Judge John J. Gibbons's rationale for trial by jury remains a powerful one. "It is often said that the judicial process involves the search for objective truth," the federal appeals court judge once observed in an opinion. "We have no real assurance, however, of objective truth whether the trial is to [a judge] or to a jury. The judicial process can do no more than legitimize the imposition of sanctions by requiring that some minimum standards of fair play, which we call due process, are adhered to. . . . In the process of gaining public acceptance for the imposition of sanctions, the role of the jury is highly significant."[10]

If one appreciates the advantages of letting jurors decide he-said, she-said cases, the main issue raised by the Schneider case becomes how to ensure that jurors are trained, or at least instructed, to become more discerning judges of witnesses' credibility.

Certainly, much is already known within the academic community that would be useful to anyone trying to make an intelligent choice between witnesses' contradictory stories.[11] The research, usually done in an experimental setting using college students as subjects, shows that people tend to believe one witness over another on the basis of who is more likable, assertive, secure, and capable of sticking to his story under intense cross-examination. Here, it seems, was Kevin Schneider's big advantage over Marisol.

The most reliable indications that a person is lying turn out to be quite different. Studies show that compared with truth tellers, liars typically make fewer hand gestures, move their heads less, speak more slowly, and sit more rigidly, but that they betray their anxiety by shifting their feet or tapping their fingers. In addition, liars tend to relax their facial muscles and affect pleasant expressions, as if aware that observers will be watching their faces for signs of deceit. Partly because untrained observers seem to watch for the wrong signals, they often reach the wrong results. In one often cited academic study of 715 observers, a truthful speaker was judged to be lying by 74.3 percent of the subjects, and a lying witness was judged truthful by 73.7 percent.

As if liars don't create enough trouble for the earnest juror, witnesses who intend to provide accurate testimony but whose memories are faulty also can present serious obstacles. The problem is that human memory isn't like a videotape recording that stays constant each time it's replayed. Rather, as psychologist Elizabeth Loftus has put it, "Memory may be changed—colored by succeeding events, other people's recollections or suggestions, increased understanding, or a new context. Truth and reality, when seen through the filter of our memories, are not objective facts but subjective, interpretive realities."[12] The point: that a witness may think he is telling the truth but may actually be recalling the event inaccurately. Conceivably Marisol or Kevin might have actually believed aspects of their stories that were objectively untrue.

Social science research has shown that the accuracy of testimony decreases as the stress level of the person at the time of the remembered event increases. Specifically the presence of a weapon at the crime scene markedly reduces the witness's later ability to say what really happened. The witness tends to focus attention on the weapon and become inattentive to surrounding details.

Another reason for inaccurate testimony might be that the witness has been coached after the event and has actually come to believe the postevent version over his original memory. In one experiment that illustrates this point, a group of students listened to a teacher's lecture, about which the student newspaper then wrote an intentionally inaccurate story. Those who read the story later remembered the lecture differently from, and less accurately than, those who hadn't. Further, contrary to many lawyers' and jurors' instincts, independent studies show that the stress of cross-examination, rather than forcing truth to the surface, impairs memory and reduces the accuracy of testimony.

Judges usually share very little of these data with juries. Indeed, most jury instructions provide only the most pro forma advice on how to tell whether a witness is telling the truth. A standard instruction used by many judges is this: "In weighing the testimony of a witness, you should consider his relationship to the plaintiff or to the defendant; his interest, if any, in the outcome of the case; his manner of testifying; his opportunity to observe or acquire knowledge concerning the facts about which he testified; his candor, fairness, and intelligence; and the extent to which he has been supported or contradicted by other credible evidence." The simplest way to provide more detailed and useful information, such as that gleaned from the academic studies, would be for judges to incorporate it into their legal instructions, preferably at both the start and the end of the trial. Some judges already do so on their own initiative, as the following section of the book will show. More ambitiously, state judicial officials could collaborate on a set of standard jury instructions that reflect not an eighteenth- or nineteenth-century faith in raw common sense but a late-twentieth-century understanding of how the senses can deceive.

Such instructions might have alerted the Schneider jury to avoid irrelevant considerations and to ask the right questions about the witnesses. For example, might stress and the presence of a weapon—not to mention a week of intensive pre-trial preparation by prosecutors—have affected the accuracy of Marisol's testimony, however honest her intent? Might wishful thinking and the coaxing of a savvy defense lawyer have led Kevin to believe his version, even if untrue? Whose body language and facial expressions appeared more consistent with those of someone telling the truth?

Getting jurors to consider such questions means acknowledging that left to their own devices, many juries go astray. And that requires us to embrace, rather than run from, the lessons we have learned from opening the jury room door to reporters, scholars, and other observers. To improve juries and to realize the hope for a more reliable, trustworthy system that deserves to be preserved and venerated, we need to sacrifice the mystery of jury deliberations for a while, see the jury clearly, and then make changes.

Part III

THE HOPE

—

W E count on juries more than 150,000 times a year to resolve disputes, deliver justice, tell us what to believe.[1] Yet none of the juries in the previous section of this book did much to justify our extraordinary reliance on the jury system. Instead, they reinforced our doubts about the competence, fairness, and even much-vaunted common sense of jurors. At times these cases seemed to bolster the argument that we should cancel the jury's contract and sign up for another sort of system. From now on a judge or a panel of judges could render all decisions, or we could move civil disputes out of courts into the hands of arbitrators or bureaucrats. Nearly every other nation has shunned the jury; with some constitutional engine work, we could, too.

But not so fast. Even in the cases in which the juries we observed performed woefully, it seemed clear that there were powerful reasons to want a jury to make the decision. In the Marcos case a group of obscure, mostly middle-class New Yorkers took a break from their jobs with the post office and the phone company to pass judgment on two of the world's wealthiest people with close ties to some of the nation's most powerful politicians. The message: We are still, through the jury, a government of and by the ordinary people. In the Pizza Hut and Quintana cases as well, the juries were equalizers, capable of bridging the power gap between a big company and an injured person and thereby reflecting our distinctively American respect for the individual. The Liggett jury, too, had a worthy challenge: to apply community values to complex matters of commerce, a democratization of business rules attempted in few other nations. But it was in the Schneider trial, in which one witness's word was set against another's, that the vision of the jury was clearest. This was a case in which the truth could never be known but would have to be declared nonetheless, so that society could have an answer with which it could work. Kevin Schneider had to be either treated as guilty or accepted as innocent and allowed to move on. The people who made that choice sprang from, and then would return to, the community that had to live with the decision—a satisfying prospect in a nation that takes democracy seriously.

The nature of the kinship between democracy and trial by jury was pinpointed some years ago by Patrick Devlin, the British justice and jury scholar. "In a democracy, law is made by the will of the people and obedience is given to it not primarily out of fear but from good will," Devlin said. "The jury is the means by which the people play a direct part in the application of the law."[2]

The hope to be explored in this section of the book is that what disappoints us about juries' actual performance can be fixed—or at least vastly improved—so we can preserve all that remains inspirational. A justice system can't just look marvelous in theory; it has to work day after day in case after case.

To create such a system, we urgently need to build a better jury, one with the potential to be more competent, fairminded, and deliberative than many of those we are currently assembling. This means making dramatic changes in the way jurors are summoned, sifted, excluded, and selected—changes that many trial lawyers and jury consultants will passionately oppose. We also need to bridge the information gap between the courtroom professionals and the frequently befuddled amateurs we enlist as jurors. After all, people in powerful positions typically demand as much information and guidance as possible before they make decisions. Yet jurors, who briefly assume among the most powerful positions in America, have no way of insisting that their needs be met. Juries do their work and then dissolve. The institution of which they are a part has no constant membership, no offices, no support staff, no public relations department. Such an institution can't fight to change the rules that govern it. Its proxies in debates over its future are usually members of the legal profession, who, with their separate professional and financial interests, have proved to be no proxies at all.

To build a better jury system, we need to grant jurors the perquisites of power: reasonable creature comforts, practical training in the nature of their endeavor, and easier access to information about the particulars of the cases before them. None of the changes proposed in the next chapter are impractical or prohibitively expensive; all are necessary to make the American jury system worthy of faith and of preservation.

7

ORDER IN THE COURT

——

W HAT makes for a better jury? Just thirty years ago
many people would have said that a better jury was
one from which the poor, the uneducated, and the unrefined
were excluded. The emphasis was on entrance requirements,
as if the jury pool were a social club or an institution of
higher learning. Indeed, many communities relied on civic
club leaders to pick others from their clubs and churches to
fill out the jury rolls. And as late as 1965 the clerk's office in
New York City was administering oral exams to evaluate character and intelligence. In particularly complicated cases, jury
pickers in New York and elsewhere put together what they
called blue-ribbon juries, which were made up of people with
an extra measure of education or expertise.[1]

But thanks to much-needed civil rights legislation in 1968,
there's no going back to such an exclusionary, elitist, and frequently racist approach.[2] The law now says jury pools must
represent a fair cross section of the population. The trick to
seating the best possible juries today is to make sure that the
promise of inclusion is fulfilled, that all of the community's
strengths are tapped. That means eliminating all the ways in
which otherwise qualified individuals—ironically including

many people who would have been selected in the days of blue-ribbon juries—are removed before they can become jurors.

The most obvious problem is that jury notices simply don't reach everyone who is eligible. Voter registration records, the most common source from which jury lists are compiled, include only about 70 percent of the adult population. And in an increasingly mobile society even many registered voters slip through the cracks. In recent years many court systems have addressed the problem by culling potential jurors from a greater variety of lists, including driving, property, welfare, and tax records. That's the easy part. More problematic is getting around laws in about half the states that exclude broad categories of people from the requirement of jury service.

These laws were passed partly to ensure that people in essential professions such as medicine wouldn't be pulled from their urgent tasks to serve as jurors. But self-interest also played a role, as more and more occupational groups lobbied successfully to be removed so that their members wouldn't have to submit to the inconvenience of jury duty. New York State's judiciary law reflects the degrading result: Automatically exempted from jury duty are lawyers, physicians, clergy, dentists, pharmacists, optometrists, psychologists, podiatrists, registered and practical nurses, Christian Science practitioners and nurses, embalmers, police officers, correctional officers, firefighters, sole business proprietors, prosthetists, orthotists, and licensed physical therapists.[3]

As a result, the jury system has lost access to these people's special perspectives, their education and expertise, their contribution to the community profile. And the community has lost the benefit of having such people serve as jurors and then emerge, as many jurors do, as more alert and active participants in public affairs. As a result, it is now more difficult to assert, as de Tocqueville once did so eloquently, that jury service makes all Americans "feel the duties which they are bound to discharge towards society . . . [and] rubs off that private selfishness which is the rust of society."[4]

Eliminating the exemptions legislatively would go a long way toward seating more distinguished juries and placing renewed value on the universality of jury service. But many individuals would still seek to avoid the draft by ignoring jury notices or by convincing a judge or clerk that it would be too inconvenient for them to serve. In some jurisdictions as many as two thirds of the people who receive jury-related notices simply ignore them. The national no-show rate is about 55 percent. Despite the warnings about contempt of court printed on jury notices, in almost no instance does anybody suffer any consequences.[5]

In some courthouses jury duty is so lengthy, tedious, and inconvenient that it's difficult to blame anyone for wanting to steer clear of it. It's up to court officials to package jury duty more attractively if they want more people to participate. Requiring people on jury duty to serve on only one jury is one good approach; if they are not chosen, they are dismissed after just one day. An alternative is to let people call the courthouse each day for a week or so to see if they will be needed that day and to let them go about their business if they're not. In recent years a number of communities have discovered the virtues of one approach or the other.[6]

But convenience must be accompanied by firmness. Building a better jury means treating jury duty like military service in wartime; the requirement of service should be, for the most part, nonnegotiable. Judges already have the power to insist that people serve and, after giving fair warning, to fine or even jail those who don't. But this power is exercised so rarely that it's a national cause célèbre when it is. Court officials in Essex County, New Jersey, attracted incredulous press coverage a few years ago when they dispatched sheriff's officers to roust a dozen no-shows from their beds before dawn and drag them to court, where fifty-dollar fines were dispensed.[7] The jury scofflaw culture has become so broadly accepted that such occasional enforcement efforts are still viewed as tantamount to arresting people for jaywalking or failing to recycle.

This needs to change. The same people who ridicule the acquittal of Imelda Marcos or the hung juries of the Menendez brothers should by rights embrace a jury system in which everyone is required to show up for jury duty periodically and in which jury evasion is taken seriously. In such a system, enforcement costs spike initially, but soon all law-abiding people —the kind who file tax returns every year—are also fulfilling their jury obligations. The community, with its psychologists, clergymen, business owners, and embalmers, as well as with its bus drivers, teachers, clerks, and postal workers, is well represented in the jury assembly room. The culture accepts jury service, and everyone participates.

Unfortunately there's still something wrong with the picture. Many qualified prospects continue to get excluded from serving as a result of the lawyers' ultimate poker game, exercising peremptory challenges. As we have seen, these lawyers' exclusions target people whom the judge considers fair-minded enough to serve but who a lawyer suspects may not favor his client. Of the eighty million living Americans who have been called for jury duty, about 30 percent—or some twenty-four million—have been sent home because a lawyer for one side or the other made such a strategic judgment. And as the voir dires in the Marcos case and others have illustrated, many of those who are removed appear to be more alert and unbiased than many who are seated.[8]

Peremptory challenges have been undermining the integrity of a jury system for a long time. Mark Twain addressed the problem in his nineteenth-century travel narrative *Roughing It,* saying even then that these challenges removed well-informed people from juries and ensured that we "swear in

juries composed of fools and rascals, because the system rigidly excludes honest men and men of brains."[9] He also said
reforming the jury law was a legislative program that he supported but that was unlikely to catch fire.

It didn't then, and it may not now. Nonetheless, there are
hopeful signs. Bar groups exploring jury reform in several
states are considering reducing the number of peremptory
challenges permitted to lessen the impact of the lawyers' strategic war. In addition, there may be constitutional grounds
for change. Though peremptory challenges are presented by
lawyers as mere hunches, in fact, as the Marcos case demon-
strated, many such exclusions are rooted in racial, ethnic,
and sex discrimination. If a defense lawyer excludes all
Irish-Americans because "they" tend to be proprosecution,
Irish-Americans lose the opportunity to serve as jurors. Recog-
nizing this invidious aspect of peremptory challenges, courts
in recent years have begun placing restrictions on lawyers'
ability to make such exclusions. In 1986, in the Batson case,
the Supreme Court got the ball rolling by barring prosecutors
from using such challenges to remove black jurors from criminal cases involving black defendants. Since then courts have
expanded on the reasoning in *Batson* to bar any lawyer's use
of peremptory challenges if the purpose is to remove blacks
or any other racial group from any criminal or civil case. In
1994, the Supreme Court made a great leap by finally declaring that lawyers can't remove prospective jurors solely on the
basis of sex. In one of Justice Harry Blackmun's last opinions,
the Court held that under the Equal Protection Clause, "gender, like race, is an unconstitutional proxy for juror competence and impartiality."

But there are limits to how effective such rulings can be. In
general, they require only that a lawyer provide a neutral,
nonracial explanation for any peremptory challenge to which
the opposing counsel objects. And trial lawyers have become

extremely adept at offering such neutral rationales, even when the true motive for a challenge is race or ethnicity. As a result, some legal scholars are now predicting that the Supreme Court will eventually order a more radical solution. That's just what Justice Thurgood Marshall proposed in a concurring opinion in *Batson* in which he noted that prosecutors in Texas had once been instructed not to take "Jews, Negroes, Dagos, Mexicans or a member of any minority race on a jury." The late justice concluded: "The inherent potential of peremptory challenges to distort the jury process by permitting the exclusion of jurors on racial grounds should ideally lead the Court to ban them entirely from the criminal justice system."[10]

Another alternative would be for Congress and state legislatures to enact such a ban themselves. This would be exceedingly difficult to achieve, given trial lawyers' extraordinary power as a lobbying and political fund-raising force. But at least there's a model for such an act of legislation: The British Parliament did the deed in 1988.

Peremptory challenges were once popular with British lawyers, too; at the turn of the century defense lawyers were sometimes allotted as many as thirty challenges, enough to engross the most avid strategist. But British legal reformers objected strenuously to the way the challenges were distorting the fundamental nature of juries. The allotment was cut to just three in 1977, then eliminated entirely in 1988. Now jury selection in criminal cases is a streamlined affair. Potential jurors are picked at random from voter lists. As few as twenty prospects are called to court to be considered for a routine case. A clerk shuffles the index cards on which their names and addresses are written. The first twelve take their seats. The lawyers are permitted neither to ask them questions nor to begin arguing the case before a jury is sworn in, as Marty Cohen did so effectively in the Pizza Hut trial. If a lawyer sees a juror who he happens to know has a conflict of interest, he can challenge that juror "for cause." But the lawyer can't even ask general questions to find out whether such a conflict exists. And of course, peremptory challenges are not an option. The process takes a matter of minutes or hours, instead of the days or even weeks that are consumed by voir dire in many American trials.

The British may have shrunk their jury system by eliminating juries in nearly all civil cases. But they have moved closer to the core principles of jury trial in criminal cases by insisting that jurors be chosen as randomly as possible. And lawyers who once craved the chance to take the field of battle in voir dire have gotten used to the change; some have even become converts. "The whole principle of the jury in England," reflects prominent London solicitor Andrew Nitch-Smith, "is that, as far as possible, it should be random selection and just luck of the draw."

Eliminating peremptory challenges means destroying the only means through which lawyers can, in Nitch-Smith's words, "get a jury you like the look of." In the United States it would also mean destroying the huge market for jury consultants who promise not only to pack juries but to do so scientifically. It would mean the end of primers, courses, and conferences on how to assemble a winning jury. And it would mean that decades of stereotypes about how people of various ethnic groups are likely to vote would become moot. Black and white, fat and skinny, young and old, transit worker and physicist all would be treated alike. And rather than wonder why they were excluded and doubt the fairness of the system, millions among the formerly spurned would finally get their due: the chance to exercise true power in a democracy.[11]

Building a better jury takes us only partway toward building a better jury system. The other half of the equation is making it possible for a conscientious jury, whatever its makeup, to understand its task and perform it well. The cases in this book reflect the interplay between poorly picked juries and poor courtroom practices; both factors together produced the disappointing verdicts.

But most of the courtroom practices that prove so detrimental to jurors are built on convention and tradition rather than on any legal or constitutional foundation. It's the judges themselves, or the court functionaries who work for them, who maintain the routines. Because of habit, lack of imagination, and lawyers' and colleagues' expectations, this has typically meant that the courtroom has been set up as a convenient, functional workplace for lawyers, judges, and clerks. As a rule, these people work in reasonably comfortable, occasionally opulent quarters. They have some control over their schedules. And even in underfunded court systems they usually get the basic tools they need in order to get their jobs done: access to lawbooks or electronic research services, typewriters or computers, basic office supplies.

In contrast, jurors are often treated like annoying interlopers. They wait in shabby, crowded assembly rooms, frequently staffed by hostile or condescending clerks. They are supposed to follow directions, ask no questions, make no demands. When they move from room to room, they go as a group, escorted by men in uniform. Many jurors complain that they feel as if they are on trial, that they are not there to judge but to be judged. "It was the closest I've ever been to being in jail," Marcos juror Sandra Alberts observed.

Mary Timothy, the forewoman of the jury in the 1972 criminal trial of black activist Angela Davis, describes her own frustration this way:

> With all its formal language and ritualistic procedures, the court pushed and fitted us into the mold of THE JURY so that the mechanics of the trial could proceed. . . . We were

never consulted about the hours we were to report, or whether dismissal at a certain time was convenient for us. We were never given any reasons for delays or early dismissals, other than the vague statements that court business needed to be taken care of.

We were told just where to sit and when to come and what we must not read and who we must not talk to. . . . Most importantly, we were not informed as to what actions on our part would lead to our dismissal from the jury, or cause a mistrial. Not knowing the limits put a lot of pressure on us. Everyone else in the courtroom knew his or her job. They knew what they were doing—everyone except us. We were overwhelmed.[12]

Timothy could have been writing about nearly any jury trial in the United States, even today. Court practices that stymie the work of juries are responsible for much of the disorder in our courts. This, in a way, is encouraging. The jury system can be improved dramatically if judges and court administrators simply insist, as they nearly always have the power to do, that jurors receive a level of respect and resources commensurate with their power and importance.

More vital than creature comforts is knowledge. Jurors need more of it, and they need it as early in the process as possible. As was obvious in the Liggett and Marcos cases, jurors can't function effectively if they don't understand from the very start what laws have allegedly been broken, the meaning of key terminology, and how witnesses' testimony is intended to relate to the charges. Yet court procedures dictate that jurors won't be briefed on these issues, if at all, until after all the evidence is in. In the Marcos case, for example, jurors weren't instructed on the subject of mail fraud until page 55 of the final instructions, delivered after almost three months of testimony. They didn't understand the highly technical explanation, had no way to measure it against what they had heard earlier or even to remember which evidence was relevant to the charge. Quite reasonably they declined to consider it in their deliberations.

Though illogical and inefficient, this is the way court cases have been organized for a very long time. One reason is that deferring substantive legal instructions until the end of the case is convenient for those who labor full-time in the workshop. The practice gives lawyers a greater opportunity to shift legal theories midstream, or to abandon arguments that the evidence doesn't support, without the jury's discovering that they have done so. Leaving instructions until the end also helps judges by letting them begin the trial with minimal preparation. Many judges prefer to hear the evidence themselves and to study the law during the trial before telling the jury what questions it must answer to decide the case properly. As we saw in the Liggett case, Judge Bullock even told the lawyers before trial that he didn't know much about antitrust and that he'd be cramming as the trial progressed. Such an approach, unfortunately, meant that the jury would receive no useful guidance on the meaning or relevance of seven months of testimony about highly technical economic matters. And it would ensure the jury's eventual disillusionment and failure.

As early as 1960 the absurdity of waiting until the end of a trial to instruct the jury on the law was apparent to some judges. That year the federal appeals court judge E. Barrett Prettyman blasted his judicial colleagues for failing to address the problem. He wrote in the *American Bar Association Journal:*

> What manner of mind can go back over a stream of conflicting statements of alleged facts, recall the intonations, the demeanor, or even the existence of the witnesses, and retrospec-

tively fit all these recollections into a pattern of evaluation and judgment given him for the first time after the events? The *human* mind cannot do so. . . . The fact of the matter is that this order of procedure makes much of the trial of a lawsuit mere mumbo jumbo. It sounds all right to the professional technicians who are the judge and the lawyers. It reads all right to the professional technicians who are the court of appeals. But to the laymen sitting in the box, restricted to listening, the whole thing is a fog.[13]

Fortunately, for judges who recognize the problem and are willing or able to do their homework on legal issues in advance, a solution is readily at hand: Provide legal instructions at the start of the trial so that juries can learn the rules before they play the game. No law anywhere in the nation prevents judges from doing so. B. Michael Dann of Phoenix is one of the relatively few judges who have recognized this and responded.

Though not well known nationally, Dann has studied how the jury works both in his own courtroom and in academic settings and is emerging as an important figure in the evolution of the modern jury system. A bit paunchy at fifty-four, with a bland, round face and curly brown hair shading to gray, he appears quiet and studious; the stars of the academic symposia that he attends don't always register who he is. But Dann has something on all the law professors, trial consultants, psychologists, pollsters, and lawyers who generally make more of an impression at these meetings: He can apply his growing understanding of jurors' needs, and of their strengths and weaknesses, in his own courtroom.

A recent case in Judge Dann's courtroom illustrates his innovative approach to jury instructions. The case was a routine criminal prosecution of a twenty-eight-year-old man named Freddy Burrow, who was accused of exposing his genitals to an eleven-year-old girl. As soon as the jurors were picked,

Dann distributed a nineteen-page set of instructions that served throughout the trial as a practical how-to manual and viewers' guide for the jury. He read the instructions aloud, then told the jurors that they could keep them and refer to them whenever they wanted.

Among other things, the instructions made absolutely clear what crime was alleged, how it was defined, and precisely what evidence would have to be presented to prove that the crime had occurred. As a result, when a witness approached an issue the jurors knew would be important, they were able to concentrate more closely and make more of an effort to remember the testimony. By understanding the legal context, they became more sophisticated decision makers.

Others of Dann's preliminary instructions were aimed at introducing court procedures to the jurors in language they would be likely to understand. One instruction presented the order of the trial, laying out the sequence of events that seems so obvious to lawyers but is often perplexing to people who have never been in a courtroom. Another distinguished between statements of lawyers, which are not to be viewed as evidence, and witnesses' testimony and exhibits, which the jurors are supposed to consider. Many jurors in posttrial interviews in other cases reveal that they have learned of this distinction for the first time when it has been stated in jury instructions at the end of the trial; often this is too late because they haven't been sifting information with this in mind as the trial has progressed, and they no longer remember who said what. Because of Judge Dann's simple preliminary instruction, the jurors in the indecent exposure case didn't share this confusion.

It's not enough, of course, that legal instructions be presented early. They also have to make sense. Frequently they do not. When jurors can't understand their marching orders, it doesn't matter when they receive them; there's little chance that justice will prevail.

Yet jury instructions have been confounding jurors for well over a century, indeed pretty much since these judicial pronouncements emerged as an important part of the jury trial. In our nation's earliest years judges acted primarily as masters of ceremonies; they either gave no legal instructions or provided them only on an advisory basis. But by the end of the nineteenth century a movement had gathered force to place restrictions on the jury's discretion to decide legal questions. Among the reasons was that a more complex economy seemed to require a more consistent, predictable application of commercial laws than uninstructed juries appeared able to offer. As a consequence, states began mandating that the judge instruct the jurors on what the law required. And appeals courts got in the habit of throwing out judgments if the instructions didn't follow the precise wording of the legal rules. To avoid getting reversed on appeal, trial judges made their instructions ever more technical, verbose, and—to most jurors—incomprehensible.

Even lawyers and judges could see that this was so, and in the 1930s a movement developed to simplify the instructions and to make them uniform. Committees of judges began writing model jury instructions that appeared to be clearer and more consistent than those that had preceded them. But these so-called pattern instructions, too, usually proved too technical for juries because they were taken from the language of appellate opinions, which were written for legal audiences.[14]

Now that social scientists have turned their attention to analyzing jurors' comprehension of legal instructions, they have discovered that the most modern ones, even updated in supposedly simpler language, often still leave jurors at a loss.

Terms such as *liability, damages, inference, execute, representation, immaterial, preponderance of the evidence, admissibility,* and *burden of proof,* which seem self-evident to lawyers, baffle jurors. Instructions are thick with complex, multiclause sentences, passive constructions, and multiple negatives. Jurors often either ignore the instructions or misapply them, as at least some of the jurors did in each of the trials described in the preceding chapters. In Chicago in 1992 a death sentence was thrown out on the basis of a study showing that as many as 75 percent of jurors in the local courts didn't understand parts of the instructions. But the sentence was restored by a federal appeals court. Indeed, the jury's verdict usually stands, and judges continue to dish out the same indigestible fare in their next cases.[15]

Judge Jerome Frank, a trenchant critic of the jury system, once characterized the phenomenon this way: "What a crop of subsidiary semi-myths and mythical practices the jury system yields! Time and money and lives are consumed in debating the precise words which the judge may address to the jury, although everyone who stops to see and think knows that those words might as well be spoken in a foreign language. Yet, every day, cases which have taken weeks to try are reversed by upper courts because a phrase or sentence, meaningless to the jury, has been included in, or omitted from the judge's charge."[16]

The fear of getting reversed on appeal—much like having a pass intercepted, failing a test, or having a sales presentation ripped to pieces by one's boss—naturally deters judges from getting too creative with jury instructions. To enable all jury instructions to be made understandable to nearly all jurors, appeals courts, too, will have to change. Appellate judges will have to cease demanding that the precise wording of court decisions and statutes be parroted by a trial judge's instructions. The new question will have to be merely whether the instructions were faithful to the law in spirit and meaning and whether they made sense to the jury.

People who seek this sort of change bemoan the fact that the lawyers and judges who run the justice system have no stake in making it happen and that jurors have no power to do so. Proposals for plain-language instructions, drafted by legal academics, generally lie on the shelf.

Here again Judge Dann of Phoenix is an exception. His preliminary instructions in the Burrow case set the stage for a well-run trial and aided the jurors' comprehension. But before the jury deliberated, Dann needed to give them a more detailed set of instructions that also reflected any issues that had arisen during the case. It was in his method of drafting these final instructions, which are the only instructions most judges provide, that Dann deviated the most from traditional courtroom practices.

Toward the end of any trial the lawyers for the two sides typically submit proposed legal instructions to the judge, usually gleaned from the state's pattern instructions. Each side tries to pick a mix of instructions on the various legal issues to benefit its cause. The judge chooses between them and perhaps tailors the standard instructions a bit to fit the facts of the case more closely.

But when prosecutor Lynn Krabbe and defense lawyer Jeffrey Phillips arrived in Dann's chambers, each set to fight for a separate set of pattern instructions in the Burrow case, the judge handed each a version of his own. This would be the draft, he told them, from which they would work.

Dann's draft strayed far from RAJI, Recommended Arizona Jury Instructions. To Dann, rewriting the pattern instructions was more than just a matter of cleaning up awkward sentences and providing simpler definitions of terms. It also involved incorporating social scientists' understandings of how witnesses perceive and remember, the kinds of understandings that might, for example, have especially benefited the jurors in the Schneider love triangle case.

This is hardly what Krabbe, an intense, even cantankerous advocate, had in mind. She had what appeared to be a very weak case that relied heavily on the sometimes inconsistent testimony of an eleven-year-old and on the girl's identification of Burrow in a photo lineup in which Burrow's picture had been the first one she had been shown. But Krabbe was intent on pursuing the case aggressively because she was convinced that Burrow was guilty of this crime and that he was a repeat sex offender, a man best kept off the streets for a very long time. To get him convicted here, she needed legal instructions that gave the jury plenty of room to believe that Burrow's accuser had properly identified him as her assailant.

From Krabbe's standpoint, Dann's proposed instruction on eyewitness identification was a disaster. For one thing, it told the jurors that they could consider the possibility that the photo lineup through which Burrow had been identified had been unfairly staged. This was a virtual invitation, she believed, to acquit. The instruction also told the jurors that they could consider all relevant factors in determining whether the girl had identified the right man and then suggested specific factors to consider. These included the suggestion that the girl might have been under stress at the time she saw the flasher and that her perception might therefore have been clouded. The instruction also advised jurors to consider that the accuser had made a cross-racial identification: She was a white girl fingering a black man and perhaps, as research suggested, would have trouble telling one black from another.

After reviewing the instructions, Krabbe was in the judge's face, thundering. Arizona law provided for a perfectly neat five-part instruction for eyewitness identification, following the language of a Supreme Court case called *Neil* v. *Biggers*. The jury was supposed to consider the witness's original opportunity to view the suspect, the witness's degree of attention at the time, the accuracy of any prior description the witness had provided, the witness's level of certainty, and the length of time between the crime and the identification. That was all. *Neil* v. *Biggers* said nothing about a witness's level of stress or the racial differences between the defendant and the witness. "This isn't Arizona law," Krabbe nearly shrieked. "This comes out of the clear blue sky."[17]

Judge Dann had seen lawyers react to his instructions this way before. It was ironic. He was the judge, the member of the established order. The lawyers, usually younger, generally full of fire, should be pushing him to try new things. Instead, in his chambers and his courtroom, Dann was usually the maverick, while the lawyers were the protectors of the faith. Yet he knew from the academic research that a witness's certainty bore no relationship to the accuracy of his or her testimony, so he saw no reason to include such an instruction. His own offerings, on the other hand, were aimed to guide the jurors to a more intelligent decision. "It's not part of RAJI, but is it warranted? Is it helpful?" he asked Krabbe, referring to his proposed instruction. "It is well known today in the social science research that making cross-racial identifications is much more difficult than within the same ethnic group."

Krabbe angrily repeated her citation of the Neil case, seemingly aghast that Judge Dann didn't see what a mess he'd made of the instruction. Defense lawyer Jeffrey Phillips was in just his second year of legal practice, but he quickly recognized that the instructions helped his client, and not surprisingly he decided to offer his support to the judge in the battle with Krabbe. "All the factors listed are things the jury might reasonably consider," he interjected, "and our job is to help the jury." Krabbe gave him a withering look.

Seemingly in desperation, she finally suggested that the instruction on stress was sexist. It suggested, she said, that a girl would get too flustered to remember what she'd seen. Judge Dann replied patiently that the academic literature shows that stress reduces a witness's ability to perceive events accurately.

The next day Judge Dann told the lawyers that he was sticking to his eyewitness identification instruction, with a few minor modifications. Then he reminded them that he would read the final instructions to the jury *before* the lawyers' closing arguments. In the traditional courtroom, as it has appeared in the previous chapters, the lawyers speak first, then the judge instructs. But Judge Dann believes that jurors get more out of the closings if they have the legal instructions already in hand. Both lawyers said that they had seldom, if ever, encountered this reverse order before. But they had also never been in a jury-centric courtroom before.

Back in court that afternoon the jurors found a copy of the final instructions on their chairs. Judge Dann read them aloud; then each side wrapped up its case. Taking advantage of the favorable instructions, Phillips emphasized the issue of cross-racial identification. "Can we convict Mr. Burrow because he is the only black man in the courtroom?" he asked. "Is this what our society is about?" The verdict that came back was surely the right one, given the thinness of the evidence: not guilty.

Jurors who have been instructed early and well have much of the information they need in order to understand most cases. But what if they are still confused about a witness's testimony or about an issue that seems important but hasn't been addressed? Whom can they ask? Can they ask at all? The traditional answers—nobody and no—no longer suffice as we strive to build a better jury system. An alert, responsible jury needs a voice in the courtroom.[18]

The concept of the inquisitive jury is hardly new. During

the first few centuries of the jury system in England jurors were active participants in court cases. They sometimes investigated the charges themselves by interviewing witnesses in their communities and then reporting the results in court. When trial procedures evolved so that witnesses were brought into court to testify, jurors continued to play a role in questioning them. But as a well-organized legal profession developed in the sixteenth and seventeenth centuries and a professional judiciary emerged, jurors were pushed to the periphery. The workshop didn't belong to them. And the opportunity to ask questions—an important way to control the proceedings as well as to gather information—all but disappeared.[19]

Today in the United States most judges surveyed never allow question asking by jurors. And lawyers race to the appeals courts to challenge the practice whenever it is tried without their advance consent.[20]

The prohibition was a recurring problem for jurors in the cases in this book, and it was an important contributor to the disappointing results. Because she couldn't ask questions, Sandra Alberts never received a clear enough explanation of the financial crimes that Imelda Marcos had allegedly committed. Pauline Hurley didn't find out what *market power* really meant and thus couldn't figure out whether Brown & Williamson had it in the Liggett case. Beth Chapman was left wondering aloud, "What's the Robinson-Patman Act?" Mike Poremba didn't learn why the first emergency worker to arrive after Fabio Hernandez had been shot wasn't called as a witness, adding to his doubts about the competence of the prosecutors in the Schneider case. And the jurors in the Quintana blood bank lawsuit didn't find out whether they were permitted to pad the damage award to cover legal fees, so they did so, wrongly.

Antipathy to permitting jurors to ask questions seems

mostly to reflect lawyers' commitment to the adversarial trial process, through which each side presents its best case and strictly controls the questioning of its witnesses. Many lawyers believe that jurors' questions break that lawyers' lock on the pace and rhythm of the trial. Lawyers argue that if a clarifying question is needed, the judge, schooled in law and sympathetic to the lawyers' development of their case, can ask it. Other common concerns are that lawyers will be afraid to object to jurors' questions for fear of offending them, even if the questions are harmful to their client; that jurors' questions will disrupt courtroom decorum; and that the questions might not be relevant.

But judges who have experimented with permitting jurors to ask questions have devised procedures that seem to dispose of these potential concerns. Judge Dann, in fact, spells out such procedures in his preliminary instructions: He tells jurors to write down questions when they arise and hand them, unsigned, to the bailiff during a recess. Then the judge and lawyers get to review the questions outside the jurors' presence and decide whether they address any relevant issues and are permissible under the evidence rules. With the lawyers' help, Judge Dann edits the questions to accommodate any of the lawyers' concerns before reading them to the witness. This way neither the jurors nor the witnesses know which juror asked a particular question or which lawyer may have been responsible for any changes in the way the question was posed to the witness. The important thing is that procedure isn't allowed to get in the way of substance. Usually the questions get answered, and jurors get information they otherwise would have been denied.

That's what happened in a big, complicated case against Johnson & Johnson in Chicago in 1990, in which use of a tampon was blamed for a death from toxic shock syndrome. Judge Warren D. Wolfson sought jurors' questions after each witness had testified. More than forty questions, some with multiple parts, were asked by the jurors during the trial, and Judge Wolfson asked witnesses to respond to twenty-seven of them. "They were good, sensible questions," the judge said afterward. Not only did jurors get answers that they needed, but merely by asking the questions, they were able to provide the lawyers with ongoing guidance on which aspects of the testimony jurors understood and which were proving to be confusing.[21]

In endorsing the use of jurors' questions in his own courts, Robert W. Landry, presiding judge of the criminal division of the Circuit Court for Milwaukee County, has written convincingly that "the present system composed exclusively of two adversaries limits the inquiry to each of their special interests; but the jury, composed of 12 disinterested people sworn to perform their duty, is not confined to the exclusive cause the respective lawyers are championing. They enter the courtroom fresh from the streets, untainted by self-interest and impressed with their duty to search for the truth."[22]

It's one thing to supply jurors with the information they need. It's another to expect them to remember it all. This is a particular problem in complex cases. The Marcos case lasted three months; the Liggett case more than seven. The California murder trial of the Menendez brothers was a seven-month affair. The World Trade Center bombing case spanned five months before the guilty verdicts in March 1994. A broader terrorism case that was scheduled to go to trial in the fall of 1994 was projected to last a year or more.

How can jurors remember the facts and the law in cases such as these? One answer is that no case should last so long. Judge William Schwarzer, who directs the Federal Judicial Center, argues powerfully that trials can be shortened if judges sharply define the relevant issues before trial and deal in advance with any procedural and legal disputes that are likely to arise. In addition, judges can set time limits for witnesses and can deter the parties from introducing repetitious testimony.[23]

A parallel strategy involves helping jurors remember what they have heard. The simplest way for jurors to remember the legal instructions is to bring written copies into the jury room during deliberations, something that many judges unaccountably do not permit. The most obvious way to improve jurors' recollections of testimony is to permit them, even encourage them, to take notes.[24]

The Liggett jury, like so many others, was badly handicapped by its not being allowed to take notes; the jurors had to store in their heads 108 volumes' worth of testimony from the twenty-three witnesses who appeared in court and from the eighty-five others whose depositions were read into the record during the long, tedious afternoons of trial. In addition to making jurors' jobs more difficult, the ban on note taking underscores the gap in respect and resources between jurors and everyone else laboring in the courtroom. The disparity hardly escapes jurors: Liggett juror Rocky Phillips remembers struggling to keep the witnesses' testimony in his head while he watched the judge and lawyers scribbling feverishly on their own notepads.

That note taking is helpful to jurors is intuitively obvious to anyone who has ever sat through a lecture course and then tried to prepare for exams without the benefit of notes. It's also been verified in several significant courtroom studies. Nonetheless, according to one survey, 37 percent of judges nationally join Judge Bullock, the Liggett judge, in not allowing note taking by jurors. Many other judges technically allow the practice but do not provide paper and pens and purposely fail to announce that it is permitted, and many jurors therefore assume that it isn't.[25]

Some judges who bar note taking say they fear that note

takers will become too influential in deliberations and that inaccurate notes will be accepted as gospel. Others argue that note takers often fall behind the testimony and miss important statements because they are still taking notes on something that was said earlier. But jurors disagree. When given the chance, two thirds of all jurors choose to write things down during a trial. And when judges try permitting it, even they seem to come around to the idea. In thirty-one trials in which note taking was allowed in a New York experiment, judges in twenty-six of the cases said note taking by jurors proved to be helpful, and none said it was unhelpful.[26]

In his juror-centric courtroom, Judge Dann not only permits note taking but seeks to impel it. Pencils and notebooks are waiting for jurors at their places in the jury box. And in his preliminary instructions the judge advises them that although note taking isn't mandatory, "if you take no notes at all, you run the risk of forgetting important testimony needed for your verdict." Having received this instruction, all but one of the jurors in the Burrow case chose to take notes.

The innovations described in this chapter provide a road map for changing courtroom practices to empower the jury and thus to reinvigorate the justice system. They also provide a guide to answering the question that began this book: Can the jury system be improved enough to make it worth preserving, cherishing, perhaps even fighting for, as our nation's founders once did?

Dann's work reflects his faith that it can. And taken together, the changes proposed here offer hope that we can create a better jury system, one that looks a good deal more like the one that acquitted an innocent defendant in *12 Angry Men* than the one that sparked riots in Los Angeles. The vision is still there, as is the most basic ingredient: the commitment of those who end up on juries to work hard and reach a verdict they believe is just.

None of the suggested approaches to helping them do this job better is particularly difficult to pursue. Many, though, are politically chancy because they siphon power from lawyers or require judges to work harder or, at least, differently. The thorniest and probably the most important effort will be to eliminate peremptory challenges and make the jury truly representative.

Yet awareness of flaws in the jury system is at an all-time high thanks to televised trials on Court TV and CNN. The Rodney King case alone raised the profile of the jury and turned its performance into a national issue. Perhaps a program to improve the jury will finally generate interest in the 1990s. A hint that this may prove to be so is already being provided by a rather offbeat group, the Fully Informed Jury Association, that has managed to get parts of its jurors' rights amendment introduced in more than twenty states. This group's main goal—to inform jurors of their power to disregard the law and vote their consciences—is a controversial one. Yet FIJA, despite a limited budget and libertarian roots, has struck a chord with its projury rhetoric, generating hundreds of sympathetic articles and editorials in mainstream publications and capturing the loyalty of many dozens of energetic volunteers in every state. A broader-based, better-funded effort aimed at eliminating peremptory challenges, broadening the jury pool, abolishing most juror exclusions, and providing more information and resources for jurors might do even better.

Most jurors are, after all, voters. And we—as individuals who count on our legal system to do justice, as jurors and potential jurors, and as potential plaintiffs and defendants—have a huge stake in the future of the jury. Though we sometimes duck jury service and deride the verdicts we see on TV, jury service remains one of our most precious birthrights and, for most of us, our greatest source of direct political power. It's a right we cannot afford to lose.

A defendant's right to trial by jury in a criminal case remains one of our people's strongest protections against tyranny; the government can't keep any of us behind bars unless it convinces a jury to do so. The American jury's role in civil trials, though under attack, continues to support our uniquely American vision of ordinary people brokering the disputes of their neighbors. And the jury's opportunity to write so much of our official history—from what happened amid a blur of baton blows on a dark Los Angeles street to who bombed the World Trade Center—is a testament to how much deference we're still prepared to pay to the common sense of the common man and woman.

Moreover, for many of the millions of Americans who have exercised the power and experienced the responsibility, jury service turns out to be an unforgettable, even transforming experience. Although a majority of people try to avoid service, nearly three quarters of those who do serve come away with a more favorable view of the system than they had before. They eagerly tell war stories from the jury room; many decide to write about what they saw and accomplished. Nearly every juror interviewed for this book is proud of the job he or she did, proud of the seriousness of deliberations, proud of having exercised power soberly, proud—rightly or wrongly— of the verdicts that were reached. More than when they vote, or pay taxes, or attend a parade, they are realizing the democratic vision that still sustains our nation: They are governing themselves.[27]

There's disorder in the court but not despair. The jury system can be saved and is, for all our disappointments, well worth saving.

NOTES

INTRODUCTION

1. About 45 percent of Americans who are sent jury notices actually appear at the courthouse, according to studies conducted by the National Center for State Courts. G. Thomas Munsterman, director of the state courts' Center for Jury Studies, says the percentage varies enormously from place to place. In big cities the yield is generally much lower. In Los Angeles, for example, about 25 percent of the notices can't be delivered; another 25 percent are ignored by the recipients; and an additional 35 to 40 percent of potential jurors get themselves excused. As a result, he says, the yield there is just 10 to 15 percent.

   Nationally, about two thirds of those who do respond to the call ultimately avoid service as a result of work needs and other conflicts or purported infirmities or because they are excluded through a lawyer's challenge, according to *The Defense Research Institute's Report on Jury Service in the United States* (Chicago: June 1990). Other studies of jurors' efforts to avoid service are reported in Shari Seidman Diamond, "What Jurors Think: Expectations and Reactions of Citizens Who Serve as Jurors," *Verdict:*

Assessing the Civil Jury System, ed. Robert E. Litan (Washington, DC: The Brookings Institution, 1993), pp. 282–305.

2. A cross-cultural perspective on the use of juries is provided in Marcus Gleisser, *Juries and Justice* (Cranbury, NJ: A. S. Barnes, 1968). The decline of the jury in England is charted in Sir Patrick Devlin, *Trial By Jury* (London: Stevens & Sons, 1956).

3. Jury awards are altered by judges in at least 20 percent of all civil cases. Though available data aren't comprehensive, it appears that punitive damage awards may be reduced or eliminated on appeal more often than not. For further discussions, see Robert MacCoun, "Inside the Black Box: What Empirical Research Tells Us About Decisionmaking by Civil Juries," in Litan, pp. 137–80.

PART I: THE VISION

1. Maude's story is related in Gerry Spence, *With Justice for None: Destroying an American Myth* (New York: Times Books, 1989), pp. 89–90.

2. Alexis de Tocqueville, *Democracy in America* (New York: Vintage Books, 1990), pp. 280–87.

3. The spiritual, if not historical, ancestor of our modern jury was born in Athens, the first great democracy, during the fifth century B.C. The extraordinary Athenian jury courts were called dicasteries, and the jurors—all 501 of them for any single case —were known as dicasts. A majority of these jurors was needed to reach a verdict, and the jurors generally decided both the outcome and the sentence. They voted by dropping a bean or pebble into one of two urns, and were paid three obols a day— enough, scholars say, to pay for three salted fish.

   A more formalized Roman version of the dicasteries featured smaller juries and often rhetorically sweeping arguments by professional advocates, including Cicero. This system may have been transported to the rest of Europe by the Roman conquerors, but it faded between A.D. 300 and 500, apparently because it was too democratic for the tastes of the increasingly despotic emperors.

The next stage in jury history is far murkier because few records of court procedures exist from the Middle Ages. Historians generally agree, though, that community courts with nonprofessional judges thrived for long periods in Germany and some Scandinavian countries. In addition, the Anglo-Saxons left records of a system known as compurgation, which bears some resemblance to the modern jury. When a person was accused of a crime and claimed that he was innocent, he would be permitted to bring to court a number of friends, often twelve, to swear to his honesty. The compurgators were neither witnesses nor jurors in that they didn't ordinarily have independent knowledge of the facts of the case and did not hear evidence. Rather, they merely put their oaths on the line.

Some jury scholars have argued that compurgation evolved into trial by jury. Most now insist that the true precursor to the modern jury trial was imported to England from Normandy by William the Conqueror in 1066. A compromise view is that the experience with compurgation may have prepared the vanquished Anglo-Saxons to accept the Norman model. This latter system began as a way for the king to compile data on the population, with particular emphasis on who owned various parcels of land—and thus who should be taxed for them. Typically a group of residents of each county was brought to court to swear to the proper land titles, in what was called a recognition. The panelists were presumed to know the facts, in essence to be witnesses to the proper titles, and to report truthfully what they knew.

King Henry II, famous for his great battle with Thomas Becket over the power of the church and for his marital wars with Eleanor of Aquitaine, is probably the true father of the modern jury. In the middle of the twelfth century, he expanded the jurisdiction of the recognition panels so that they could decide property disputes between private parties. The process, which was extended gradually to other types of disputes and to criminal matters, appears to have marked the beginning of the direct evolution of our current system.

At least until the seventeenth century, though, some jury verdicts were subject to the influence, and even the direction, of government officials. The trial of William Penn and William Mead at the Old Bailey courthouse in London in 1670 marked a turning point in the development of the jury as an independent popular voice. With the jury in the case deadlocked over charges that the defendants had illegally preached in the streets, court officials invaded the jury room to determine which jurors favored acquittal. Finding four, the officials locked them up without food or water. When they refused to convict, they were fined and then imprisoned, as was still the custom.

But in this case, one of the dissenters, a man named Bushell, took the matter back to court and won a ruling that jurors could no longer be punished for their verdicts. If the judge could compel a jury to find one way or another, wrote Chief Justice Vaughan with seemingly self-evident logic, then "the jury is but a troublesome delay, a great charge, and of no use." Thanks in part to Bushell's case, the jury became recognized as an ever-present check against abuses by the authorities.

The Athenian and Roman systems are described in William Forsyth, *Hortensius: An Historical Essay on the Office and Duties of an Advocate* (London: John Murray, 1879). A long, comprehensive history of the jury appears in James B. Thayer, "The Older Modes of Trial," 5 *Harvard Law Review* 45 (May 1891); Thayer, "The Jury and Its Development I," 5 *Harvard Law Review* 249 (January 1892); Thayer, "The Jury and Its Development II," 5 *Harvard Law Review* 295 (February 1892); and Thayer, "The Jury and Its Development III," 5 *Harvard Law Review* 357 (March 1892). Also see William Forsyth, *History of Trial By Jury* (New York: Cockcroft, 1878), and Morris S. Arnold, "Law and Fact in the Medieval Jury Trial: Out of Sight, Out of Mind," 18 *American Journal of Legal History* 267–80 (1974).

4. The trial of John Peter Zenger is described in James Alexander, *A Brief Narrative of the Case and Trial of John Peter Zenger*, ed. Stanley Nider Katz (Cambridge, MA: The Belknap Press of Harvard University Press, 1972).

5. Judge Gibbons's remarks about the jury's role as an "ad hoc

parliament" are from his dissent in the *Japanese Electronic Products Antitrust Litigation*, 631 F.2d 1069, 1093 (3rd Cir. 1980).

6. A jury in Indianapolis convicted former world heavyweight boxing champion Mike Tyson of rape on February 10, 1992, and the judge imposed a ten-year prison sentence. The case stemmed from Tyson's 1991 sexual assault of a contestant in the Miss Black America pageant. William Kennedy Smith was acquitted by a West Palm Beach, Florida, jury on December 11, 1991. He had been accused of raping a woman he had met at a Palm Beach nightspot after returning with her to the Kennedy family's beachfront home.

7. The Soviet Union relied on panels of professional and lay judges in lieu of juries, the system that's still prevalent in Europe. In politically sensitive cases Soviet courts deferred to the dictates of political officials. The strengths and weaknesses of the European model are explored in John H. Langbein, "Mixed Court and Jury Court: Could the Continental Alternative Fill the American Need?" *American Bar Foundation Research Journal* 195 (1981). Post–Soviet Russia's move to introduce trial by jury was reported in "Russia to Bring Back Jury Trials in Regions," *The New York Times*, October 29, 1993, p. A7; and Judith Ingram, "An Innovation in Russia: Courts Offer Jury Trials," *The New York Times*, December 19, 1993, p. A18.

1. THE AWFUL COURT OF JUDGMENT

1. British essayist G. K. Chesterton's comments on "the awful court of judgment" are quoted in Shirley S. Abrahamson, "A View from the Other Side of the Bench," 69 *Marquette Law Review* 463 (Summer 1986).

2. New York University law professor Stephen Gillers discusses possible reasons behind the jury's central role in death penalty cases in "Deciding Who Dies," 129 *University of Pennsylvania Law Review* 1, 15 (November 1980).

3. One among many cogent critiques of capital punishment in the United States is offered in Ronald J. Tabak and J. Mark Lane, "The Execution of Injustice: A Cost and Lack-of-Benefit Analysis of the Death Penalty," 23 *Loyola of Los Angeles Law Review* 59

(November 1989). A leading book on the subject is Charles L. Black, Jr., *Capital Punishment: The Inevitability of Caprice and Mistake* (New York: W. W. Norton, 1981).

4. How death qualification affects the composition of juries is discussed in Robert Fitzgerald and Phoebe C. Ellsworth, "Due Process vs. Crime Control, Death Qualification and Jury Attitudes," 8 *Law and Human Behavior* 31 (1984). Polling data on public attitudes toward the death penalty are provided in "Legal Beat," *The Wall Street Journal,* April 19, 1993, p. B2.

5. The leading U.S. Supreme Court case on the qualifications of jurors in death penalty cases is *Witherspoon* v. *Illinois,* 391 U.S. 510, 522–23, n. 21 (1968).

6. Aristotle's comments about Athens's jurylike institution, the dicastery, are quoted in Raymond S. Rodgers, "The Wasps in Court: Argument and Audience in the Athenian Dicasteries," 28 *American Journal of Legal History* 147, 162 (April 1984).

7. In the Robertson case, the Texas death penalty format required the jury to answer two questions. In cases in which there is an allegation that the victim provoked the attack, a question on this issue is also provided for. The U.S. Supreme Court upheld Texas's death penalty law in *Jurek* v. *Texas,* 428 U.S. 262 (1976).

8. Texas's faith in the ability of jurors to decide whether there is a "probability" that a convicted murderer will pose a future danger to society was endorsed by that state's Court of Criminal Appeals in *Granviel* v. *State,* 552 S.W. 2d 107 (1976). A pessimistic assessment of whether even trained professionals can predict future dangerousness is offered in Robert Wayne Gordon, "Crystal-Balling Death?" 30 *Baylor Law Review* 35 (1978).

9. The McMartin Preschool child sex-abuse case, which ended in acquittals and mistrials, at one time involved sixty-five counts of alleged molestation of young children by the school's director and a number of teachers. The case is described in Ann Hagedorn, "McMartin Trial Ends in Deadlock, Case Is Now Dead," *The Wall Street Journal,* July 30, 1990, p. B6; and by Robert Safian, "McMartin Madness: Ten Days in the Life of the Longest, Most Gruesomely Difficult Criminal Trial Ever," *The American Lawyer,* October 1989, p. 46.

10. Coincidentally, the author of this book also wrote *The Wall Street Journal*'s article on jury nullification that Robertson juror Sue Warner had read just before the trial had begun. See Stephen J. Adler, "Courtroom Putsch? Jurors Should Reject Laws They Don't Like, Activist Group Argues," *The Wall Street Journal,* January 4, 1991, pp. A1, A4. A further discussion of nullification is provided in Valerie P. Hans and Neil Vidmar, *Judging the Jury* (New York: Plenum Press, 1986), pp. 149–60, and Alan W. Scheflin and Jon M. Van Dyke, "Merciful Juries: The Resilience of Jury Nullification," 48 *Washington and Lee Law Review* 165–83 (Winter 1991).

11. The authority of a federal judge to withhold from the jury the fact that it has the power to defy the judge's legal instructions was asserted by the U.S. Supreme Court in *Sparf and Hansen* v. *U.S.,* 156 U.S. 51 (1895).

12. The Texas Court of Criminal Appeals upheld Mark Robertson's death sentence on December 8, 1993. A motion for a rehearing before that court was denied on March 9, 1994, after which the separate federal appeals process began.

13. John Galsworthy's "The Juryman," appears in *Law In Action: An Anthology of the Law in Literature* (New York: Bonanza Books, 1947) p. 472.

PART II: THE DISAPPOINTMENT

1. Twain's nineteenth-century rap against the jury system bemoaned the effects of pretrial publicity in an age in which news traveled fast via "telegraphs and newspapers." See Mark Twain, *Roughing It,* Volume II (New York: Harper and Brothers, 1913), pp. 55–58. More contemporary concerns about pretrial publicity are explored in Newton N. Minow and Fred H. Cate, "Who Is an Impartial Juror in an Age of Mass Media?" 40 *The American University Law Review* 631–64 (Winter 1991).

2. Aristophanes' mocking play *The Wasps* was produced in Athens in 422 B.C. It remains a primary source of historical information about the ancient jury. One modern translation, by Douglass

Parker, appears in *Three Comedies by Aristophanes* (Ann Arbor, MI: The University of Michigan Press, 1969).

3. The so-called ploughman's rule was set out in the case of *Clench v. Tomley*, 21 Eng. Rep. 13 (1603).

4. Corporate litigator Patrick Lynch argued for using judges instead of juries in "The Case for Striking Jury Demands in Complex Antitrust Litigation," 1 *The Review of Litigation* 3 (1980). For the opposing view, see Maxwell M. Blecher and Howard F. Daniels, "In Defense of Juries in Complex Antitrust Litigation," 1 *The Review of Litigation* 47–91 (1980).

5. The Texaco-Pennzoil fight is richly detailed in Thomas Petzinger, Jr., *Oil & Honor* (New York: G. P. Putnam's Sons, 1987). Also see Stephen J. Adler, "How to Lose the Bet-Your-Company Case," *The American Lawyer*, January–February 1986.

6. The conflicting verdicts in the Bensonhurst trial were described in Howard Kurtz, "Bensonhurst Ringleader Acquitted on Murder Counts," *The Washington Post*, May 19, 1990, p. 1.

7. Differing views of the first Rodney King trial appeared in Roger Parloff, "Maybe the Jury Was Right," *The American Lawyer*, June 1992, pp. 7, 78–80; and in D. M. Osborne, "Reaching for Doubt," *The American Lawyer*, October 1992, pp. 62–69. In June Parloff concluded after watching the videotape of the beating as well as the tape of the entire trial that the jury may have reached a reasonable result, based on the evidence. In September, after interviewing seven jurors and two alternates and reconstructing the deliberations, Osborne determined that some jurors' own biases may have affected their verdicts. She wrote: "Their reverence for police officers as guardians of the social order colored their view of the entire case. At the same time, the jurors' low regard for the likes of Rodney King—a paroled felon, driving drunk and resisting arrest—made it inconceivable that they could sympathize with him as the victim of an alleged crime."

8. The estimate of 1 million jury verdicts between 1986 and 1993 is based on the figure of more than 150,000 a year provided by G. Thomas Munsterman of the National Center for State Courts.

9. The study by the American Bar Association's litigation section, called "Jury Comprehension in Complex Cases," was made public in September 1989. The project was overseen by Daniel H. Margolis, chairman of the litigation section's Committee on Jury Comprehension.

2. LAWYERS' POKER

1. The quote about rational jury decision making appears in the *Japanese Electronic Products Antitrust Litigation,* 631 F.2d 1069, 1079 (3rd Cir. 1980).
2. The Jury Selection and Services Act of 1968, which applies to federal civil and criminal jury selection, requires selection from a fair cross section of the population. The U.S. Supreme Court made clear that the fair-cross-section requirement also applies to state courts in *Taylor* v. *Louisiana,* 419 US 522 (1975).
3. For the best available figures on how many people have been called for jury duty and how many have actually served, see *The Defense Research Institute's Report,* pp. 3, 8. According to the report, 45 percent of adult Americans had been called for jury duty at some time in their lives. There were 186 million adults in the United States in 1989, meaning that the number called for jury duty approximated eighty million. Slightly more than one third of these people actually have sat as jurors through an entire trial. Separately, federal court data from the Administrative Office of the U.S. Courts show that roughly 29 percent of federal jurors who are present for voir dire are actually selected to serve on juries. About 37 percent are removed via lawyers' challenges and 34 percent turn out not to be needed. Although about 95 percent of all jury trials occur in state courts, it seems likely that the federal figures on exclusion rates are within the ballpark for state courts as well.
4. The nearly systematic exclusion of college-educated jurors from the conspiracy trial of John Mitchell and Maurice Stans in 1974 was documented in Hans Zeisel and Shari Seidman Diamond, "The Jury Selection in the Mitchell-Stans Conspiracy Trial," *American Bar Foundation Research Journal* 151 (1976).
5. Sir John Hawles, a prominent lawyer who lived from 1645 to

1716, explains to a citizen why he shouldn't want to avoid jury duty in *The Englishman's Right: A Dialogue In Relation to Trial By Jury* (Boston: Soule and Bugbee, 1883 edition). Among other things, Hawles declares that jury trial "is brought down to us as our undoubted birth-right, and the best inheritance of every Englishman."

6. The purpose of peremptory challenges is laid out by the U.S. Supreme Court in *Swain* v. *Alabama,* 380 U.S. 202, 219 (1965).

7. The advertisement that advocates "packing" the jury was for a Shepard's, McGraw-Hill Inc., jury primer and was mailed, among other places, to the in-house legal department at Dow Jones & Company, publisher of *The Wall Street Journal.*

8. The opinion of the 7–2 majority in *Batson* v. *Kentucky,* 476 U.S. 79 (1986), was written by Justice Lewis F. Powell, Jr. Peremptory challenges based on race were prohibited in civil cases by the U.S. Supreme Court in *Edmonson* v. *Leesville Concrete Co.,* 111 S.Ct. 2077 (1991); criminal defense lawyers were barred from making racial exclusions in *McCollum* v. *Georgia,* 112 S.Ct. 2348 (1992). Gender-based challenges were invalidated in *J.E.B.* v. *Alabama Ex Rel. T.B.,* No. 92-1239 (April 19, 1994).

9. Jurors' failure to admit their biases in voir dire is illustrated by a study conducted by the consulting company Litigation Sciences Inc., based on the facts of the Ford Pinto product liability case. In a case involving injuries from gas tank explosions during rear end collisions, 63 percent of the subjects answered during a mock jury selection that they could decide the case fairly. But when asked much more specific questions concerning their attitudes, 60 percent said they believed Ford was cutting corners in safety precautions; 73 percent said Ford was negligent and careless; 79 percent said Ford should pay damages for pain and suffering; 64 percent said Ford should pay huge damages for its disregard of safety; and 18 percent went so far as to accuse Ford and its executives of being murderers. The study is described in Donald E. Vinson, *Jury Trials: The Psychology of Winning Strategy* (Charlottesville, VA: The Michie Company, 1986), pp. 76–78.

10. Ferdinand Marcos's tumultuous affair in the 1970s with an American starlet named Dovie Beams, documented through sex

tapes she made and allowed to be broadcast on radio, is described in Sterling Seagrave, *The Marcos Dynasty* (New York: Fawcett Columbine, 1988), pp. 214–17; and in Stanley Karnow, *In Our Image: America's Empire in the Philippines* (New York: Ballantine Books, 1989), p. 379. Karnow wrote of the tapes that they gave "the public a heavy dose of Marcos grunting, breathing obscenities, crooning love songs and revealing Imelda's sexual inadequacies."

11. In an interview with the author, Judge John F. Keenan said he was surprised and disappointed that jurors had become aware of his comments outside their presence regarding whether the Marcos case should have been brought in the United States. "I don't know how you can insulate the jury without locking up all the jurors," he said. "And if you lock up juries, it makes jury service intolerable for them."

12. Four jurors in the Marcos case said they saw fellow juror Alan Belovsky clipping newspaper stories about the trial while in the jury room. When confronted during the trial by juror Ted Kutzy, Belovsky said he was keeping a scrapbook, the jurors said. In an interview soon after the trial, Kutzy said of Belovsky, "At one point, he even wanted to talk about what he'd read. I said, 'Do anything you want at home but not here.' " After the trial, Belovsky wouldn't comment directly on whether he had read about the case. "Some of us were aware of some of what was in the paper," he said, adding that nothing in any newspaper report had any effect on how he or the others reached their verdict.

13. The University of Chicago Jury Project, an enormous research undertaking in the 1950s, remains the most important academic study on the jury. Many of its findings appear in Harry Kalven, Jr., and Hans Zeisel, *The American Jury* (Boston: Little, Brown, 1966). One part of the project involved interviewing juries on their deliberative processes. The authors determined that a lone juror, or even two or three, rarely holds out against the wishes of the rest of the panel. In seventy-nine criminal cases in which between nine and eleven jurors (out of twelve) voted guilty on the first ballot, not a single hung jury resulted.

Similarly, hung juries were extremely rare when no more than three jurors initially favored conviction. This showed, wrote the authors, "that juries which begin with an overwhelming majority in either direction are not likely to hang. It requires a massive minority of four or five jurors at the first vote to develop the likelihood of a hung jury." Ibid., p. 462.

14. The Welsh barrister's comments on peremptory challenges are quoted in Hans and Vidmar, p. 48.

3. THE WIZARDS OF ODDS

1. The revenue estimate of two hundred million dollars for jury consulting appears in Stephen J. Adler, "Litigation Science: Consultants Dope Out the Mysteries of Jurors for Clients Being Sued," *The Wall Street Journal,* October 24, 1989, pp. A1, A10.
2. The pioneering social science work performed for the defense in the Harrisburg Seven case is described in Jay Schulman, Phillip Shaver, Robert Colman, Barbara Emrich, and Richard Christie, "Recipe for a Jury," *In the Jury Box: Controversies In the Courtroom,* eds. Lawrence Wrightsman, Saul M. Kassin, and Cynthia E. Willis (Newbury Park, CA: Sage Publications, 1987), pp. 13–47.
3. The origin of the shadow jury in the IBM antitrust litigation is described in Adler, "Litigation Science." Additional reporting comes from interviews with David Boies and Donald Vinson.
4. Arthur Patterson's homegrown consulting company was acquired by an engineering-consulting and courtroom-animation firm that was called FTI in 1992 and became FTI Jury Analyst Group. It has since entered into a strategic partnership with the accounting and consulting giant Arthur Andersen.
5. A few well-publicized cases in the early 1990s—including the Menendez mistrials and the acquittal of Lorena Bobbitt—suggested to some observers that juries were becoming all too eager to let people avoid responsibility for their own acts. But the best available data contradict this view. A nationwide study of jury verdicts, conducted by Jury Verdict Publications, found that juries are much less willing than they used to be to let personal injury plaintiffs blame their accidents on someone else. See

1994 Current Jury Awards (Horsham, PA: LRP Publications, 1994), p. 65.

6. The important role of jurors' attitudes in predicting their behavior is discussed in Vinson, pp. 1–21.

7. Ibid., p. 138.

8. In his masterful voir dire speech to prospective jurors in the Pennzoil-Texaco case in 1985, Pennzoil lawyer Joseph Jamail sought to make the complex takeover fight turn on the seemingly simple question whether Texaco would be required to abide by a handshake agreement. He asked potential jurors if they agreed with Texaco's position (as he described it) that "a handshake in New York is meaningless," and then answered the question himself: "I take it you do not." Petzinger, p. 302.

9. Sociologist Amitai Etzioni gave his critique of jury consultants in a personal interview.

10. De Tocqueville, p. 283.

4. WHAT'S A BLIVET?

1. John Adams's prerevolutionary valentine to the jury is quoted in *Diary and Autobiography of John Adams,* ed. L. H. Butterfield (Cambridge, MA: The Belknap Press of Harvard University Press, 1961), Vol. 1, p. 298.

2. Harvard Law School Dean Erwin Griswold's now famous critique of jury trials appeared in his dean's report of 1962–63. In a telephone interview on November 20, 1989, he said this: "I still feel that way about jury trial in complex [civil] cases. . . . I think it's gotten worse as the country has grown and gotten more litigious, the cases have grown, and the nature of litigation in commercial cases has become more complex."

3. Warren Burger, speech at Loyola University, New Orleans, November 10, 1984.

4. The IBM case in which the jurors proved so hopelessly overmatched was called *ILC Peripherals Leasing Corp.* v. *IBM Corp.; Memorex Corp., MRX Sales and Service Corp.* v. *IBM Corp.,* 458 F. Supp. 423 (U.S. Dist. Ct., N. Dist. of Calif., Aug. 11, 1978).

5. *Williams* v. *Florida,* 399 U.S. 78 (1970) upheld the use of six-person juries in criminal cases. *Colgrove* v. *Battin,* 413 U.S. 149

(1973) approved such juries in civil cases. Juries of fewer than six were declared unconstitutional in *Ballew* v. *Georgia*, 435 U.S. 223 (1978).

6. The observation that a jury trial is like a baseball game in which the players don't learn the rules until the end of the game is in William W. Schwarzer, "Reforming Jury Trials," 1990 *University of Chicago Legal Forum* 119, 130 (1990).

7. The statement about the need to make lay jurors understand the jury charge is by Judge Charles Wyzanski, in *Cape Cod Food Products Inc.* v. *National Cranberry Assn.*, 119 F. Supp. 900, 907 (D. Mass. 1954).

8. The U.S. Supreme Court ruled, by a 6–3 vote, against Liggett in *Brooke Group Ltd.* v. *Brown & Williamson Tobacco Corp.*, 113 S. Ct. 2578 (June 21, 1993).

9. The U.S. appeals court in Philadelphia is the only federal appellate court to find a "complexity exception" to the Seventh Amendment right to jury trial in civil cases. *Japanese Electronic Products Antitrust Litigation*, 631 F.2d 1069, 1084 (3rd Cir. 1980).

10. Warren Burger, speech at Loyola University, New Orleans, November 10, 1984.

11. Judge Jerome Frank delivered his stinging critique of jurors' competence in *Skidmore* v. *Baltimore & Ohio Railroad*, 167 F.2d 54, 60 (2d Cir. 1948). Further concerns about the justice system are laid out in his book *Courts on Trial: Myth and Reality in American Justice* (Princeton, NJ: Princeton University Press, 1950).

12. Richard O. Lempert, "Civil Juries and Complex Cases: Let's Not Rush to Judgment," 80 *Michigan Law Review* 68, 84 (1981).

5. BLOOD MONEY

1. Quayle carried his complaints about lawyers, lawsuits, and soaring jury awards right to the lion's den. He announced the Bush administration's legislative "civil justice reform" program at the annual meeting of the American Bar Association on August 13, 1991. An impromptu debate ensued when ABA president John J. Curtin, Jr., followed the vice president to the microphone and offered a rebuttal. Ralph Nader responded to Quayle's pitch by accusing him of "pandering to powerful corporate in-

terests" with "a pastiche of shopworn" proposals. David Broder, "ABA President Disputes Quayle on Litigation Proposals," *The Washington Post*, August 14, 1991, p. 1.

2. The Chicago study of nine thousand jury trials is reported in Audrey Chin and Mark Peterson, *Deep Pockets, Empty Pockets, Who Wins in Cook County Jury Trials* (Santa Monica, CA: Rand Institute for Civil Justice, 1985).

3. The Jones Corporation/Mr. Jones experiment is discussed in Valerie P. Hans and M. David Ermann, "Responses to Corporate Versus Individual Wrongdoing," 13 *Law and Human Behavior* 151 (1989). Experimental jurors treated the individual and corporate defendants roughly equivalently when doling out damages for easily quantifiable doctors' and hospital bills for an injured plaintiff. Only when presented with the flexible category of pain and suffering did their tougher treatment of the corporate defendant emerge.

4. A National Center for State Courts study of personal injury trials in twenty-seven state trial courts produced the data showing that plaintiffs win 50 percent of the time against corporations and 61 percent of the time against individuals. Brian Ostrom, David Rottmann, and Roger Hanson, "What Are Tort Awards Really Like? The Untold Story from the State Courts," 14 *Law and Policy* 77, 83 (1992).

Moreover, the data from Jury Verdict Publications show that plaintiffs are winning jury trials much less frequently than they used to. Through most of the past thirty years, plaintiffs have won about 60 percent of their cases. But since 1989 the percentage has been dipping: In 1990 it was down to 58 percent, and in 1992 it had slipped to 52 percent. One possible reason: Widespread publicity of the sort generated by Quayle and big business groups has affected jurors and made them more reluctant to award damages to plaintiffs. A study published in 1992 found that 83 percent of jurors questioned believed that "there are far too many frivolous lawsuits today." Valerie P. Hans and William S. Lofquist, "Jurors' Judgments of Business Liability in Tort Cases: Implications for the Litigation Explosion Debate," 26 *Law & Society Review* 85, 95 (1992).

5. The debate over how much litigation costs the economy is reported in Milo Geyelin, "Tort Bar's Scourge: Star of Litigation Reform Kindles Controversy but Collects Critics," *The Wall Street Journal,* October 16, 1992, p. A1.

6. The figure for median jury verdicts in Chicago is provided in Stephen Daniels and Joanne Martin, "Myth and Reality in Punitive Damages," 75 *Minnesota Law Review* 1 (October 1990). The later study of other courts, with similar results, is reported in Ostrom, Rottmann, and Hanson.

7. The absolutist attitudes of jurors toward companies' safety standards emerged from interviews with 141 jurors in 18 personal injury cases against businesses, as reported in Hans and Lofquist, p. 85.

8. The more than two-thousand-year history of damages for bodily injuries is traced in Jeffrey O'Connell and Rita James Simon, "Payment for Pain & Suffering: Who Wants What, When & Why?" 1972 *University of Illinois Law Forum* 1. The authors write that Table 8 of the Roman Law of 12 Tables (450 B.C.) provided for the payment of 300 asses (copper coins) for a broken limb of a free man; 150 for a broken limb of a slave; and 25 for lesser bodily injuries. The citation for the important British case of *Ash* v. *Lady Ash* is 90 Eng. Rep. 526 (K.B. 1696).

9. Different modern approaches to establishing the amount of damages for pain and suffering are analyzed in Randall R. Bovbjerg, Frank A. Solan, and James F. Blumstein, "Valuing Life and Limb in Tort: Scheduling 'Pain and Suffering,' " 83 *Northwestern University Law Review* 908–76 (Summer 1989). One commonly used jury instruction on pain and suffering provides "that the law cannot give you a precise formula or yardstick . . . but the law contemplates that twelve intelligent jurors, exercising common sense and calling upon their experiences in life, can satisfactorily fix and determine a proper award of money. . . ." 8 *American Jurisprudence Pleading & Practice Forms* 278 (1982).

10. "No market place exists": *Botta* v. *Brunner,* 26 N.J. 82 (1958).

11. Historical discussions of loss of consortium appear in Susan G. Ridgeway, "Loss of Consortium and Loss of Services Actions: A

Legacy of Separate Spheres," 50 *Montana Law Review* 349–70 (Summer 1989); and Nancy C. Osborne, "Loss of Consortium: Paradise Lost, Paradise Regained," 15 *Cumberland Law Review* 179–209 (1984–85).

12. *Guy* v. *Livesey,* 79 Eng. Rep. 428 (1618). The court ruled that a lawsuit could be brought by a husband because "he lost the company of his wife, which is only a damage and loss to himself, for which he shall have this action as the master shall have for the loss of his servant's service."

13. The U.S. court case that finally allowed a woman to sue for loss of her husband's marital services was *Hitaffer* v. *Argonne Co.,* 183 F.2d 811 (D.C. Cir., 1950).

14. The experiment in which many mock jurors inappropriately added legal fees to their damage award is reported in Jane Goodman, Edith Greene, and Elizabeth F. Loftus, "Runaway Verdicts or Reasoned Determinations: Mock Juror Strategies in Awarding Damages," 29 *Jurimetrics Journal of Law, Science and Technology* 285, 303 (Spring 1989).

15. *Charles Newman* v. *Johns-Manville* was tried in U.S. District Court in East Texas in 1984. The jury believed that the plaintiffs had become ill because of exposure to asbestos and awarded four individuals a total of $3.9 million in compensatory damages and $4 million in punitive damages. Posttrial interviews with jurors revealed that they had added about 40 percent to each plaintiff's award to cover attorneys' fees. Molly Selvin and Larry Picus, *The Debate Over Jury Performance: Observations from a Recent Asbestos Case* (Santa Monica, CA: Rand Institute for Civil Justice, 1987).

16. United Blood Services agreed in late 1993 to pay the Quintanas an undisclosed sum in exchange for dropping its appeal of the jury award. Such postverdict settlements are a common way of resolving civil lawsuits.

17. In its brief supporting its motion for a new trial (which wasn't granted), United Blood Services cited the average damage award figures for medical malpractice and AIDS-related transfusion cases.

18. The Texaco worker's case is *Martin* v. *Texaco Refining and Market-*

ing Inc. in Los Angeles Superior Court. The actual and punitive damages were awarded, respectively, on September 25 and October 3, 1991. The Illinois hospital case is *Tierney* v. *LaGrange Memorial Hospital,* Cook County Circuit Court, Chicago; the verdict was reached on December 2, 1991. Both cases were reported in *The National Law Journal*'s annual feature, "1991's Largest Verdicts," January 20, 1992, pp. S-2, S-7, S-12. The motel mirror case against the Cantebury Inn in Coralville, Iowa, was decided in Johnson County District Court on June 24, 1992. The verdict was reported by the Gannett News Service the following day.

19. The study showing the wide variation among damage awards for equivalent injuries appears in Bovbjerg, Solan, and Blumstein, pp. 908–76.

20. Various proposals aimed at reducing the unpredictability of jury damage awards are discussed in Bovbjerg, Solan, and Blumstein.

21. The median verdict in personal injury cases nationally has declined from seventy thousand dollars in 1989 to sixty-two thousand dollars in 1993, according to *1994 Current Jury Awards,* p. 4. Consultant Arthur Patterson's jury polls as of March 1994 showed that about 75 percent of jurors believed that jury awards were too high. And about 70 percent believed that too many lawsuits were being filed. Patterson's results closely track those of the Metricus National Jury Opinion Survey, conducted a few years earlier by Metricus Inc., a Palo Alto, California, jury research firm.

22. The salary arbitration approach to damages is explained by Judge Robert Satter in *Doing Justice: A Trial Judge At Work* (New York: American Lawyer Books/Simon & Schuster, 1990), p. 138. Based on his experience as a trial judge, he also observes: "Damage verdicts are damaging when they are as random as lottery numbers. That quality, more than any other, brings the system into disrepute." Ibid., p. 135.

6. Love and Death in New Jersey

1. Robert G. Ingersoll's memorable jury address on credibility and probability is preserved in *Famous American Jury Speeches,* ed., Frederick C. Hicks (Littleton, CO: Fred. B. Rothman, 1990), p. 232. The case, a high-stakes will contest, was tried in Butte, Montana, in 1891.

2. The study on witnesses' use of hypercorrect speech is in John M. Conley, William M. O'Barr, and E. Allan Lind, "The Power of Language: Presentational Style in the Courtroom," *Duke Law Journal* 1375 (1978).

3. Jurors' tendency to deny, even to themselves, that they have acted out of sympathy or prejudice was reported in Kalven and Zeisel, p. 165. The authors wrote: ". . . the jury does not often consciously and explicitly yield to sentiment in the teeth of the law. Rather, it yields to sentiment in the apparent process of resolving doubts as to evidence. The jury, therefore, is able to conduct its revolt from the law within the etiquette of resolving issues of fact."

4. "outcome predetermined": Ibid., p. 462.

5. The columnist who was so skeptical of the Schneider acquittal was Peggy Wright, "Schneider Drama: Only Players Know Real Story," *Morris County Daily Record,* March 6, 1992, p. A3.

6. The article quoting Marisol Schneider as saying, "Dead men don't speak," is by Cort Parker, Jr., "Marisol Schneider of Victim: 'I Always Thank God for the Day I Met Him,' " *The Echoes-Sentinel,* March 12, 1992, p. 1.

7. Judge Nicholas A. Politan's decision was reported and analyzed in Wade Lambert, "After the Verdict: Will Juror Interviews Skew the Deliberations in Future Trials?" *The Wall Street Journal,* December 30, 1993, p. B1.

8. Trial by battle and by ordeal are described in Thayer, "The Older Modes of Trial," pp. 65–68. Ordeals involved various medieval tortures designed to sort out the innocent from the guilty. Accounts from the period refer to the accused being forced to walk over hot plowshares or to carry a glowing piece of iron or to plunge his hand into a pail of boiling water. If the defendants burned, they were guilty. Dunking also was popular:

If the tightly bound defendant floated, he was spared because the pure element of water "would not receive into its bosom anyone stained with the crime of a false oath." The conviction rate was obviously high. Until the beginning of the thirteenth century, many of the trials were conducted, for a price, in ordeal pits on church grounds and in monasteries. But the ordeal system lost its crucial religious endorsement in 1215 when Pope Innocent III banned churchmen from participating. The pendulum thus swung to the most practical remaining trial mode—the jury.

9. The importance of jury trial in maintaining public faith in the justice system is stressed in Robert J. MacCoun and Tom R. Tyler, "The Basis of Citizens' Perceptions of the Criminal Jury, Procedural Fairness, Accuracy, and Efficiency," 12 *Law and Human Behavior* 333 (September 1988). The authors of the article write: "Decisions in criminal and civil cases typically require judgments about community norms concerning reasonable conduct, standards of proof, and appropriate compensation or sanctions. By entrusting such judgments, at least in part, to juries, there is an assurance that legal verdicts are consistent with community values. This larger political role of the jury evolved during a historical period in which English and American citizens were concerned with maintaining checks and balances on the power of political authorities."

10. Judge Gibbons gives his rationale for jury trial in his dissent in the *Japanese Electronic Products Antitrust Litigation,* 631 F.2d 1069, 1093 (3rd Cir. 1980).

11. Research on how untrained observers judge witnesses' credibility is described in A. Daniel Yarmey, *The Psychology of Eyewitness Testimony* (New York: The Free Press, 1979); Elizabeth F. Loftus, *Eyewitness Testimony* (Cambridge, MA: Harvard University Press, 1979); and Steven I. Friedland, "On Common Sense and the Evaluation of Witness Credibility," 40 *Case Western Law Review* 165–225 (1989/1990).

12. Elizabeth F. Loftus and Katherine Ketcham, *Witness for the Defense: The Accused, the Eyewitness, and the Expert Who Puts Memory on Trial* (New York: St. Martin's Press, 1991), p. 20.

NOTES

PART III: THE HOPE

1. No one knows for certain how many jury trials occur each year in thousands of state and federal courtrooms around the country. The estimate of more than 150,000 comes from research conducted by the National Center for State Courts and is based on extrapolations from states in which precise data are available.
2. Devlin explains the connection between juries and democracy in *The Judge* (Oxford, England: Oxford University Press, 1979), p. 127.

7. ORDER IN THE COURT

1. Until the late 1960s, some courts picked juries by the so-called keyman system, under which certain pillars of the community were designated to select those who were worthy to serve on juries. These jurors may have brought diverse business and professional backgrounds to their task, but socially they tended to be quite homogeneous—and, more often than not, noticeably different from the people they were asked to judge. In one midwestern court that used this keyman system and that was studied in the 1950s, virtually all members of the jury pool voted Republican, attended church, and were active in community service groups. Dale W. Broeder, "Voir Dire Examinations: An Empirical Study," 38 *Southern California Law Review* 503 (1965).

   Information about oral exams for jurors in New York City comes from an interview with Norman Goodman, the clerk of courts for New York County. He said that examiners made subjective judgments about intelligence and character before clearing individuals to become eligible jurors. "I remember a couple of employees who treated this as though they were making very important decisions and got great pleasure out of telling people they didn't measure up," Goodman said.
2. The federal civil rights law covering juries is the Jury Selection and Services Act of 1968.
3. There has been a powerful backlash in many states against automatic exemptions of professional groups. As of 1992 twenty-six states had no professional exemptions; and while twenty-four

states maintained exemptions, they were very limited in nine of those states. H. Lee Sarokin and G. Thomas Munsterman, "Recent Innovations in Civil Jury Trial Procedures," *Verdict: Assessing the Civil Jury System,* in Litan, pp. 378, 380. Also see Jan Hoffman, "New York Casts for Solutions to Gaping Holes in Juror Net," *The New York Times,* September 26, 1993, p. 1.

New York's statute excluding so many professional groups from service is the Judiciary Law Section 512. A jury reform commission, appointed by Chief Judge Judith S. Kaye, has recommended eliminating all these exemptions. See "The Jury Project: Report to the Chief Judge of the State of New York," March 31, 1994, p. 31.

4. "the rust of society": De Tocqueville, p. 285.
5. Court officials' difficulties getting prospective jurors to the courthouse, even in the most political of all cities, Washington, D.C., are related in Garry Sturgess, "Dire Days for Voir Dire," *Legal Times,* September 10, 1990, p. 1.
6. About 25 percent of the U.S. population now lives in jurisdictions in which jury duty is limited to one trial or, if the person isn't selected, just a single day's availability. Sarokin and Munsterman, in Litan, p. 381.
7. For the get-tough measure taken in Essex County, N.J., see Arthur S. Hayes, "Solving the Case of the Missing Jurors," *The Wall Street Journal,* March 12, 1990, p. B1.
8. In criminal cases 22.7 percent of prospective jurors are removed by defense lawyers and 7.4 percent are removed by prosecutors, according to studies reported in Hans and Vidmar, p. 74.
9. "fools and rascals": Twain, *Roughing It,* p. 56.
10. *Batson* v. *Kentucky,* 476 U.S. 79, 103, n. 3; 107 (Marshall concurring).
11. London solicitor Andrew Nitch-Smith and barrister Geoffrey Robertson described the British jury selection system in personal interviews. British jury picking is discussed in Sarah McCabe, "Is Jury Research Dead?" in *The Jury Under Attack,* eds. Mark Findlay and Peter Duff (London: Butterworths, 1988), pp. 27–39; Devlin, *Trial By Jury,* pp. 28–29, and Valerie P. Hans,

"Jury Selection in Two Countries: A Psychological Perspective,"
2 *Current Psychological Reviews* 283–300 (1982).

12. Mary Timothy, *Jury Woman* (Palo Alto, CA: Glide Publications/
Emty Press, 1974), pp. 127–28.

13. E. Barrett Prettyman, "Jury Instructions—First or Last?" 46
ABA Journal 1066 (1960).

14. The history of the use of jury instructions is traced in William
W. Schwarzer, "Communicating with Juries: Problems and
Remedies," 69 *California Law Review* 731 (1981).

15. The Illinois court case in which a death sentence was thrown
out because of incomprehensible instructions but then reinstated is *Free* v. *Peters*, Nos. 92-3618, 92-3711, and 93-2517, 7th
U.S. Circuit Court of Appeals, December 21, 1993.

   The U.S. Supreme Court addressed the issue of the compre-
hensibility of jury instructions in the combined cases of *Sandoval* v. *California* and *Victor* v. *Nebraska*, 1994 U.S. Lexis 2490
(1994). In *Sandoval* the justices upheld the constitutionality of
California's standard instruction defining "reasonable doubt,"
even though in concurring opinions justices called it "ambiguous," "archaic," and "unhelpful" to jurors (Lexis, p. 38). The
California instruction states: "Reasonable doubt is defined as
follows: It is not a mere possible doubt; because everything re-
lating to human affairs, and depending on moral evidence, is
open to some possible or imaginary doubt. It is that state of the
case which, after the entire comparison and consideration of all
the evidence, leaves the minds of the jurors in that condition
that they cannot say they feel an abiding conviction, to a moral
certainty, of the truth of the charge." Lexis, p. 12.

16. Jerome Frank, *Law and the Modern Mind* (Magnolia, MA: Peter
Smith, 1930), p. 181.

17. *Neil* v. *Biggers*, 409 U.S. 188 (1972).

18. The impact of jurors' asking questions has been studied closely
in recent years by researchers. One of the biggest and most
important research projects, based on interviews with 550 jurors, 95 lawyers, and 63 judges in 67 cases, is reported in Larry
Heuer and Steven D. Penrod, "Increasing Jurors' Participation
in Trials: A Field Experiment with Jury Notetaking and Ques-

tion Asking," 12 *Law and Human Behavior* 231–62 (September 1988). Research on jurors' questioning is also explored in depth in Hedieh Nasheri and Richard J. Rudolph, "An Active Jury: Should Courts Encourage Jurors to Participate in the Questioning Process?" 16 *American Journal of Trial Advocacy* 109 (1992).

19. The history of the relationship between jurors and witnesses was spelled out by Thayer in "The Jury and Its Development II," pp. 302–17. Initially jurors were, in essence, witnesses who were presumed to know or be able to find out the facts at issue. But, Thayer wrote, by the thirteenth century, a mixed system had evolved under which jurors were called along with separate witnesses to the actual deed. They conferred together, in effect acting as one body. Witnesses did not generally testify in open court; rather, they communicated privately with the jurors. By the fourteenth century a greater distinction had developed among witnesses and jurors. A witness was supposed to say only what he or she had seen or heard, and an actual witness wasn't allowed to be seated on the jury. Actual witness testimony in open court was established by 1465, according to Thayer, as evidenced by a reported case in which witnesses testified openly.

20. A survey of hundreds of judges nationwide found that 77 percent never allow jurors to ask questions of witnesses. Larry Heuer and Steven D. Penrod, "Some Suggestions for the Critical Appraisal of a More Active Jury," 85 *Northwestern University Law Review* 226, 302 (Fall 1990). In allowing jurors to ask questions, the Fifth U.S. Circuit Court of Appeals wrote: "Trials exist to develop truth. It may sometimes be that counsel are so familiar with a case that they fail to see problems that would naturally bother a juror who is presented with the facts for the first time." *U.S.* v. *Callahan*, 588 F.2d 1078, 1086 (1979).

21. The Johnson & Johnson case in which jurors' questions were allowed was reported in John Flynn Rooney, "Lawyers Laud Questions of Toxic Shock Jury," *The Chicago Daily Law Bulletin*, January 29, 1990, p. 1.

22. Robert W. Landry, "Let the Jurors Ask!" *The National Law Journal,* January 29, 1990, pp. 13–14.

23. Judge Schwarzer, in "Reforming Jury Trials," writes that federal trials of twenty days or more increased from eighty-three to a hundred and seventy per year between 1976 and 1988.

24. The argument against allowing written instructions into the jury room is that jurors may focus too heavily on a single word or passage rather than on the gist of the entire text, as it has been read to them. When instructions run to fifty pages or more, however, it seems unlikely that jurors will remember the gist—or much of anything else—unless they can review the manuscript. See discussion in B. Michael Dann, " 'Learning Lessons' and 'Speaking Rights': Creating Educated and Democratic Juries," 68 *Indiana Law Journal* 1229, 1259 (Fall 1993).

25. The extensive research that has been done on jury note taking is reviewed in Sarokin and Munsterman, pp. 386–388. The survey of judges on note taking is in Heuer and Penrod, p. 302.

26. The New York note taking experiment appears in the *Report of the Committee on Juries of the Judicial Council of the Second Circuit,* August 1984, pp. 65–73.

27. The research on how jurors' views of the jury system change after they have served is summarized in Diamond, "What Jurors Think: Expectations and Reactions of Citizens Who Serve as Jurors," in Litan, pp. 284–88.

BIBLIOGRAPHY

Abrahamson, Shirley S. "A View from the Other Side of the Bench." *Marquette Law Review* 69 (Summer 1986), 463–93.

Adams, John. *Diary and Autobiography of John Adams.* Ed. L. H. Butterfield. Cambridge, MA: The Belknap Press of Harvard University Press, 1961.

Adler, Stephen J. "Courtroom Putsch? Jurors Should Reject Laws They Don't Like, Activist Group Argues." *The Wall Street Journal,* January 4, 1991, p. A1.

Adler, Stephen J. "How to Lose the Bet-Your-Company Case." *The American Lawyer,* January–February, 1986, pp. 27–30, 107–10.

Adler, Stephen J. "Litigation Science: Consultants Dope Out the Mysteries of Jurors for Clients Being Sued." *The Wall Street Journal,* October 24, 1989, pp. A1, A10.

Alexander, James. *A Brief Narrative of the Case and Trial of John Peter Zenger.* Ed. Stanley Nider Katz. Cambridge, MA: The Belknap Press of Harvard University Press, 1972.

Aristophanes. "The Wasps." *Three Comedies by Aristophanes.* Trans. Douglass Parker. Ann Arbor, MI: The University of Michigan Press, 1969.

Arnold, Morris S. "Law and Fact in the Medieval Jury Trial: Out of

Sight, Out of Mind." *American Journal of Legal History* 18 (1974), 267–80.

Attorney for the Damned: Clarence Darrow in the Courtroom. Ed. Arthur Weinberg. Chicago: University of Chicago Press, 1989.

Black, Charles L., Jr. *Capital Punishment: The Inevitability of Caprice and Mistake.* New York: W. W. Norton, 1981.

Blecher, Maxwell M., and Howard F. Daniels. "In Defense of Juries in Complex Antitrust Litigation." *The Review of Litigation* 1 (1980) 47–91 (1980).

Bonner, Raymond. *Waltzing with a Dictator: The Marcoses and the Making of American Policy.* New York: Vintage Books, 1987.

Bovbjerg, Randall R., Frank A. Solan, and James F. Blumstein. "Valuing Life and Limb in Tort: Scheduling 'Pain and Suffering,' " *Northwestern University Law Review* 83 (Summer 1989), 908–76.

Brill, Steven, and the editors and reporters of *The American Lawyer. Trial by Jury.* New York: The American Lawyer/Touchstone/Simon & Schuster, 1990.

Broder, David. "ABA President Disputes Quayle on Litigation Proposals." *The Washington Post,* August 14, 1991, p. 1.

Broeder, Dale W. "Voir Dire Examinations: An Empirical Study." *Southern California Law Review* 38 (1965), 503–28.

Chin, Audrey, and Mark Peterson. *Deep Pockets, Empty Pockets, Who Wins in Cook County Jury Trials.* Santa Monica, CA: Rand Institute for Civil Justice, 1985.

Conley, John M., William M. O'Barr, and E. Allan Lind. "The Power of Language: Presentational Style in the Courtroom." *Duke Law Journal* (1978), 1375–99.

Daniels, Stephen, and Joanne Martin. "Myth and Reality in Punitive Damages." *Minnesota Law Review* 75 (October 1990), 1–64.

Dann, B. Michael. " 'Learning Lessons' and 'Speaking Rights': Creating Educated and Democratic Juries." *Indiana Law Journal* 68 (Fall 1993), 1229–79.

The Defense Research Institute's Report on Jury Service in the United States. Chicago: June, 1990.

de Tocqueville, Alexis. *Democracy in America.* New York: Vintage Books, 1990.

Devlin, Sir Patrick. *The Judge*. Oxford, England: Oxford University Press, 1979.

Devlin, Sir Patrick. *Trial By Jury*. London: Stevens & Sons, 1956.

Diamond, Shari Seidman. "What Jurors Think: Expectations and Reactions of Citizens Who Serve as Jurors." *Verdict: Assessing the Civil Jury System*. Ed. Robert E. Litan. Washington, DC: The Brookings Institution, 1993, pp. 282–305.

Famous American Jury Speeches. Ed. Frederick C. Hicks. Littleton, CO: Fred. B. Rothman, 1990.

The Federalist Papers. Ed. Roy P. Fairchild. Garden City, NY: Anchor Books, Doubleday & Company, Inc., 1966.

Fitzgerald, Robert, and Phoebe C. Ellsworth. "Due Process vs. Crime Control, Death Qualification and Jury Attitudes." *Law and Human Behavior* 8 (June 1984), 31–51.

Forsyth, William. *History of Trial By Jury*. New York: Cockcroft, 1878.

Forsyth, William. *Hortensius: An Historical Essay on the Office and Duties of an Advocate*. London: John Murray, 1879.

Frank, Jerome. *Courts on Trial: Myth and Reality in American Justice*. Princeton, NJ: Princeton University Press, 1950.

Frank, Jerome. *Law and the Modern Mind*. Magnolia, MA: Peter Smith, 1930.

Friedland, Steven I. "On Common Sense and the Evaluation of Witness Credibility." *Case Western Law Review* 40 (1989/1990), 165–225.

Fukurai, Hiroshi, Edgar W. Butler, Richard Krooth. *Race and the Jury: Racial Disenfranchisement and the Search for Justice*. New York: Plenum Press, 1993.

Galanter, Marc. "The Civil Jury as Regulator of the Litigation Process." *The University of Chicago Legal Forum* (1990), 201–71.

Galsworthy, John. "The Juryman." *Law In Action: An Anthology of the Law in Literature*. New York: Bonanza Books, 1947.

Geyelin, Milo. "Tort Bar's Scourge: Star of Litigation Reform Kindles Controversy but Collects Critics." *The Wall Street Journal*, October 16, 1992, p. A1.

Gillers, Stephen. "Deciding Who Dies." *University of Pennsylvania Law Review* 129 (November 1980), 1–124.

Gleisser, Marcus. *Juries and Justice*. Cranbury, NJ: A. S. Barnes, 1968.

Goodman, Jane, Edith Greene, and Elizabeth F. Loftus. "Runaway Verdicts or Reasoned Determinations: Mock Juror Strategies in Awarding Damages." *Jurimetrics Journal of Law, Science and Technology* 29 (Spring 1989), 285–309.

Gordon, Robert Wayne. "Crystal-Balling Death?" *Baylor Law Review* 30 (1978), 35–64.

Guinther, John. *The Jury in America.* New York: Facts on File, 1988.

Hagedorn, Ann. "McMartin Trial Ends in Deadlock, Case Is Now Dead." *The Wall Street Journal,* July 30, 1990, p. B6.

Hans, Valerie P. "Jury Selection in Two Countries: A Psychological Perspective." *Current Psychological Reviews* 2 (1982), 283–300.

Hans, Valerie P., and M. David Ermann. "Responses to Corporate versus Individual Wrongdoing." *Law and Human Behavior* 13 (June 1989), 151–66.

Hans, Valerie P., and William S. Lofquist. "Jurors' Judgment of Business Liability in Tort Cases: Implications for the Litigation Explosion Debate." *Law & Society Review* 26 (1992), 85–116.

Hans, Valerie P., and Neil Vidmar. *Judging the Jury.* New York: Plenum Press, 1986.

Hawles, Sir John. *The Englishman's Right: A Dialogue In Relation to Trial By Jury.* Boston: Soule and Bugbee, 1883.

Hayes, Arthur S. "Solving the Case of the Missing Jurors." *The Wall Street Journal,* March 12, 1990, p. B1.

Heuer, Larry, and Steven D. Penrod. "Increasing Jurors' Participation in Trials: A Field Experiment with Jury Notetaking and Question Asking." *Law and Human Behavior* 12 (September 1988), 231–62.

Heuer, Larry, and Steven D. Penrod. "Some Suggestions for the Critical Appraisal of a More Active Jury." *Northwestern University Law Review* 85 (Fall 1990), 226–39.

Hoffman, Jan. "New York Casts for Solutions to Gaping Holes in Juror Net." *The New York Times,* September 26, 1993, p. 1.

Horwitz, Morton J. *The Transformation of American Law 1780–1860.* Cambridge, MA: Harvard University Press, 1977.

Ingram, Judith. "An Innovation in Russia: Courts Offer Jury Trials." *The New York Times,* December 19, 1993, p. A18.

Kalven, Harry, Jr., and Hans Zeisel. *The American Jury*. Boston: Little, Brown, 1966.

Karnow, Stanley. *In Our Image: America's Empire in the Philippines*. New York: Ballantine Books, 1989.

Kurtz, Howard. "Bensonhurst Ringleader Acquitted on Murder Counts." *The Washington Post*, May 19, 1990, p. 1.

Lambert, Wade. "After the Verdict: Will Juror Interviews Skew the Deliberations in Future Trials?" *The Wall Street Journal*, December 30, 1993, p. B1.

Landry, Robert W. "Let the Jurors Ask!" *The National Law Journal*, January 29, 1990, pp. 13–14.

Langbein, John H. "Mixed Court and Jury Court: Could the Continental Alternative Fill the American Need?" *American Bar Foundation Research Journal* 195 (1981), 195–219.

"Legal Beat." *The Wall Street Journal*, April 19, 1993, p. B2.

Lempert, Richard O. "Civil Juries and Complex Cases: Let's Not Rush to Judgment." *Michigan Law Review* 80 (November 1981), 68–132.

The Liability Maze: The Impact of Liability Law on Safety and Innovation. Eds. Peter W. Huber and Robert E. Litan. Washington, DC: The Brookings Institution, 1991.

Loftus, Elizabeth F. *Eyewitness Testimony*. Cambridge, MA: Harvard University Press, 1979.

Loftus, Elizabeth F., and Katherine Ketcham. *Witness for the Defense: The Accused, the Eyewitness, and the Expert Who Puts Memory on Trial*. New York: St. Martin's Press, 1991.

Lynch, Patrick. "The Case for Striking Jury Demands in Complex Antitrust Litigation." *The Review of Litigation* 1 (Winter 1980), 3–45.

McCabe, Sarah. "Is Jury Research Dead?" *The Jury Under Attack*. Eds. Mark Findlay and Peter Duff. London: Butterworths, 1988, pp. 27–39.

MacCoun, Robert. "Inside the Black Box: What Empirical Research Tells Us About Decisionmaking by Civil Juries." *Verdict: Assessing the Civil Jury System*. Ed. Robert E. Litan. Washington, DC: The Brookings Institution, 1993, pp. 137–80.

MacCoun, Robert J., and Tom R. Tyler. "The Basis of Citizens' Perceptions of the Criminal Jury: Procedural Fairness, Accuracy, and Efficiency." *Law and Human Behavior* 12 (September 1988), 333–52.

Massaro, Toni M. "Peremptories or Peers?—Rethinking Sixth Amendment Doctrine, Images, and Procedures." *North Carolina Law Review* 64 (1986) 501–64.

Minow, Newton N., and Fred H. Cate. "Who Is an Impartial Juror in an Age of Mass Media?" *The American University Law Review* 40 (Winter 1991), 631–64.

Nasheri, Hedieh, and Richard J. Rudolph. "An Active Jury: Should Courts Encourage Jurors to Participate in the Questioning Process?" *American Journal of Trial Advocacy* 16 (Summer 1992), 109–50.

1994 Current Jury Awards. Horsham, PA: LRP Publications, 1994.

"1991's Largest Verdicts." *The National Law Journal,* January 20, 1992, pp. S-2, S-7, S-12.

O'Connell, Jeffrey, and Rita James Simon. "Payment for Pain & Suffering: Who Wants What, When & Why?" *University of Illinois Law Forum* (1972), 1–120.

Olson, Walter K. *The Litigation Explosion: What Happened When America Unleashed the Lawsuit.* New York: Truman Talley Books/Dutton, 1991.

Osborne, D. M. "Reaching for Doubt." *The American Lawyer,* September, 1992, pp. 62–69.

Osborne, Nancy C. "Loss of Consortium: Paradise Lost, Paradise Regained." *Cumberland Law Review* 15 (1984–85), 179–209.

Ostrom, Brian, David Rottmann, and Roger Hanson. "What Are Tort Awards Really Like? The Untold Story from the State Courts." *Law and Policy* 14 (January 1992), 77–106.

Parker, Cort, Jr. "Marisol Schneider of Victim: 'I Always Thank God for the Day I Met Him.' " *The Echoes-Sentinel,* March 12, 1992, p. 1.

Parloff, Roger. "Maybe the Jury Was Right." *The American Lawyer,* June, 1992, pp. 7, 78–80.

Petzinger, Thomas, Jr. *Oil & Honor: The Texaco-Pennzoil Wars.* New York: G. P. Putnam's Sons, 1987.

Prettyman, E. Barrett. "Jury Instructions—First or Last?" *ABA Journal* 46 (October 1960), 1066.

Ridgeway, Susan G. "Loss of Consortium and Loss of Services Actions: A Legacy of Separate Spheres." *Montana Law Review* 50 (Summer 1989), 349–70.

Rodgers, Raymond S. "The Wasps in Court: Argument and Audience in the Athenian Dicasteries." *American Journal of Legal History* 28 (April 1984), 147–63.

Rooney, John Flynn. "Lawyers Laud Questions of Toxic Shock Jury." *The Chicago Daily Law Bulletin,* January 29, 1990, p. 1.

"Russia to Bring Back Jury Trials in Regions." *The New York Times,* October 29, 1993, p. A7.

Safian, Robert. "McMartin Madness: Ten Days in the Life of the Longest, Most Gruesomely Difficult Criminal Trial Ever." *The American Lawyer,* October, 1989, pp. 46–55.

Sarokin, H. Lee, and G. Thomas Munsterman. "Recent Innovations in Civil Jury Trial Procedures." *Verdict: Assessing the Civil Jury System.* Ed. Robert E. Litan. Washington, DC: The Brookings Institution, 1993, pp. 378–98.

Satter, Robert. *Doing Justice, A Trial Judge At Work.* New York: American Lawyer Books/Simon & Schuster, 1990.

Scheflin, Alan W., and Jon M. Van Dyke. "Merciful Juries: The Resilience of Jury Nullification." *Washington and Lee Law Review* 48 (Winter 1991), 165–83.

Schulman, Jay, Phillip Shaver, Robert Colman, Barbara Emrich, and Richard Christie. "Recipe for a Jury." *In the Jury Box: Controversies In the Courtroom.* Eds. Lawrence Wrightsman, Saul M. Kassin, and Cynthia E. Willis. Newbury Park, CA: Sage Publications, 1987, pp. 13–47.

Schwarzer, William W. "Communicating with Juries: Problems and Remedies." *California Law Review* 69 (May 1981), 731–69.

Schwarzer, William W. "Reforming Jury Trials." *University of Chicago Legal Forum* 1990 (1990), 119–46.

Seagrave, Sterling. *The Marcos Dynasty.* New York: Fawcett Columbine, 1988.

Selvin, Molly, and Larry Picus. *The Debate Over Jury Performance: Observations from a Recent Asbestos Case.* Santa Monica, CA: Rand Institute for Civil Justice, 1987.

Spence, Gerry. *With Justice for None: Destroying an American Myth.* New York: Times Books, 1989.

Sturgess, Garry. "Dire Days for Voir Dire." *Legal Times,* September 10, 1990, p. 1.

Sugarman, Stephen D. *Doing Away with Personal Injury Law: New Compensation Mechanisms for Victims, Consumers, and Business.* New York: Quorum Books, 1989.

Tabak, Ronald J., and J. Mark Lane. "The Execution of Injustice: A Cost and Lack-of-Benefit Analysis of the Death Penalty." *Loyola of Los Angeles Law Review* 23 (November 1989), 59–146.

Thayer, James B. "The Jury and Its Development I." *Harvard Law Review* 5 (January 1892), 249–73.

Thayer, James B. "The Jury and Its Development II." *Harvard Law Review* 5 (February 1892), 295–319.

Thayer, James B. "The Jury and Its Development III." *Harvard Law Review* 5 (March 1892), 357–88.

Thayer, James B. "The Older Modes of Trial." *Harvard Law Review* 5 (May 1891), 45–70.

Timothy, Mary. *Jury Woman.* Palo Alto, CA: Glide Publications/Emty Press, 1974.

Twain, Mark. *Roughing It,* Volume II. New York: Harper and Brothers, 1913.

Vinson, Donald E. *Jury Trials: The Psychology of Winning Strategy.* Charlottesville, VA: The Michie Company, 1986.

Wishman, Seymour. *Anatomy of a Jury.* New York: Penguin Books, 1986.

Wright, Peggy. "Schneider Drama: Only Players Know Real Story." *Morris County Daily Record,* March 6, 1992, p. A3.

Yarmey, A. Daniel. *The Psychology of Eyewitness Testimony.* New York: The Free Press, 1979.

Zeisel, Hans, and Shari Seidman Diamond. "The Jury Selection in the Mitchell-Stans Conspiracy Trial." *American Bar Foundation Research Journal* (1976), 151–74.

INDEX

ABOUT THE AUTHOR

STEPHEN J. ADLER, law editor of *The Wall Street Journal,* is a graduate of Harvard College and Harvard Law School and a member of the District of Columbia Bar. Before launching the *Journal*'s law page in 1988, he was editor of *The American Lawyer*. He lives in New York City with his wife and daughter.